The Japanization of British Industry

The Japanization of British Industry

Nick Oliver and Barry Wilkinson

Basil Blackwell

Copyright © Nick Oliver and Barry Wilkinson 1988

First published 1988

Basil Blackwell Ltd
108 Cowley Road, Oxford, OX4 1JF, UK

Basil Blackwell Inc.
432 Park Avenue South, Suite 1503
New York, NY 10016, USA

British Library Cataloguing in Publication Data
Oliver, Nick
    The Japanization of British industry
    1. Great Britain. Japanese multinational
    companies
    I. Title   II. Wilkinson, Barry
    338.8'8952'041

    ISBN 0-631-16022-1

Library of Congress Cataloging-in-Publication Data
Oliver, Nick
    The Japanization of British industry / Nick Oliver and Barry Wilkinson
        p.   cm.
    Bibliography: p.
    Includes index.
    ISBN 0-631-16022-1
    1. Corporations, Japanese—Great Britain. 2. Investments,
    Japanese—Great Britain. 3. Industrial management—Japan.
    4. Industrial relations—Japan.   I. Wilkinson, Barry.   II. Title.
    HD2845.043 1988
    338.8'8952'041—dc19   88-10503
                        CIP

Typeset in 10 on 11½ pt Times
by MHL Typesetting Ltd, Coventry
Printed in Great Britain by Bookcraft Ltd, Bath, Avon

'Not that bloody book again' is dedicated to Sandra and Karen, for their endurance during its just-in-time production

Contents

List of Figures

List of Tables

Foreword

The British have for long looked overseas for ways of raising their industrial game. First it was to the Americans and, to an extent, it still is: politicians, industrialists, advisers and some royalty are still running breathlessly down the gangways at Heathrow to tell us the good news of the enterprise culture. Others, and in large numbers, have looked to Germany since the heady days of the *Wirtschaftswunder* as the model for industrial revival and industrial relations discipline. Now they have all been joined by messengers from Japan — as well as the Japanese themselves, whose electronics and car companies have settled and subdued the supposedly hostile territories of Wales and the Northern Earls, where the dreaded unions once roamed the land. The Japanese have brought with them not only jobs but also a penchant for removing the slack said to be traditionally associated with British manufacturing methods; an insistence upon greater work discipline; and a strong preference for those single-union, strike-free agreements which have caused such a jumble in the TUC's cupboard. The single-union deals may even be *faute de mieux*, and *mieux* from the Japanese perspective may mean no unions at all — as the advocates of single-union deals in and out of the unions repeatedly maintain. Indeed, the AEU in the much-discussed Nissan plant at Sunderland can claim no more than 20 per cent in membership and a recent study of electronics plants in Scotland reports that none of the Japanese-owned are unionized.*

Curiously though, many of the modern gifts from the Orient are of Western provenance. Some prominent US companies are far from recent converts to the supposed non-union option and the large Japanese firms do at least seem to have positive feelings about the company unions. Nor are the new techniques necessarily Japanese. Quality circles, for example, were imported into Japan from the United States to be suitably modified and then re-exported with Japanese companies or enthusiastically re-imported into the United States. Nor is 'Japanization' exclusively Japanese. The term, to my knowledge, was first used in the *Industrial*

---

*Paper given by John McInnes to an Edinburgh conference, reported in the *Financial Times* 30 March 1988.

Relations Journal† and of the six revealing and important case studies chosen for this book only two are Japanese and one (IBM) has its own special brew of motivational and personnel practices.

According to Oliver and Wilkinson what is different about the British 'emulators' of the Japanese is that whilst in manufacturing their policies and methods follow those of Japanese companies this is generally not the case in their approach to their workers. Nor should this surprise us. Japanese companies in Japan are a vast flotilla of ships, large and small, bobbing upon their own cultural and institutional sea. The success of their personnel policies in their large corporations is greatly assisted by a supportive complex of customs and mores in the wider society. Naturally, when Japanese businessmen venture abroad they take with them enough of their personnel practices to underwrite their manufacturing methods. The wider cultural and institutional support must be left behind although in some cases there have been attempts by Japanese companies to recreate some elements of it, in Britain, in the immediate environment of their factories. They also seem, as this book shows, to be more successful in meeting their objectives than their British corporate emulators. The argument of the book is that they can more easily combine new directions in manufacturing *and* personnel. This is persuasive. But they are also usually operating in regions of recent industrial failure, for whatever reasons, by British companies. Local civic leaders and trade union officials have an honourable, as well as a vested, interest in their success. Labels are of course less important than contents. The term 'Japanization' may subsume a battery of characteristic techniques − carefully described in this book − to which British workers are widely being urged to adapt. But inward-investing Japanese, or 'Japanizing' British or American companies claiming to be looking for improvements in their competitiveness, are all likely to be welcomed by the long-term unemployed. Perhaps they always should.

The trouble is that free lunches are just as scarce in Swansea and Dundee as in Tokyo and Detroit. Or, as Oliver and Wilkinson more precisely argue, Japanization has important implications both for the manner in which people pass their individual working lives and the nature and degree of their collective strength. Maybe jobs are all; but history *does* tell us that the living replace the dead and that unorganized individuals − even organized communities and governments − are frail breakwaters against the tide of corporate power. These issues are far too important to go by default and the imperative of having paid work. This book brings sound analysis to bear upon the range of manufacturing and personnel practices associated with Japanization. It also reminds us of the equation of benefits *and costs* associated with 'Japanese' innovations. We have already set out upon the journey: we should at least be discussing where we want to go. I am pleased that the *Industrial Relations Journal* has helped to keep this debate alive.

Brian Towers
Editor, *Industrial Relations Journal*

---

†In an article by Peter Turnbull (vol. 17, no. 3, 1986), followed by a special issue of articles on the Japanization of British industry (vol. 19, no. 1, 1988), which was edited by the authors of this volume.

Acknowledgements

In producing this book, we have incurred many debts, especially to all those who gave generously of their time to talk to us about their experiences of Japanization — workers, trade unionists, managers and other practitioners.

The material in the book benefited from the contributions of staff and students both at the Cardiff Business School and other institutions. Thanks go to Annette Davies, John Hassard and Steve Sloan who, along with the first-named author, were involved in a pilot project under the New Technologies and the Firm Initiative of the ESRC. Data from this project have enriched the book. Jon Morris generously shared information from his own survey of Japanese companies in Britain, enabling us to extend our coverage of this area. A number of our MBA students in the 1986—7 year also deserve mention — in particular Simon Gleave, Jonathon Lewis, Ken Khi Pang and Richard Spiridion — whose research added extra dimensions to our own knowledge. Joyce Fortune, with whom the first-named author worked whilst at the Open University, is deserving of mention, as is Mike Bresnen for his helpful comments on the draft of this book.

The lively debates which took place at the *Japanization of British Industry* conference helped us to crystallize our ideas. Some of the arguments are referenced in this book, and our thanks go to all who participated.

Finally, we would like to thank Joyce Brown of the Aberconway Library at Cardiff, who fed us a never-ending stream of references, articles and books; and Brian Towers who, by accident or design (we're still not sure which!), prodded us into writing this book in the first place.

Japanese-style organizations seek co-operation simultaneously with accountability. In keeping with this, we extend our gratitude to those who co-operated with us, but accept sole responsibility for any errors or omissions.

Nick Oliver
Barry Wilkinson

List of Abbreviations

ACAS: Advisory, Conciliation and Arbitration Service
APEX: Association of Professional, Executive, Clerical and Computer Staff
ASTMS: Association of Scientific, Technical and Managerial Staffs
AEU: Amalgamated Engineering Union
CBI: Confederation of British Industry
EEC: European Economic Community
EETPU: Electrical, Electronic, Telecommunication and Plumbing Union
GMB: General, Municipal, Boilermakers and Allied Trades Union
IBM: International Business Machines
JETRO: Japan External Trade Organization
MATSA: Managerial, Administrative, Technical and Supervisory Association
NEDO: National Economic Development Organization
NUPE: National Union of Public Employees
TASS: Technical, Administrative and Supervisory Section (of the old AUEW)
TGWU: Transport and General Workers' Union
TUC: Trades Union Congress
UDM: Union of Democratic Mineworkers

Introduction

We first encountered the term 'Japanization' in an article by Peter Turnbull which appeared in the *Industrial Relations Journal* in early 1986. The author was using the term to refer to organizational changes which Lucas Electrical, suppliers of components to the motor industry, were then in the process of implementing. These changes were described as 'Japanization' largely because they were based on methods of production used by many large Japanese corporations. What was particularly interesting about Turnbull's article was his suggestion that the changes in manufacturing methods were creating pressures for changes in the *social* arrangements of production. He argued that the success of the Japanese style production techniques at Lucas was:

> dependent on a social organization for the production process intended to make the workers feel obliged to contribute to the economic performance of the enterprise and to identify with its competitive success. (Turnbull 1986, p. 203)

This observation was consistent with those we had made ourselves during visits to other UK companies which were attempting to use Japanese-style production methods. It suggested that the attempts many Western companies were making to emulate Japanese industrial practices – particularly manufacturing techniques – carried wider social and political implications than was commonly realized, and this prompted us to explore the area further.

A second phenomenon currently receiving considerable attention is direct investment in manufacturing plants in Britain by the Japanese. This is taking the form of subsidiary companies which are wholly Japanese-owned, and an increasing prevalence of joint ventures. Honda's collaboration with the Rover Group and Isuzu's joint venture with Bedford Vans are two of the better known of these.

Sensing that something widespread and significant was sweeping across the British industrial scene, at the beginning of 1987 we put out a call for papers for a conference entitled 'The Japanization of British Industry'. The call brought forward thirty papers on the subject. At the conference, which was held in

September 1987, many ideas crystallized, and in this book we have drawn widely on material which was presented there. Additional material for this book comes from our own surveys, from our many interviews with managers, trade unionists and public office holders, from the endeavours of our postgraduate students, and from published sources. Without wishing to be melodramatic, the evidence we have collected suggests British industry is undergoing a fundamental transformation, the nature of which is neatly captured by the term 'Japanization'.

The Concept of Japanization

The term Japanization has two potential uses: as a summary term to describe the attempts of British companies to emulate Japanese practices, and as a term to describe the process and impact of Japanese direct investment. Both these processes will be explored in this book, although the emphasis is on the former rather than the latter on the grounds that the implications of this are of import for a larger proportion of British employees.

However convenient as a shorthand way of describing a whole gamut of changes currently taking place in British industry, the term Japanization is not without its problems, nor its critics. At one extreme it has been argued that 'the Japanization of British industry is now unequivocal' (Turnbull 1987). At the other, some commentators have dismissed the very idea of Japanization, suggesting it is neither useful as a concept nor reflects any patterns discernible within British industry. Japanization has hence been described as a 'chaotic conception' and a 'bad abstraction':

> A bad abstraction arbitrarily divides the indivisible and/or lumps together the unrelated and the inessential, thereby 'carving up' the object of study with little or no regard for its structure or form. (Dickens and Savage 1988, p. 63)

In a critical, but somewhat more constructive vein, others have attempted to refine the concept in order that it can be used more precisely and therefore usefully. Ackroyd et al. (1988) have described three types of Japanization which they have labelled 'direct', 'mediated' and 'full' or 'permeated' Japanization. *Direct* Japanization refers to Japanese companies setting up operations — particularly manufacturing operations — in the UK and the effects that this is having on the wider British industrial situation. Ackroyd et al. divide *mediated* Japanization into two sub-categories, labelled mediated Japanization I and mediated Japanization II. The former covers the attempts of British companies to emulate Japanese practice, or at least Western perceptions, correct or otherwise, of Japanese practice. Figures such as those in table 1, which show the competitive advantage of Japanese firms engaged in the manufacture of electro-mechanical components, reinforce the idea that the Japanese are doing something right, and that Western industry has much to gain by emulating their practices.

In contrast, Ackroyd et al.'s 'mediated Japanization II' refers to what might

Table 1 Japanese and Western business performance in the electro-mechanical components industry

Performance indicator	Japan	Western
Sales per employee per annum	$150K	$85K
Stock turnover ratio	15	5
Ratio indirect : direct labour	1 : 2	3 : 2
Lead-times (development and manufacture)	50%	100%

Source: adapted from Parnaby (1987b)

be considered the *hidden agenda* behind Western companies' use of Japanese practice, which is the association Japanese practice has with international competitiveness. By linking new production methods and working practices to Japan and hence to competitiveness, one instils an imperative likely to legitimate change in the eyes of those who will be affected by such changes. This argument has also been put forward by Graham (1988), who points out that many of the benefits accruing from a shift to just-in-time (JIT) production are the types of things which managers have been looking for for some time. In support of this Graham has analysed the results of a survey by Voss and Robinson (1987a), which examines the extent to which the elements of Japanese-style production management techniques are currently in use, being implemented or are planned by British companies. Noting that flexible working comes top of this list in terms of its prevalence as a Japanese technique in use in the UK, Graham concludes:

> The most striking point about the results of this survey is that the JIT techniques which are being most widely considered are not in themselves novel. Manufacturing managers have recognized the inefficiencies caused by task specialization which exist in both craft and Taylorist manufacturing systems and have sought to remove or reduce demarcation, without this being seen as a copying of practice in Japan. (Graham 1988, p. 76)

Similarly, in discussing Ford's 'After Japan' programme, Ackroyd et al. describe it as essentially 'a process of giving publicity to the need to face up to the competition', but nonetheless involving many changes to existing practices at all levels in the company.

The final type of Japanization identified by Ackroyd et al. is *full* or *permeated* Japanization. They argue that this would be evidenced by Britain developing strategies similar to those of Japan in terms of investment patterns and strategic marketing in the international trade arena. In emphasizing these elements of the Japanese industrial situation, they ascribe much of Japan's remarkable economic success to the country's economic structures, arguing that comparisons between Britain and Japan, if one is to talk sensibly about the convergence of one with the other, should therefore be conducted at this level. These ideas are further explored in chapter 1.

Our own analysis, though primarily conducted at the organizational level, considers the role of economic structures and economic policy, and as we shall see, notes that the structure of finance to British industry may indeed be an important limiting factor in its attempts to emulate Japanese practice. Nonetheless, there is strong evidence of a move towards Japanese-style practices at the level of the firm, as companies pursue international competitiveness. If British-owned industry fails to achieve such competitiveness it is probable that foreign-owned companies with more adequate financial arrangements — Japanese or otherwise — will come to play an even more important role in home and overseas markets at the expense of British firms.

We see Japanization as a fundamental transformation because it brings with it a whole set of assumptions about, and demands on, the whole range of the corporation's constituents — not just labour but also trade unions, suppliers, and other actors in the broader polity of Britain. As we shall see, those organizations failing to take account of the social and political dimensions of Japanization are unlikely to make the transformation, their plans blocked by resistance from trade unions and middle managers, and hampered by supplier inability and unpreparedness to meet its demands. Japanization is not simply a matter of implementing total quality control and just-in-time (JIT) production processes — it entails the adoption of particular work practices and personnel and industrial relations systems as well, and the whole package of change is most likely to succeed where the organization has some degree of control over its external environment.

The term 'Japanization' may grate with some people, though we consider it to be appropriate. This is because although some Western companies *have* successfully adopted total quality management and JIT principles and practices, and despite the fact that Japanese industry borrowed many of their ideas from the West — group technology and quality circles being well known examples — it is Japanese industry which has most widely put the principles to use. This may be partly because, as the popular conception has it, the Japanese are proficient at operationalizing new ideas and innovations. However, if we are correct in our analysis a more important reason may be that Japanese industry, in the early 1960s when the ideas were rapidly diffusing throughout Japan, already had the social and political arrangements conducive to these practices. Of course this is a hypothesis in need of scrutiny by historians. The important point here is that the Japanese certainly refined these practices, demonstrated their practical effects, and now the West is importing (or re-importing) the system.

About the Book

We have endeavoured to make the book of relevance and accessible to practitioners as well as academics, and hence it is worth beginning with a word of warning on chapter 2. Here we develop a theory of Japanization drawing on ideas and concepts which may be unfamiliar and abstract to some readers. We have therefore tried to make each chapter more or less self-contained, so that the second chapter can be skipped without seriously compromising the impact of the others.

Having said that, we do hope that readers will explore chapter 2 as it contains important ideas on how — and why — Japanese practices fit together as a package.

We begin in chapter 1 with a review of the industrial practices found in Japan. This is made difficult because of the relative scarcity of detailed descriptions of Japanese industry — or at least of English versions — but we have attempted to separate the myth from the reality, and the chapter is useful for referral in order to make comparisons and contrasts between the Japanese and British situations. One thing which emerges from chapter 1 is the apparent 'fit' between manufacturing practice, personnel and industrial relations practice, and wider economic and political conditions, and it is this fit which is the subject of exploration in chapter 2. Here we develop a theory of *dependency relations* which suggests that the process of Japanization is based on the successful management of high-dependency relationships. Put simply, because Japanese industrial practice places the organization in a situation of high dependency on its constituents — trade unions, suppliers, customers, and so on — the organization must find ways of exerting sufficient influence over its constituents so as to prevent them from taking advantage of the organization's dependency. The rest of the book could be read as demonstrating how this is achieved, what the consequences are, and what happens when organizations fail to manage their dependencies.

Chapters 3, 4 and 5 discuss the experiences of Japanese and Japanizing companies in the UK, drawing on a range of empirical evidence. Chapter 3 is a set of short case studies — two Japanese, three British and one American-owned — which we hope give a 'feel' for what Japanization entails. Chapters 4 and 5, on the other hand, take a systematic look at the broader evidence for Japanization, detailing progress (and problems) with regard to the various elements of the 'package'. What becomes clear here is that although potential problems and pitfalls are substantial, attempts to emulate Japanese-style practice are widespread and a determination to do so is there. The stakes in the transformation are high. These two chapters — the first on Japanizing companies of British ownership and those multinationals well established in the UK, and the second on inwardly-investing Japanese companies — draw their evidence from the authors' own surveys of the extent of the adoption and use of Japanese-style manufacturing and personnel practices, and this is supported by a range of other survey, case study and anecdotal evidence.

Chapter 6 considers the special implications of Japanization for trade unions, demonstrating how fundamental union adjustment is likely to be. Also described is the union response to date which, it seems, has been largely a defensive one in the context of trade union decline. It has also been a response largely to the manifest, or overt, aspects of Japanization, to questions of union recognition for instance, rather than to the latent but equally salient implications, such as the establishment of communication channels which bypass shop stewards. A failure to properly attend to these, we would suggest, could lead to the undermining of trade unions as we know them in the 1980s. Nonetheless, it seems that unions still could resist, and occasionally have resisted what they consider to be the more unsavoury aspects of Japanization, and to the extent that they remain independent they pose problems for Japanizing organizations.

Finally, in chapter 7, we draw together our evidence and arguments in order to address the policy questions which are raised, and to suggest where British industry and British industrial culture is heading. Here we point to the British system of support to industry (or rather the lack of it in a situation of City dominance) as an important limiting factor on the process of Japanization. We conclude with a discussion of the likely consequences of Japanization for the individuals and institutions involved in British industry.

1

Japanese Industrial Practice

The secret of Japan's undoubted economic success has been ascribed to many things, different aspects coming in vogue at different times. These include culture (Pascale and Athos 1982), collaboration between government and industry (Wolf 1985), strategic marketing (Dace 1987; Wong, Saunders and Doyle 1987), manufacturing methods (Schonberger 1982), their prowess at manufacturing systems engineering (Parnaby 1987a) and personnel practices (Pucik 1985). This chapter describes these practices under the categories of manufacturing methods, personnel practices, and economic and political context. We would argue that a proper understanding of Japan's economic success must take into account all these things. In chapter 2 we generate a theory of Japanization which argues that the successful introduction of the 'Japanization package' of interdependent manufacturing and personnel practices is facilitated by, if not dependent upon, a particular set of economic and political circumstances.

Manufacturing Methods

Although many manufacturing practices are currently being ascribed to the Japanese, one theme that runs through most of these practices concerns their quality control techniques. Particularly striking is how considerations of quality are linked not just to customer satisfaction but to the efficiency of the production process itself. This contrasts with the traditional Western view in which the maintenance of high quality standards has been construed as adding cost to a product. In Japan, maintenance of high standards of quality is seen to make a net reduction in costs, for reasons which we shall explore shortly. First, we shall consider one of the key elements of the Japanese production process, namely total or company-wide quality control.

Total Quality Control
In common with many of the ideas currently in vogue in the contemporary management literature, the total quality concept (also referred to as company-wide quality
control) is frequently assumed to be Japanese in origin. In fact the idea may be
traced to an American, J.M. Juran, who was invited to Japan in 1954 by a branch
of JUSE (the Union of Japanese Scientists and Engineers) specializing in quality
control. Juran's philosophy was that quality control should be conducted as an
integral part of management control, in contrast to the traditional situation in which
responsibility for product quality is vested in the hands of a quality control department which acts as 'policeman' to production. Between 1955 and 1960, these ideas
spawned the company wide quality control movement (Ishikawa 1984).

Interestingly, Juran and other American quality control experts such as Deming
and Feigenbaum were also peddling these ideas in Europe and America at this
time but their ideas were largely ignored in the West. Schonberger (1982) suggests
the fact that by and large they were only taken up in Japan can be explained by
two factors. First, resource scarcity in Japan created stronger pressure for the
elimination of waste caused by the production of bad output in the form of scrap
or products requiring rectification work. Second, in Japan there exists a culture
in which the dysfunctions of specialization in organizations — in particular the
lack of concern or sense of responsibility for any area other than one's own —
do not fit in. This, Schonberger suggests, has led to responsibility for quality
remaining in its 'natural' place, namely where production is performed. This stands
in marked contrast to the traditional 'policeman' role of quality control departments in the West, the legacy of highly segregated, specialized organizational
forms based on scientific management principles.

In the West, the expression 'quality control' has traditionally carried distinct
connotations, raising images of inspectors with measuring instruments standing
at the end of production lines policing the production workers. The total quality
concept is antithetical to this, and it is worth spelling out in some detail exactly
what the phenomenon encompasses. The first point to note is the broad conception of control used in this context. Within the context of company wide quality
control, control has been described as 'A process for delegating responsibility
and authority for a management activity while retaining the means of ensuring
satisfactory results' (Feigenbaum 1983, p. 10).

A second important point to note is the use of the term *quality*. Although many
authors emphasize the traditional view of quality as simply a question of conformity to a specification, a wider definition, and one which underpins the total
quality concept is one of *fitness for purpose*. One such conception is provided
by Feigenbaum (1983, p. 7) who defines quality as 'The total composite product
and service characteristics of marketing, engineering, manufacture and maintenance through which the product and service in use will meet the expectation
of the customer.' Notable in this definition of quality is the emphasis on the meeting
of customer needs and expectations — a distinctive feature of total quality organizations. This customer orientation typically extends *inside* the organization as well,
with individuals and departments having internal 'customers' whose requirements

it is their job to satisfy. Although it is the major Japanese corporations who are generally associated with total quality control principles, some Western companies have applied these principles for many years. Notable are many of the so-called 'excellent' American companies (Peters and Waterman 1982) who also merit the title 'total quality' organizations. The key philosophy behind total quality control has been summarized by Feigenbaum (1983) as a management approach 'which regards the quality of products and services as a primary business strategy and a fundamental determinant for business health, growth and economic viability'. Quality in this sense does not necessarily mean the 'best' in the sense in which one thinks of say, Rolls-Royce cars. It rather means best for particular customer requirements, these requirements being determined by the use to which the product is put and the price at which it is sold. Total quality control thus comprises the systems which 'enable marketing, engineering, production and service at the most economical levels which allow for full customer satisfaction' (Feigenbaum 1983, p. 7).

These aims imply a tightly integrated organization, efficient in its use of resources so that it is price competitive, but simultaneously flexible enough to respond to customer requirements. The types of organizational structures and control mechanisms required to meet these performance criteria have as yet attracted little attention from organizational researchers, although Peters and Waterman (1982) and Kanter (1985) have put forward some preliminary ideas and popularized the issue. Schonberger's (1982) view is that total quality control is a 'fundamental production function' utilizing many of the other aspects of Japanese manufacturing methods such as quality circles (which employ elementary problem-solving and statistical techniques), just-in-time production, and tight in-process controls. We shall now briefly describe each of these practices.

Quality Circles

Quality circles are a significant component of the total quality control concept. The quality circle movement in Japan started in 1962 with the publication of *Genba-To-QC* (quality control for the foremen), and it was in this year that the first quality circles were set up in various factories (Ishikawa 1984). Quality circles are small groups of people, usually between five and ten in number, who meet voluntarily to try to improve quality and productivity in their work areas. The leaders of quality circles in Japan are typically foremen, assistant foremen or work team leaders, although this role may be performed by shopfloor workers. JUSE has defined a quality circle as:

> A small group to voluntarily perform quality control activities within the workshop to which they belong. This small group with every member participating to the full carries on continuously, as part of company-wide quality control activities, self development and mutual development, control and improvement within the workshop utilizing quality control techniques. (Fortune and Oliver 1986, p. 24)

In Japan, quality circle members are trained in the use of simple statistical analysis and problem-solving techniques. The 'seven statistical tools' typically employed by circles are Pareto analysis, cause and effect (fishbone) diagrams, scatter diagrams, stratification, tally cards, histograms, scatter diagrams and Shewhart control charts. In 1981 there were claimed to be 130,000 quality circles registered with JUSE, with a total membership of over one million people (Wolf 1985).

Although quality circles were the first of the Japanese manufacturing practices to really catch the eye of the West in the late 1970s and early 1980s, Schonberger suggests that their significance in Japan itself has been overrated. In support of this he claims that many Japanese companies had enviable reputations for high quality products before they introduced quality circles, and that circles are not universally popular among the leading Japanese companies. He further argues that workers and foremen are only in a position to solve approximately 15 per cent of quality problems, their impact being most significant in addressing relatively minor quality problems.

Claims have also been made for the significance of quality circles regarding motivation and commitment. Here it is suggested that quality circles are a 'participative mechanism' creating shopfloor involvement and leading to (among other things) job satisfaction, good management−employer relations, increased commitment, improved morale and opportunities for 'self-actualization' (Yap 1984; Ishikawa 1984). From a more critical perspective writers such as Briggs (1988) have pointed to the pressure that workers may be put under to take part in such activities. Describing quality circles as another 'instrument of management' in the employers' arsenal of 'coercive techniques', Briggs cites Kamata's (1983) account of quality circles at Toyota, where weekly postings of employee suggestion rates pressure workers into committing themselves to the scheme.

In-process Controls

Of the techniques used to assist in the control of production processes, statistical process control (SPC) has recently received much attention in the West. The basic principles on which SPC is based are relatively simple, although some of the more detailed texts on the subject are enough to make a non-mathematician's head spin. The principle of SPC is that in any production process there are basically two sorts of variation; variation that is natural to a process (which ought not to create any product that is out of tolerance) and unnatural or unassigned variation that is due to a specific cause, for example excessive wear in a tool, a machine out of adjustment and so on. If uncorrected the latter type of variation will cause products to fall outside specified tolerance.

SPC involves first working out the extent of a machine's natural variation, and then the regular sampling of the machine's output. These samples are used to chart the behaviour of the process, and elementary probability theory is used to detect trends indicating that the machine is starting to produce output which falls outside its 'natural' variability, although such output may still be within design tolerances. This information is used to trigger corrective action − for example a machine reset − *before* the process generates bad product (outside design tolerances) and hence scrap or rework costs.

SPC thus involves operators periodically sampling their own production, not with a view to accepting it or rejecting it, but in order to produce a chart of how the process itself is behaving. In addition to reducing scrap and rework costs, minimizing variation in components can significantly improve the performance of products. A senior quality manager from an international car manufacturer described to one of the authors how the same automatic gearbox was manufactured in North America and Japan, using identical plant. The Japanese units, however, were consistently more reliable and smoother in operation, simply because the Japanese better controlled their processes resulting in less variation in the components used to build the gearbox. It was not that more non-conforming components were being fitted to the North American gearbox — simply that variation *per se* (even within the specified tolerances) affected performance.

Just-in-time Production

As the name suggests, just-in-time (JIT) systems of production are those in which goods are produced just in time for them to be used. The principle underpinning JIT has been described as follows:

> The JIT idea is simple: produce and deliver finished goods just-in-time to be sold, sub-assemblies just-in-time to be assembled into finished goods, fabricated parts just-in-time to go into the sub-assemblies and purchased materials just-in-time to be transformed into fabricated parts. (Schonberger 1982, p. 16)

A little more provocatively, the goal of JIT has been described as:

> To produce instantaneously, with perfect quality and minimum waste. (Bicheno 1987, p. 192)

The above quotations highlight a number of critical elements of JIT production. Given that ideally products are produced perfectly matched to market demand, at least one of two conditions is implied if production is to be performed at the last minute. Either demand is uniform — or at least predictable — and so plans can be made in advance, or the production process itself must be inherently very responsive. The latter condition is obviously necessary if production is to take place at the last minute *and* be profitable. The goal of perfect quality requires tight control of the production process itself, as illustrated in the preceding section on statistical process control. Minimizing waste typically involves removing any non-value added operations from the process; examples of such operations are storage, inspection and movement within a factory, all of which add cost, but not value to a product.

Just-in-time systems of production are sometimes considered synonymous with Kanban systems of production. In fact Kanban represents one particular aspect of Toyota's just-in-time production system. Under the Kanban system materials are moved between the various stages of the production process in purpose-built containers. At Toyota every component has its own special container designed to hold a precise (and usually fairly small) number of those components. There are two cards for each container. These cards are known as Kanban, and it is from these that the system derives its name. These cards initiate production and accompany the materials as they pass through the factory. This arrangement serves to limit the amount of stock in a system; if there is no container with a Kanban attached then no components will be produced. A container with no Kanban attached is ignored. The amount of stock in the system can thus be varied by altering the number of cards in the system. In this way materials are 'pulled' through the system on a daily basis according to the demands of final assembly rather than 'pushed' through by an inflexible production plan.

To create the stability necessary for production to (successfully) take place at the last minute, production schedules are 'smoothed' over a monthly period. A forecast for the month's production of finished vehicles is made, and the total required number of each component calculated. This is then divided by the number of operating days in the month — say 20 — and that becomes the daily base-line target for each production unit. Kanban orders thus function primarily to 'fine-tune' the system around this base line (Sugimore et al. 1977; Monden 1981a, 1981b; Burbidge 1982).

Requirements are modified as the month goes on, according to whether orders are conforming to the forecast or not. There is little published evidence of the system having to cope with significant periods of slack demand; Kamata's account of life at Toyota suggests that manning levels are such that overtime is an integral part of the system if output is to meet targets. Increases in demand are met by even more overtime. A just-in-time system, Kanban controlled or otherwise, is not limited simply to the operations of a particular plant or even a particular company, but may stretch from final assemblers, to their suppliers, to their suppliers' suppliers and so on.

There are a number of accounts as to the origins of the JIT practice. Schonberger suggests that the concept was first applied in the late 1950s or early 1960s in the Japanese shipbuilding industry, and followed an over-expansion of the Japanese steel industry. Because of excess capacity shipbuilders were able to get steel delivered virtually on demand, and as a consequence dropped their stocks down from about one month's requirements to three days. The idea spread to other companies, and was applied to the holding of stocks between the different manufacturing operations within companies, as well as to bought-in supplies. Voss (1987) on the other hand claims that JIT originated at Toyota. According to Voss, Toyota had been developing a range of new approaches to manufacturing management, including the just-in-time concept. This development was spurred on by the oil shock of the early 1970s. By the mid-1970s the 'Toyota manufacturing system', as it was known, had attracted widespread attention within Japan, and other Japanese companies began to emulate it.

Another explanation for the development of JIT in Japan that has been put forward centres on the country's economic circumstances. As a small nation with little in the way of natural resources, geographically isolated, and with scarce land space, Japanese manufacturers were at a relative disadvantage compared with some of their Western competitors. JIT evolved as a response to these resource constraints (Sugimore et al. 1977). Again, Toyota is credited with developing the technique under the guidance of its then vice-president Taiichi Ohno.

For a JIT system to work effectively, a number of conditions must be met. Indeed, some of the benefits of this system of production may be attributable to companies being forced to create these conditions, as will be described shortly. The conditions necessary for Kanban work to work effectively are: swift machine set-ups (Burbidge 1982; Schonberger 1982); simple uni-directional material flow, typically achieved by line layouts or group technology and the product form of organization (Burbidge 1982); and total quality control (Schonberger 1982).

If materials are to be produced just-in-time, then a capability to produce relatively small batches is necessary. The problem with very small batches is that one is likely to run up against cost constraints in terms of smallest economic batch sizes. Typically a compromise is reached by calculating the batch size which will give the lowest unit cost by balancing the *economies* of large batches (set-up costs are spread over more units in the case of long production runs) with the *costs* of large batches (the costs of having large amounts of capital tied up in inventories). For example, fitting a machine with the appropriate tools and then setting it up, running off trial pieces and readjusting it may take several hours, hence creating a pressure for a long production run to justify the lengthy set-up. However, a significant part of Japan's success with JIT systems has stemmed from their determination not to accept set-up times as given, but to devote effort to reducing set-up times in order to approach a (theoretical) economic batch size of one. Table 1.1 shows set-up times at Toyota compared with those typically found in Western companies.

Conventional Western practice has tended to regard set-up times as given in the economic batch size equation. JIT attacks the basic premises of the cost curves in such equations by bringing set-up time — and hence cost — down. Typical strategies for reducing set-up times are machine standardization, pre-kitting, the development of special tools and intensive training of operators.

A second requirement for the successful use of a Kanban system is that there should be a relatively simple workflow. Burbidge (1982) comments that all successful applications of the Kanban system have been based on a form of production organization where operations are organized on a product, as opposed to a process, basis. In factories organized on a process or functional basis people and machines are grouped according to the function they perform. Thus in, say,

Table 1.1   Set-up times for heavy power presses

	Toyota	USA	Sweden	W. Germany
Set-up time (hours)	0.2	6.0	4.0	4.0
Set-ups per day	3.0	1.0	—	0.5
Lot size (days use)	1.0	10.0	31.0	—

Source: Burbidge (1982)

an engineering factory laid out on such a basis one would probably find lathes grouped together in one area, milling machines in another and so forth. In a factory organized on a product basis people would be grouped around the products they produce (output-based groupings) rather than around the functions they perform (input-based groupings). 'Families' of machines, dedicated to the production of specific, and usually similar, products are characteristic of the product form of organization. Examples are group technology and cellular production, which we shall discuss in more detail shortly. In organizations which are organized on a process or functional basis the Kanban system does not work so well, as materials may have to re-visit a work station a number of times. The Japanese use of Kanban has largely been confined to mass produced components, predominantly in the vehicle industry, where production layout is based on flow lines.

A third, and crucial aspect of JIT production is the aforementioned condition of total quality control. As JIT systems run with virtually no margins for error, it is obviously essential that the various upstream work stations deliver to their downstream ones not only on time and in the right quantity, but that the goods are also of the right quality. For this reason it is suggested that JIT systems will only work effectively within the wider context of total quality control. This relationship between quality and JIT production is not a one way dependency of the latter on the former. As we shall see later, JIT not only requires total quality control, it is also one device by which total quality may be realized.

In terms of the effects of JIT, a number of beneficial outcomes have been posited to follow from just-in-time methods of production. The most common ones are a more efficient use of working capital, a reduction in lead times, and improvements in quality and reductions in waste. JIT permits more efficient utilization of working capital essentially by reducing the levels of inventories and stocks. Materials lying around in this form add cost (for example interest charges on the capital thus tied up), but not value to a product. By reducing stocks, capital can be released and may be used more productively elsewhere. A second strength of JIT, albeit an indirect one, is that the reduction in machine set-up times which form an integral part of the package permit reduction in batch sizes. As batch size is a major determinant of lead-time, just-in-time systems can permit greater responsiveness to customer demands — assuming that the system stretches all the way up the supply chain. Switches in demand can be accommodated by 'pull' systems of production control better than under highly centralized 'push' systems, although it should be recalled that Kanban is essentially a fine-tuning device, used in combination with smoothed production schedules. According to Toyota, demand variations of about 10 per cent can be handled by the Kanban system. In the case of greater fluctuations, either the number of Kanban (and hence the amount of material in the system) must be increased or adjustments to the production process made. For example, more overtime working may be demanded, temporary workers may be taken on (or laid off), or production lines rearranged (Monden 1983). Such demands carry obvious implications for personnel policy, which we will explore later in this chapter.

The flexibility of this system may provide a company with a crucial competitive advantage where market environments are unstable, and where there is a premium on customized goods or short lead-times. Finally, JIT systems can encourage quality and minimize waste because of the greater visibility which the small amount of stock in the system bestows upon the production process. Machine or human errors are rapidly detected, simply because the components at one stage are quickly used in the next. Thus sources of problems tend to be quickly detected, and the problem corrected before expensive scrap or rework costs are incurred. The practice of line stop or 'Jidoka' is central to this process. 'Jidoka' is a term used at Toyota and means 'to make the equipment or operation stop whenever an abnormal or defective condition arises' (Sugimore et al. 1977, p. 557). It refers to the practice of giving operators the power to stop a production line if they detect a problem which is producing bad product. If something is wrong the line will quickly be stopped and the problem corrected at source. Under this system the 'insurance policies' of buffer stocks, reserve staff and so on (which allow part of a process to go wrong without total disaster striking) are construed as obstacles to improvement. By permitting one to live with a problem, such spare resources remove the imperative to correct it.

Work Organization

In line with the demands of a flexible production system, a flexible and responsive workforce is also required. This is particularly the case when group technology or cellular manufacture, which could be considered adjuncts of just-in-time production systems, are adopted. Group technology contributes towards the sorts of advantages sought through JIT because it can simplify work flow, hence permitting reductions in work-in-progress and improving throughput (Edwards 1974; Burbidge 1979). The basic idea, which derives originally from the Soviet Union in the 1950s (Graham 1988) is to group machines by family rather than by function — that is, the machines necessary for the production of a family of components are grouped together so that machine tooling can be specialized to a family of components and so that production flows are simple rather than components having to follow tortuous routes through different functional areas around the factory. An added advantage is that responsibility (technical or human) for substandard components is more easily identified as 'ownership' for a product, or a set of operations upon a product, tends to be concentrated within cells or teams rather than dispersed among a range of different functional groups. If used in tandem with a just-in-time system errors quickly surface — if things go wrong feedback from the next cell or 'neighbour' is immediate.

In the Toyota production system the flexibility of labour to meet fluctuations in demand is termed 'shojinka'. There are two key methods by which such flexibility is attained: a particular type of machine layout and the use of multiskilled workers. The machine layout used in Toyota's flexible workshops is based on U-shaped assembly lines, and is represented in figure 1.1. According to Monden (1983) this layout enables the range of jobs for which each worker is responsible to be widened or narrowed very easily. A worker in the enclosed area could theoretically tend two (or more) machines, and is also well positioned to assist others who may be falling behind or who are having difficulty with their work. Thus the balancing of the various operations on the line can be achieved via the

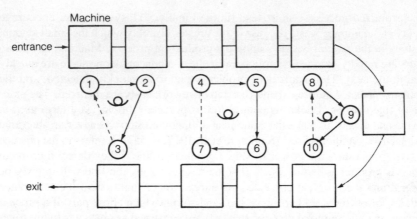

Figure 1.1   U-shaped production lines at Toyota
Note: Numbered discs represent worker operations
Source: Monden (1983, p.101) ©*Toyota Production System*, Institute of Industrial
Engineers, 25 Technology Park, Atlanta Norcross, Georgia 30091, USA

flexibility of labour deployment, rather than by having buffers to accommodate fluctuations in work rate at the various stations along the line. This of course assumes that the workers possess the necessary skills, which is where the requirement of multiskilling comes in. At Toyota multiskilling is developed by a high degree of job rotation, with workers being rotated through different jobs several times a day. This job rotation, and the relatively high degree of ownership and responsibility which the system confers on workers has led some commentators (Sugimore et al. 1977; Monden 1983) to describe it as a 'respect-for-human' system. However, Kamata (1983), whose book *Japan in the Passing Lane* is an autobiographical account of life in one of Toyota's factories presents a picture of an intense, gruelling work experience. Describing his reason for producing the book he writes:

> I wanted to show the inhumanity of it all — not only its inhumanity but also the unquestioning adherence to such a system. Is the prosperity of a modern, industrial society worth such a cost, such a cruel compulsion of robot-like work? (Kamata 1983, p. viii)

Clearly there are differences in how commentators view the Toyota production system.

Japanese manufacturers may be considered fortunate in that traditions of teamwork and collective responsibility had been maintained in Japanese organizations despite the advent of Taylorism in the early part of this century. Littler (1982) describes how Taylorism became popular in Japan in the 1920s and 1930s, but unlike in the US and the UK did not result in a rigid separation of planning and execution of tasks, nor in social fragmentation. Rather, although some aspects of job analysis and work procedures were adopted, they were adapted and diluted in order to leave workteams with their internal flexibility intact, and the foreman retained most production planning responsibilities rather than their being relocated in a separate planning department. Littler attributes this preservation of team-work and foreman responsibilities to the political strength of the *oyakata* histori-cally (the *oyakata* were the internal subcontractors common in the late nineteenth and early twentieth centuries who employed teams of workers). This strength meant that the subcontractor was not, as in Britain, destroyed, but incorporated into the company structure. Hence over the last two or three decades when Japan adopted the manufacturing techniques described in this section, it found itself already with the basis of the concomitant work organization.

Personnel Practices

It is the employment and personnel practices of the major Japanese corporations which have, at least until recently, most captured the attention of Western observers. Here the arguments rest on a line of reasoning in which the success of the Japanese in certain world markets is attributed to 'progressive' personnel policies such as single status terms and conditions, consultative management styles, lifetime employment guarantees, and company-based welfare schemes. This section details these practices under the categories of employment contracts; selec-tion, induction and socialization; payment and reward systems; and consultation and communication.

Employment Contracts

Perhaps *the* most celebrated aspects of personnel management in Japan are the provision of lifetime employment and company-based welfare. These are frequently, if erroneously, presented as stemming directly from Japanese Confucianism and the feudal legacy (Morishima 1982; Nakane 1973), and are held to create a commitment and loyalty to the organization not commonly found in the West.

The origin of lifetime employment provision has been related back to the days of the *zaibatsu* — the huge family-owned and controlled conglomerates which dominated Japanese industry until the 1930s — when youths would join firms as apprentices and eventually rise into the ranks of management (Sethi et al. 1984). Litter (1982) describes how the system emerged during the incorporation of the *oyakata* (subcontractors) into giant corporations in the late nineteenth and early twentieth centuries. Apart from company loyalty, it is argued that a lifetime commitment to employees reduces labour mobility between firms and increases the potential for mobility within firms — these advantages being reinforced by a seniority pay and promotion system (described below). The mutual commit-ment characteristic of the system means that employees are more likely to be treated as 'assets' than 'costs', and employers are hence more willing to train and develop their human resources at their own expense.

The feudal legacy argument must, however, be read carefully, for the evidence does not suggest that lifetime employment is necessarily a culturally determined institution. Dore (1973b) argues that although the ideology of loyalty to one lord was used to underpin the system, restrictions on the mobility of labour was a conscious managerial strategy attempting to cope with an acute shortage of skilled labour following the decision to industrialize in 1867. Morishima (1982) adds that lifetime employment was also encouraged by the military — both for planned production for war, and for the preparation of workers for army life.

Further qualifications regarding the institution of lifetime employment include first, that the retirement age for the majority of Japanese is 55 (Franko 1983), though eligibility for welfare pensions does not begin until the age of 60. Pensions tend to be meagre, and the 1980 census in Japan indicated that over 80 per cent of Japanese men over 60 were still active in the labour force, and 45 per cent of males over 65 were still economically active (Sethi et al. 1984). Second, women are virtually excluded from the system. Third, the system is made viable by companies surrounding themselves with 'layers' of temporary workers (Littler 1982) — an important point which will be elaborated in a section on 'the dual economy' below. And finally, lifetime employment is not a legal or contractual obligation, but rather a matter of company policy.

Despite the latter qualification, employers have normally been able to fulfil their commitment to lifetime employment, especially since the policy has largely been restricted to very large corporations which can redeploy labour in other organizational branches when necessary. However, very recently the strong yen, anti-dumping laws in the US and Europe, and competitive pressure from other East Asian newly industrialized countries has led to slowed growth in many industries and to redundancies in the steel, coal and shipbuilding industries. The official unemployment rate, at 3.2 per cent in 1987, has reached a post-war high, and in the same year most Japanese unions accepted the lowest pay rise in 28 years. This was just over 3 per cent in the steel, automobile and electronics industries (*Financial Times* 10 April 1987). Hence despite 'rings of defence' in the form of peripheral workers the system could be under threat.

The other aspect of the Japanese employment contract associated with company loyalty in popular literature is company-based welfare provision. Characterized as paternalism, many Japanese companies offer a range of benefits which Hirschmeier and Yui (1981) divide into three categories: assistance in cases of sickness, accident or death; educational benefits for employees; and facilities to foster loyalty and community spirit such as subsidized housing, holiday homes and company provision of shops and schools. Dore (1973a) contrasts Hitachi's welfare expenditure on welfare at 8.5 per cent of labour costs with that of the median British firm at 2.5 per cent.

As with lifetime employment, the context of the emergence of corporate welfarism is crucial. Again it emerged as a conscious managerial strategy, rapidly diffusing through Japanese industry in the 1920s and 1930s as a control strategy intended to head off radical trade unionism. Littler (1982, p. 155) describes how employers at the time:

saw paternalism as a panacea for all the ills of industrial capitalism and specifically as an alternative to Western-type class struggle ... this managerial strategy received active support from the Japanese government.

Company welfarism fosters employee dependence on the company, this often being supported with subsidized leisure activities which pervade non-working hours. Paternalism is seen as desirable and potentially transferable by many in the West (Pascale and Athos 1982). Others are cynical, Briggs (1988) for instance commenting that 'the very advantages the large organizations offer their workers can become chains', and Kamata (1983, p. 57), describing Toyota, providing an illustration: 'Approximately 4,000 workers have supposedly bought houses built with the help of (company) loans, and in a very real sense these young married men are tied to the company — that is, to the assembly line — by their loan repayments until the day they retire'.

Selection, Induction and Training

Vogel (1980) suggests that 'in initially hiring employees, the company aims to be as merciless as possible in order to select people of quality'. Obviously related to the expectation that (core) employees will remain with the firm until retirement, recruitment and selection is a careful process. The vast majority of recruits are taken straight from college, people who have worked elsewhere generally being avoided. In any case, there is enormous competition among school-leavers and graduates to enter the large corporations as core workers — educational performance being the key to entry (Ouchi 1981). The major corporations recruit direct from educational institutions with the best reputations, which in turn recruit from the best high schools, and so on down the educational system. Consequently there is strong competition to gain admission even to the best kindergartens and cramming classes for four to five year olds are common (Ouchi 1981).

Close attention is also given to hiring new employees who will fit into the company culture. Careful screening ensures candidates likely to endorse the company's values and philosophy are selected, and 'moderate views' and a 'balanced personality' are a prerequisite. Radical views or an inability to 'get along with others' result in rejection regardless of ability and potential (Robbins 1983), and Pucik (1985) claims that private investigators are routinely used to check on candidates' backgrounds, as well as those of families, neighbours and friends.

Because recruitment is straight from college, employers seek potential as opposed to specific skills, job training being provided on entry. Immediately before job training, however, is a period of induction which typically begins with an entrance ceremony. The induction programme, which lasts on average about ten days (Naylor 1984) may involve group residence, team activities, physical exercise, and instruction in the history, philosophy and mottoes of the firm, and a spokesman for the new entrants may read a speech pledging the intake's best efforts. The aim is 'to make each employee realize that he is a member of the organization' (Hirschmeier and Yui 1981).

Following induction, employees are typically further socialized in an initial training programme, sometimes lasting as long as six months, whose main purpose is to familiarize them with the organization. Azumi (1969) suggests a similarity in this training to that given in religious orders or military schools, and some companies since the 1960s have sent entrants to the army or to Zen temples for periods of 'character building' (Ishida 1977). Training and socialization continues through employees' careers, and is typically on-the-job involving frequent rotation. This experience encourages an acceptance of flexibility and prepares employees for promotion by giving them generalist rather than specialist skills (Clegg 1986).

Payment and Reward Systems

The Japanese are well-known for their seniority-based pay systems. These emerged at the same time as lifetime employment when the *oyakata* was incorporated into the *zaibatsu* (Littler 1982). The *nenko joretsu* wage system meant basically that length of service and age played a more important role in determining wages than job performance or competence. It has been suggested that the system provides the advantages of the encouragement of skill development, less internal competition (Sethi et al. 1984), and the reduction of labour turnover (Dickens and Savage 1988). Monden (1983) points out how the system functions to assign a wage to an individual on the basis of age rather than job grade. He suggests that this facilitates the development of multi-functional workers by eliminating territorial arguments along the divides of job grades.

Most Japanese corporations retain a seniority wages system, but with recent changes such as the increased cost of labour, slowed economic growth and an ageing population, most are also actively considering its elimination, or at least dilution, in favour of performance-determined pay (Japan Institute of Labour 1984). In the meantime, individual competition between employees for slightly higher pay (performance does marginally affect bonuses) and for promotion is reported to be high (Pucik 1985; Robbins 1983; Moore 1987). This may be explained in part because appraisals will eventually affect the promotion prospects of an individual (Pucik 1985): typically entrants will, according to educational level, be given the same pay and status increases up to a certain point, after which only a select few will continue up the hierarchy. It may also be explained, of course, in relation to the intense competitiveness instilled during schooling.

Japanese companies appear however, to achieve teamwork at the same time as individual competition. The provision of team-building training is obviously one factor (Hirschmeier and Yui 1981), and so is the typical organization of employees into teams with group responsibilities for tasks (Littler 1982). Nonetheless, individual competition and teamwork appear to be contradictory notions. Ouchi (1981) suggests that this dilemma is resolved by frequent rotation of managers, which may prevent the formation of 'too cosy' relationships, and from the practice of including teamwork ability and quality of relations with subordinates in appraisals.

It is appropriate here to mention briefly a few other aspects of systems of motivation. Total quality control places great pressure on work group supervisors to meet quality and output targets, and with responsibility for maintenance and quality control typically delegated to the work group there is less opportunity to blame failure on anyone else, or to otherwise 'hide' productivity problems. Publicly displayed output target and feedback systems also provide motivational support — any problems are visible to the whole factory. Such work organization may be motivating because of the encouragement of the development of skills, and because of the relative autonomy of the work group (Clegg 1986). Briggs (1988), however, suggests that high effort is forthcoming for fear of 'loss of face' or shame — a view supported by Kamata (1983). Certainly Japanese management systems, as described in the previous section, heighten the visibility of behaviour and hence the possibility of errors, accidental or otherwise being 'found out'.

By all accounts workers in Japan are extremely hard workers, and the above descriptions of employment contracts, selection, induction, and work organization may give some clues as to the sources of motivation. Assumptions that motivation is related to work satisfaction which derives from the 'Japanese management style' have, however, been questioned in a number of empirical investigations (White and Trevor 1983). Hofstede (1980) suggests many Japanese employees feel tense or nervous at work, and Cooper's (1988) research places Japanese executives in a high position in an international league table of stress. Briggs (1988) explains this high degree of stress in terms of the culturally-embedded concept of *gaman* — a resigned acceptance of hardship without pain. The importance of a Japanese proclivity to accept hardship (as with a proclivity to work in groups or to be easily shamed) in explaining high levels of motivation is difficult to assess but it may have some relevance as an explanatory factor.

Consultation and Communication

The Japanese decision-making process is frequently referred to as decision-making by consensus, or *ringisei*. Literally translated this means a 'system of reverential enquiry about a superior's intentions' (Sethi et al. 1984). This process, most widely used amongst lower to middle managers, involves the circulation of documents to concerned members of an organization in order to gain their approval in advance of implementing a proposal. Typically, the process consists of four stages: proposal, circulation, approval and record. Although final decisions have to be approved at the appropriate level of authority, the process means that subordinates, right down to the level of the work team, are likely to have had the opportunity to have their views heard and perhaps to have had some influence. The process is slow, but when action is taken any potential resistance to change would (ideally) already be overcome and collective commitment given.

Supporting this system is the high incidence of face-to-face communication in the Japanese corporation. This occurs not only within the work team, but through managers spending large amounts of time on the shopfloor (White and Trevor 1983), and through the use in some organizations of open plan offices which mean all behaviour and actions — even telephone conversations — are visible. The steel company NKK, for instance, use a 'touching desk' system held to facilitate a 'group task force' mentality. Here, apart from the general manager or department head who sits apart on a raised dais (but still entirely visible) managers' desks are literally touching (Mitchell and Larson 1987). Through such devices communication tends to be informal and extensive. While systems of consultation and communication in large Japanese corporations are celebrated by some authors (for instance Pascale and Athos 1982), criticisms on the grounds of invasion of privacy and pressures for conformity are also occasionally made. That they are not necessarily culturally specific to Japan, however, is witnessed by the fact that at least some Western organizations such as IBM have successfully implemented such systems (Peters and Waterman 1982).

A final comment, to which we will return later in the book, is worth making here. The personnel practices we have described, despite the fact that most date back to earlier parts of the twentieth century, appear to 'fit' the manufacturing practices outlined earlier. Yet the manufacturing practices emerged only in the 1960s. The question is raised, therefore, as to whether the personnel practices were a prerequisite for success with Japanese manufacturing practices. The fit also appears to apply with regard to the third element of the Japanese 'package' − the economic and political context − to which attention will now be turned.

Wider Social, Political and Economic Conditions

Enterprise Unions

Unlike Britain's occupation and craft-based unions, Japan's unions are predominantly enterprise-based. Over 90 per cent of union members belong to enterprise unions, and the great majority exist in large-scale public and private enterprises employing more than 500 workers. The smaller the enterprise the less likely is union representation, and those enterprises employing less than 100 workers are approximately 95 per cent non-union. There are three main national federations: the Domei and Churitsuroren, covering the private sector, and the Sohyo, comprising public sector unions. However, these are only loosely based and relatively powerless − the enterprise level union is more or less autonomous (including financially) and self-supporting (Moore 1987). In 1980 it was estimated that there were 71,780 unions in Japan, with a total membership of 12.3 million. Approximately two-thirds of these were in the private sector, and more than half of these were confined to the large corporations (*Anglo-Japanese Economic Institute Review*, Bulletin no. 217, 1980).

Enterprise unions emerged only after the suppression of emergent independent trade unions in Japan. During a period of a rapidly growing industrial working class (in the late 1910s and early 1920s) trade unions, often led by revolutionaries, grew rapidly and industrial conflict became commonplace. The Japanese government responded with a policy of rigid suppression of 'dangerous groups' and 'dangerous thoughts', with 'toleration' (constant surveillance and spasmodic mass arrests of trade union leaders) of reformist organizations (Littler 1982). Immediately after the Second World War the American occupation encouraged trade unions as part of a 'liberalization' programme. Communists again emerged as union leaders, but were crushed in purges in the 1950s (Morishima 1982). A big turning point was the '100 day dispute' at Nissan in 1953, which was won by management and a second union (to become Nissan's enterprise union) installed (Cusumano 1986). Lifetime employment and seniority systems became more widespread in Japan in the 1950s (Morishima 1982) and gradually enterprise unions became the norm.

Hence today the enterprise union is the negotiating unit, but Whitehill and Takezawa (1978) suggest that unions' close identification with their companies weakens their ability to defend the interests of their members. Indeed, it is not unusual for supervisors also to be union representatives; the union can function as a career route into more senior management positions. Moore (1987) estimates that around one in six business executives will have been a union leader. Trade unions offices are typically provided by the company, located on the factory site. As unions are enterprise rather than occupation or trade based there is reduced scope for demarcation disputes, greatly facilitating acceptance of change and flexible labour deployment within the company. Enterprise unions together with practices such as seniority-based payment systems and the bestowing of lifetime employment on recruits serve to increase employees' identification with their companies, and restrict mobility between firms. ~ WWI growth.

Nakane (1973) goes so far as to argue that the result is a situation of *vertical* societal divisions along enterprise lines in Japanese society rather than the *horizontal* divisions characteristic of British society along the lines of occupation or social class, a perspective which suggests an egalitarian society. However, given our discussion of the emergence of enterprise unions this argument may be difficult to sustain; and in any case horizontal divisions are evident when taking into account temporary workers or workers in small firms, who are not covered by enterprise unions.

The Dual Economy

Until relatively recently Western observers have tended to focus on the more attractive aspects of the Japanese industrial system, particularly their seemingly progressive personnel practices. However, when one extends the analysis to the economy as a whole, it may be seen that the benefits enjoyed by industrial workers extend to only a minority of the working population. In short, the dual economy in Japan is very marked, and there are substantial differences in the benefits enjoyed by those on the periphery compared with core workers. This extends both across and within enterprises. We shall consider two elements here. First, the use of core and peripheral workers within the major enterprises, and secondly the use of subcontracting companies in the economy as a whole.

Estimates of how many workers in Japan actually enjoy lifetime employment vary considerably. Sethi et al. estimate that 35 to 40 per cent of the total workforce enjoy lifetime employment, with 40 to 60 per cent of the employees in the large corporations covered by this system. Other commentators have suggested that the proportion of the total workforce with lifetime employment may be as low as 10 per cent (Kendall 1984). Of those workers outside the lifetime employment system two distinct types may be discerned; workers mobile between firms who did not join the company immediately after leaving full-time education, and peripheral workers. Included in this latter category are part-time workers, and temporary workers such as seasonal or subcontracted workers. Halliday and McCormack (1973) refer to these as 'nothing but an industrial reserve army of Japan, obliged to work under less than satisfactory conditions, laid off when business becomes dull'. Women are considerably over-represented in this latter category; they are less likely to be granted lifetime employment, and are in any case required by a *de facto* rule to resign upon marriage or pregnancy (Moore 1987).

Working life for the workers on the periphery can be tough, as Kamata's (1983) autobiographical account of the life of temporary workers on the production lines at Toyota illustrates. As we mentioned earlier, the dominant images are of a relentless work-rate, along with compulsory overtime and institutionalization in the form of dormitory accommodation. In the foreword to Kamata's book Dore suggests that Kamata's experience at Toyota may have been exceptional and unrepresentative of Japanese working life, but given that Toyota has been held up as a shining example of good Japanese practice in the West, the account is of great significance. Indeed what we have termed 'Japanization' has been referred to as 'Toyotism' elsewhere. In the area of manufacturing methods in particular, when people talk about Japanese methods they are often really referring to the Toyota production system.

The second element of the dual economy concerns the widespread use of sub-contracting by the major corporations. Kendall (1984) has likened the major Japanese corporations to sharks which swim around the Japanese economy, surrounded by pilot fish (the companies to which they subcontract work). In the motor industry for example, in 1984 Japan had 11 assemblers employing 155,000 workers. Feeding these assemblers are 7,000 parts manufacturers employing 360,000 workers. Lifetime employment is less likely to exist in these subcontracting companies where there are also relatively low wages and poorer working conditions. This situation is illustrated by the figures presented in table 1.2, which describes Japanese manufacturing industry as a whole.

As table 1.2 demonstrates, the differential between the largest and the smallest companies is quite substantial — much higher than in the United States for instance (Japan Institute of Labour 1984). The significance of this differential is heightened when one considers the proportion of the Japanese labour force working in the small to medium size companies; almost half work in enterprises of less than 50 people, and nearly 80 per cent work in companies of less than 500 employees. When these figures are considered longitudinally, it appears that the proportion of the labour force employed in small to medium enterprises decreased during the economic upswings of the 1910s, late 1930s and 1960s and increased during the troughs in the 1920s and 1970s. This suggests that the small and medium scale enterprises have functioned to absorb fluctuations in the economy (Gleave 1987). This analysis is consistent with that of Kendall (1984) who also argues that in the event of the economy faltering, it will be the extended line of subcontractors which suffers, rather than the major corporations themselves.

Table 1.2   Japanese manufacturing industry wage differentials (1978)

Company size (no. of workers)	Wages[a] (%)	% of workforce[b]
1−9	33.8	
10−49	54.8	46.6
50−99	60.3	
100−499	73.4	32.9
500−999	85.5	
1000 +	100.0	20.5

Sources: [a]Katsuyo Rodo Tokei (labour statistics manual, 1981)
[b]Kojo Tokeihyo (census of manufacturers)
Both quoted in Gleave (1987)

This is not to say that the major corporations are necessarily ruthless with their suppliers. Indeed, it is interesting to note that supplier−buyer relations in Japan, at least for the primary suppliers to the big corporations, are typically of a long-term, high trust nature. We will now examine why this is the case and how it is achieved.

Buyer−Supplier Relations in Japan

Supplier−purchaser relationships in Japan are characterized by longer-term commitment (and the reciprocal obligation which that implies) than their counterparts in the West. Before looking at Japanese practice in detail it is worth considering the two types of supplier relationship; one based on competition, the other on co-operation.

In a competitive relationship both buyer and supplier attempt to secure the best deal for themselves, typically at the expense of the other party. The situation may be characterized as a zero-sum game; any gain by one party is at the expense of the other. The advantages stemming from this arrangement centre around the 'survival of the fittest' philosophy, whereby competition keeps everyone on their toes, ensuring efficient operation of the system as a whole. The drawback of the system is that frequent changes of suppliers may be required, and that the competitive nature of the relationship means that a constant policing of the relationship is necessary. An example of such policing might be heavy goods-inward inspection to ensure that the supplier does not ship below par goods to the purchaser.

In a co-operative relationship both parties have a sense of obligation to assist each other and protect the other's interests, at least to some extent. This type of relationship is described as relational or obligational contracting. Relational contracting is very common in Japan; it has been suggested that this is because Japanese companies and their subcontractors have a more developed sense of their interdependence than do their equivalents in Britain. An informative example of relational contracting from the Japanese motorcycle industry has been provided by the Boston Consulting Group (1975, quoted in Fortune 1986). The following features were described as critical elements of this practice: experience-based cost reductions due to the long-term nature of the relationship; raw materials purchase by the final purchaser on behalf of the component makers; integration of planning activities; simplification and standardization of parts design; and sharing of new technology and production methods.

In combination these elements permit a tightly integrated system of supply and assembly, with a minimum of waste in terms of inventories and inspection activities, all of which add cost but not value to a product. Dore (1983) has put forward three reasons why this system has evolved in Japan. The first concerns the financial horizons used by Japanese business which are long by Western standards. Thus, there is a willingness to forgo short-term gains on price competitiveness in order to maintain a relationship which may bear fruit in the long term. Second, the Japanese have a greater sense of obligation to the national interest, and therefore see co-operation with suppliers as one way of discharging this duty. Thirdly, Dore argues, the Japanese feel more comfortable in high trust situations and therefore automatically seek to avoid low trust situations, of which competitive purchasing relationships are one manifestation. It should be added, however, that this 'high trust' relationship could also be described as one of interference and control. The larger purchasing company places 'trust' in its supplier only in the context of a thorough knowledge of the supplier's competences, only after a lengthy probation period, and often only when financial leverage is gained through monopsony or through a direct stakeholding in the firm (Sako 1987).

Supplier—purchaser relationships of this nature also permit the use of JIT techniques between suppliers and purchasers. Toyota's suppliers typically make several deliveries of components each day, often delivering directly to the factory area where the components will be used (Monden 1981b). In these circumstances high dependability with respect to both delivery and quality is essential, as the disruption resulting from late or poor quality parts would be both swift and substantial.

Role of Government Support

An additional factor to be noted in Japan's success lies in the co-operative nature of the relationship between government and business. At the extreme this relationship has been seen as a national conspiracy and popularized by authors such as Wolf (1985). Sethi et al. suggest that the Japanese government, particularly via the Ministry of International Trade and Industry (MITI) plays an important role in planning and implementing long-term industrial and economic policy. They argue that the Japanese government systematically selects target industries, products and technologies as being of strategic importance and beneficial to the national interest, and promotes them. To achieve this it uses a combination of economic controls via the provision of public funds for research and development, capital expansion and export subsidies, and 'administrative guidance' — the shaping up of business's behaviour via denial of financial assistance or placing of bureaucratic impediments. The national interest in this sense has been furthered primarily by the creation of internationally competitive export industries. In the 1950s and 1960s shipbuilding, chemicals and synthetic fibres were promoted and more recently the development of supercomputer manufacture has been encouraged.

Government support is not limited solely to a developmental role. Boyer (1983) has described how industries in decline receive help in shifting resources to stronger sectors of the economy. Such assistance takes a variety of forms; examples are subsidies for retraining and employment benefits to tide workers over periods of employment adjustments.

Economic Structures

A final crucial element in any account of the Japanese economy must be the finance of Japanese industry, the nature of which is indicated in the use of the term 'corporate capitalism'. From the latter part of the nineteenth century onwards, in fact, the state was heavily involved in industrial policy, a policy which led in the 1920s to a heavy concentration of economic power in the *zaibatsu* with financial as well as manufacturing interests (Ackroyd et al. 1988). After the war the American occupation led to the fragmentation of *zaibatsu* into smaller units, but state support of industry was offered through the Bank of Japan and the Industrial Bank of Japan in the form of long-term credit and preferential treatment of firms rather than individuals. Gradually, the network of reciprocal share-holdings, trade oriented economic activity and banking links were regenerated (Ackroyd et al. 1988).

In considering the role of Japan's economic structures in the country's economic success it is possible to discern two views. One view, embodied in the idea of 'Japan Inc' considers there to be a conspiratorial relationship between government and industry. For example, the cover of Wolf's (1985) book, entitled *The Japanese Conspiracy* carries the subheading 'Their plot to dominate industry world-wide and how to deal with it'. The Japanese Ministry of International Trade and Industry (MITI), it is suggested, plays a key role by systematically identifying particular international markets and encouraging Japanese companies to target them. The alternative view attributes Japan's success to private economic activities, which are influenced, though not dominated by government policy. It is not within the scope of this book to explore Japan's economic structures in depth. However, what is critically important is that by all accounts financial time horizons in Japan are considerably longer than they are in Britain. Dore (1986) comments that the net effect of the financial structure of Japanese industry is:

> To very much reduce the pressure from shareholders on corporate managers — to reduce it to a degree not easily imagined by those used to thinking of the British or American economic system as a 'normal' or universal form of capitalism. This very much reduces the importance of short-term profits among corporate objectives and permits the development of a managerial

culture which makes market shares rather than profits the index through
the contemplation of which managers can massage or flagellate their egos.
(Dore 1986, p. 71)

In contrast, in the UK companies are limited by a short-term profit horizon due
to a high dependency on the stockmarket, this being compounded by the fact that
British banks are not in the business of providing long-term, low interest loans.
According to Ackroyd et al., the proportion of industrial funds contributed by
bank loans is the smallest of any highly industrialized country − 6 per cent of
total funds compared with 44 per cent in Japan − and compared with all other
industrial nations British industry has the largest proportion of ploughed back
profit as a source of funds.

Clearly, long-term strategic planning for production, human resource development and marketing − for which the Japanese are renowned − are greatly
facilitated by the close ties between manufacturing and finance capital. Whether
moves by British managements to adopt Japanese methods are limited by short-
term horizons is a question we shall return to later in the book. Suffice it to say
here that short-term profit and cost consciousness, to the extent that it dominates
British top managements, could work against the risk taking and long-term organizational development necessary if British companies are serious in re-asserting
themselves as leaders in world markets.

Having examined the key practices and conditions prevalent in Japan, we shall
now move on in the next chapter to present a conceptual framework which can
be used to explain how these ideas fit together. Readers are reminded that
chapter 2 is rather theoretical, and so some may wish to progress straight on to
the case studies in chapter 3. However, we think that most people will find the
ideas in chapter 2 useful, and for that reason recommend that it is read.

2

A Theory of Japanization

Having described the diverse elements of Japanese industrial practice, it is necessary to raise the question of Japanization as a concept. Given the mix of manufacturing methods, personnel practices, the structure of Japanese industry and indeed the nature of the Japanese economy how sensible is it to talk about their emulation in a totally different context? How far do these conditions have to be replicated before the case for the Japanization of British industry can be made?

Our view is that Japanization as a concept is useful as a shorthand term to describe an interrelated package of business strategies, but that the theoretical interrelationships among the elements of the package must be determined if the concept is to be useful analytically and escape the charge of being a 'chaotic conception'. Specifically, it is possible to identify particular clusters of practices which appear to fit together as a package, and wider conditions which facilitate the successful operation of this package. At the heart of this package, we suggest, lies a complex web of *high dependency relationships*, and it is the successful management of such high dependency relationships that is at the heart of Japanization.

Our analysis in this chapter involves first, a consideration of the areas in which Japanese industry is successful, second, an analysis of the factors apparently responsible for this success, and third, exploration of the social and political consequences of the adoption of these methods. The first process is illuminating in itself, as it immediately reveals that it is not the success of Japanese industry *per se* which we are trying to explain, but rather the success of a particular group of Japanese companies. It is really these companies that the West is trying to emulate, not necessarily Japanese industry as a whole. Indeed, Peters and Waterman's best-seller *In Search of Excellence* (1982) which describes 'excellent' (highly successful) American companies reveals significant parallels between large Japanese manufacturing corporations and some 'excellent' American ones, such as IBM. Interestingly, the Japanese translation of *In Search of Excellence* sold

50,000 copies within two days, and 320,000 within six weeks, mainly to Japanese managers, many of whom claimed important parallels between their own companies and those described in the book (Ohmae 1983). This is an important point of qualification: the production and personnel systems under consideration are not necessarily specific to Japan — indeed the Japanese appear to be continuing to look for lessons from the West in the constant refinement of their own systems. Nonetheless, the Japanese have most widely adopted total quality systems, just-in-time philosophies and so on, and it is to Japanese organizations that the West has increasingly looked in recent years for lessons in international competitiveness.

Given that these companies are serving as a model, how can their continuing international success be explained? It is clear that two factors account in large part for their success: the high quality and relatively low price of the products which they manufacture. To explain how these requirements (which according to traditional Western thinking are competing) are met, it is first necessary to consider the production process itself. The central means by which the apparent price/quality paradox is resolved is by viewing quality as 'freedom from waste', which effectively dispels the idea that quality automatically adds cost to a product. The successful Japanese corporations keep their quality up and (simultaneously or otherwise) their costs down through particular production systems and manufacturing methods. The use of total quality principles, in particular JIT production techniques are central here, representing the major tactic for meeting these requirements. However, JIT as a production system in turn generates an additional set of requirements on the wider organization, implying that its success is dependent on a set of supporting conditions.

Our theoretical framework for interpreting the processes involved in Japanization draws primarily on three related sets of ideas. These are Galbraith's (1974) theory of co-ordination and control in organizations, Marchington's (1979) analysis of power and technology and Pfeffer's (1981) ideas on power and conflict in organizations.

A Theory of Dependency Relations

Before embarking on an analysis specifically of Japanese production systems, our theoretical framework needs to be developed. What strategies and design alternatives are available to organizations, and what are their implications for power relations? In order to answer these questions, we turn our attention to a theory of organizational design originally put forward by Galbraith (1974).

Organizational Design
Galbraith's ideas revolve around the strategies organizations can use to co-ordinate and control the people and processes who comprise them. The starting point is an assumption that for an organization to perform satisfactorily it must be able to co-ordinate the activities of its various elements or sub-units — be they individuals, groups, departments or whatever — in an effective way. For routine

activities organizations typically resort to one of two strategies to accomplish this: rules and procedures to be followed, or goals and targets for the sub-units to meet. Both strategies enable co-ordinated action to take place without the need for constant (and costly) communication between the various organizational sub-units. However, as there will always be situations not covered by the existing rules and procedures, or when goals and targets cannot be met, exceptions are referred up an organization's hierarchy until (in theory) they reach a level of competence or authority where a decision can be made in the absence of rules. As situations will always arise for which there are no rules and procedures — for example if there is a sudden switch in demand for a company's product, or if there is a machine failure, or a shortage of parts due to a supplier failing to deliver — organizations must be able to cope with unanticipated contingencies. Pfeffer refers to this as an organization's *uncertainty-coping capacity*. According to Galbraith, the critical limiting aspect of an organization's structure is its ability to handle these non-routine, unprogrammed or crisis-type events. It is hence this which determines an organization's capacity to perform.

 Given that uncertainty causes organizations problems, Galbraith argues that organizations have basically three options under conditions of uncertainty: to reduce uncertainty; to develop ways of coping with uncertainty — in other words to adapt to their inability to reduce uncertainty; or to accept reduced levels of performance, which may be manifested in the form of over-runs on cost, delivery dates and so on. If one of the first two options are not adopted, then the third, reduced performance, will happen by default. Thus, if an organization cannot reduce uncertainty by exerting control over the sources of that uncertainty, then its ability to handle uncertain or unpredictable situations becomes a critical determinant of how well the organization as a whole will perform. The sources of uncertainty can be internal (for example the performance of its people and/or processes) or external (for example markets and suppliers) to an organization. The options open to organizations to cope with uncertainty are represented in figure 2.1.

 Faced with uncertainty and unpredictability, and hence (in Galbraith's terms) a need to process information, organizations can follow two basic routes. The first involves reducing the *need* to process information; the second involves increasing the organization's *capacity* to process information. Both assume that faced with an unforeseen event organizations have to begin pumping information around themselves in order to take appropriate action. An example might be an unexpected machine breakdown: information must be transmitted to the downstream work stations to warn them of the impending delay in the arrival of materials, and to maintenance to get them to come and fix the machine. If the machine is of critical importance to the whole process alternative arrangements may have to be made to make or obtain the products elsewhere until the machine is up and running again. Similar responses will be necessary in any unanticipated situation — for example if a batch of components are discovered to be faulty, or if personnel are absent or withdraw their labour. An instance of the problems such events can generate is provided by a company recently visited by one of

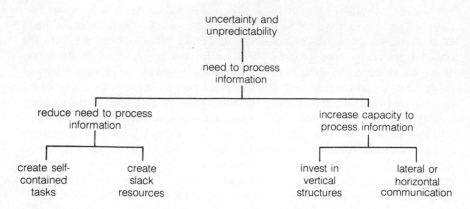

Figure 2.1   Strategies for coping with uncertainty
Source: adapted from Galbraith (1974)

the authors. The company, a supplier to the vehicle industry, was having problems meeting delivery dates and was getting three or four 'fire alarm' calls from its customers per day. The image of a fire alarm going off neatly captures the essence of what happens when unanticipated but critical events occur. Galbraith terms the ability to deal effectively with such situations as an organization's *information-processing* ability.

Methods of reducing the need for information-processing revolve around ways of reducing the *dependency* between the various elements involved in a production process; Galbraith cites the creation of slack resources and self-contained tasks as means by which this can be achieved. If one has slack resources within a production system, temporary failure of one part of the process is possible without the whole system being disabled. Obvious examples of slack resources are substantial buffer stocks between operations so that if one part of the process fails to deliver, the whole system does not immediately grind to a halt. The production of more goods than is absolutely essential in case some are below standard, the quoting of longer than necessary lead-times to allow scope for hiccups whilst still meeting delivery targets, or the possession of spare machine capacity (and/or extra staff), are further examples of methods of building slack into the system. Goods-inward inspection could also be seen as fulfilling this role of insurance policy — one is less dependent on the competence and integrity of a supplier if one devotes resources to double-checking.

Strategies such as these carry a price of course. Buffer stocks tie up working capital and can hide problems with the production process by delaying their discovery — it may be days, weeks, or even months before a batch of components is used and discovered to be faulty. Long lead-times may also incur costs as potential customers go elsewhere, where supply is swifter; the costs of surplus staff and equipment are obvious.

A second strategy to reduce the need to move information around an organization is the creation of *self-contained tasks*. To illustrate this point consider the case of an engineering company, engaged in the manufacture of fairly complex products. As we described in chapter 1, one way of laying out a factory is to have it arranged on a process basis; for an engineering works this might involve a bank of milling machines in one area of the factory, a bank of lathes in another, and so on. Each section would be under the control of a foreman, production superintendent or some similar agent. Batches of components move between processes and have various operations performed on them. Production organized in this way carries the advantages of the skill development and specialization that comes of having substantial concentrations of people and machines engaged in similar work. If one has (say) twenty people all working lathes, then there is scope for operators to become the specialists in particular types of turning jobs.

The drawback of this system is that it is typically very complex, and consequently substantial resources are required to co-ordinate the efforts of all these functional areas. Factories laid out on this basis are typically characterized by armies of progress chasers trying to urge materials through the factory, and complex vertical structures, with many layers of management.

An alternative strategy is to make the various operations within a factory more self-contained. This typically involves organizing people and machines around *products* rather than *processes*. In this way 'families' of machines (and people) perform all the work — or at least as much as possible — on particular products. Under this system workflow is simplified and ownership of the product is pinned down to a restricted set of people. The costs of this strategy lie in the loss of economies of scale and the specialization that process-based production layouts permit. Current changes at Lucas Industries, which are described in depth in chapter 3, provide an example of traditional process-based layouts being transformed into ones based around relatively self-contained tasks.

The alternative to reducing the need to process information is to increase the organization's ability to process information. This can be achieved via two mechanisms: investment in vertical structures — the means to move information up and down an organization — and mechanisms of lateral or horizontal communication. Examples of investments in vertical structures are elaborate management structures and intensive monitoring to ensure tight control. Typically this results in intensive supervision, with many foremen and first line supervisors and a high number of vertical levels in management. According to the information processing view of organizations, these layers of managers and administrators function as a gigantic system of information collection, consolidation and transmission. In a typical hierarchical organization information about problems climbs up this 'tree', and decisions (and hopefully solutions) flow down. For example, if one operation in a manufacturing system experiences a problem with components from another operation, information will flow up the management hierarchy until it reaches a level where an individual has authority (and theoretically knowledge) to resolve it — possibly until it reaches a manager whose jurisdiction covers both operations.

The costs of this system are obvious — a high proportion of indirect labour relative to direct labour, with correspondingly high overheads. Moreover, as information has to pass through many hands decision-making becomes increasingly slow, and the scope for information distortion (accidental or otherwise) goes up — the organizational equivalent of 'Chinese whispers'. For this reason some organizations go for Galbraith's second strategy to increase their capacity to process information: *lateral* or *horizontal* communication. Horizontal communication refers to flows of information in organizations which do not 'ascend' the organizational hierarchy as they pass from one functional area to another, but take a more direct route. Examples of mechanisms of lateral communication include the employment of 'progress chasers' — people whose job it is to chase materials and components through a complex manufacturing system, or liaison officers, whose job it is to shuffle information from one department to another without routing the information through the organization's hierarchy. Horizontal communication could thus be construed as a means of 'short-circuiting' the system, and often occurs informally as well as formally. Quality circles represent one way in which the hierarchy can be short-circuited, essentially by bringing problem-solving and decision-making resources to the level at which problems exist rather than vice versa. Not surprisingly, stiff resistance to quality circles has come not only from the shopfloor and trade unions, but more often from first line supervisors and middle managers, who have felt threatened by what they see as an erosion of their authority and power (Dale and Hayward 1984; Klein 1984). The system of Kanban production control clearly constitutes a mechanism of lateral communication. Although there is a centralized (smoothed) production schedule, Kanban ensures that adjustments to this (plus or minus ten per cent or so) are dealt with at shopfloor level, without the whole grand plan having to be rewritten.

Galbraith does point out that there is a third alternative to organizations making internal structural responses in order to either reduce the need for information processing or to increase their capacity to process information. This involves reaching out and controlling their environments, thus reducing the incidence of unanticipated events, and hence reducing their information processing needs. Examples of such strategies include forming cartels, developing positions of market dominance and so on.

Applying these ideas to Japanization and total quality organizations reveals a distinct configuration. Much in evidence are design characteristics which embrace heavy use of self-contained tasks, backed up by output controls based on intensive performance measurement and a 'customer-driven' ethos. Also present are strategies of horizontal communication — Kanban being one such example, quality circles another. What is particularly striking however, is the removal of one design strategy in particular — slack resources. What are the implications of removing the 'insurance policy' of slack resources?

Power and Dependency Relations
The most obvious consequence of removing slack resources — for example buffer stocks — is to dramatically increase the *dependency* between the various agencies

(mechanical and human) involved in the production process. Significantly, Pfeffer (1981) argues that dependency is a key source of power in an organizational setting:

> The power to control or influence the other resides in control over the things he values, which may range all the way from oil resources to ego support. In short, power resides implicitly in the other's dependence. (Emerson, quoted in Pfeffer 1981, p. 99)

> Power is having something that somebody else wants. (Farney, quoted in Pfeffer 1981, p. 100)

Slack resources are one way of reducing one party's dependency on another, in that they confer a degree of independence or 'loose-coupling' between operations. For example the Ford Motor Company were able to run down inventories in their UK factories by simultaneously manufacturing the same model in other European countries, inventories which had in part been kept to safeguard production in the case of isolated industrial disputes. However, with an alternative source of supply secure, the dependency of the company on its British workers was reduced; from the company's point of view, this reduced unions' ability to hold them to ransom, because supply was substitutable from elsewhere. Consequently the insurance policy of generous inventories could be dispensed with. This reveals an obvious potential problem with systems of production (such as JIT) which have little slack. They are very vulnerable to disruption, whether accidental or deliberate, machine or human based.

Focusing on human sources of disruption, Marchington (1979) has developed a set of ideas useful in analysing the relationship between the nature of production processes and the dependencies of the parties involved in them, and it is to Marchington's ideas which we now turn.

Marchington applied his theory specifically to the dependencies which particular types of production processes create, arguing that the strategic position of individuals and groups within an organization is determined primarily by the centrality of their relationship to the organization's core activities — in Pfeffer's terms, the extent to which the organization has a high dependency upon them. More specifically, Marchington suggested that the more pervasive and immediate the impact of any disruption a group could inflict on the manufacturing process, the greater would be the *power capacity* (the ability to exert influence) of the group capable of causing such disruption. 'Disruption' need not mean a total stoppage, but could also refer to problems with the production process due to lack of diligence or skill on the part of the operators, unauthorized absence, turnover and so on.

Factors outside the production process will also bear on the power capacity of groups within an organization, particularly factors such as labour market conditions, which affect the substitutability of labour. However crucial one's position in a manufacturing process, those who are expendable are unlikely to command a high dependency, and hence a strong bargaining position. Marchington thus argues that three factors are critical to explaining the social, economic and political arrangements surrounding a given production process; the potential *pervasiveness* of a disruption caused by those involved in the process; the likely *immediacy* of a disruption; and the *substitutability* of those involved in the process. When these three simple concepts are applied to an archetypal Japanese production process, especially one utilizing just-in-time production, a number of important social and political consequences are suggested, and these will be explored below. First, the three concepts themselves merit further explanation.

Pervasiveness refers to how far through an organization the effects of a disruption will be felt. Pervasiveness is closely related to the degree of interdependence between the various operations in the process. Where interdependence is high the effects of a problem at one point are likely to be widely felt at other points. Modern oil refineries and chemical processing plants provide good examples of production systems with high levels of pervasiveness, and this may explain in part the relatively high wages and good conditions found in these industries by, for instance, Blauner (1964) and Woodward (1965). That is, good wages and conditions may represent pre-emptive provisions by management as an insurance against disruptions which would be certain to be costly.

Immediacy refers to the speed with which the effects of a disruption are felt. The newspaper industry provides an example of a production process where the effects of disruption are quickly felt. The unsaleability of yesterday's news has not been overlooked, nor unexploited, by print workers.

The third critical characteristic of production processes for power and dependency relations identified by Marchington is the *substitutability* of the resources which contribute towards it. Marchington applies the idea to human resources, but the substitutability of physical resources — materials, machines and so on — will also have an impact on arrangements surrounding and supporting a production process. Taking human resources first, the substitutability principle helps explain the wage differentials between those with scarce skills — such as computer professionals — and those without. The heightened dependency of organizations on the former group gives it a better bargaining position. A strategy of deskilling makes sense in this context. An example of applying the substitutability principle to physical resources would be spreading one's requirements across a number of agencies — not putting all one's eggs in one basket, as it were. The tradition of multiple sourcing of components in the UK motor industry in the 1960s and 1970s is an illustration of this. This practice developed in the context of labour unrest within the components industry.

However, applying the substitutability principle can also carry a price. For instance, if a company spreads the risk of failure of a particular supplier by multiple sourcing, then the administrative costs for the bought-in part rise substantially, and the company has more suppliers to 'police' in terms of the quality of their supplied parts. Similarly, if workers with scarce skills are made substitutable (and therefore cheaper) through a more extensive division of labour, one cost is likely to be a need for more supervisors, inspectors, and other indirect workers to ensure production standards are met and work co-ordinated.

The mechanism which renders pervasiveness, immediacy and substitutability of such critical importance to the arrangements surrounding a production process, we suggest, is to be found in the degree of *dependency* they create between the operations and agencies comprising that process. High levels of pervasiveness and immediacy and a low level of substitutability imply a high degree of dependency in organizational relationships, and vice versa.

We suggested earlier that dependency carries important implications for power and control — dependency equates with an ability to be influenced or to influence according to whether one is depending or being depended upon by another party. In terms of technology one can take obvious steps to guard against the breakdown of machines upon which one relies. But what about the people who operate the machines? This takes us on to the final element in our theoretical framework, the conditions under which power is likely to be used, or in the terms used previously, dependency relationships exploited.

Given the existence of dependency, Pfeffer argues that two conditions determine whether or not such dependency finds expression in the exercise of power, and usually, the emergence of conflict. The first condition for the emergence of conflict lies in *goal heterogeneity* — that is the existence of goals which conflict or are inconsistent with one another. The second condition necessary for the emergence of conflict is *resource scarcity*. In situations where there are sufficient resources to satisfy everyone's goals and desires, then the fact that some of these goals may be inconsistent is not critical. However, as soon as demands exceed available resources, choices have to be made about the allocation of these resources. Under conditions of resource scarcity, such choices are likely to create winners and losers, generating conflict and hence uncertainty.

From the perspective of the organization as a whole, resource dependence gives various groups within and outside the organization the *ability* to exert an influence on it for their own benefit; in combination goal heterogeneity and resource scarcity can provide the *motivation* to utilize this ability.

Further Considerations

We have now developed the essence of our model of dependency relations which will guide our interpretation of Japanization. However, two further aspects need mentioning. First, it will be clear by now that the characteristics sought of the organization's constituents (particularly suppliers and employees but in theory potentially customers, governments, and others) will differ according to the type of production system. Second, wider social, political and economic conditions will have a bearing on the state of dependency relations and their outcome.

Taking constituent characteristics first, various pieces of research have shown that different production systems imply different types of labour. Woodward (1965) for instance, argued that small batch and process production gave rise to more stringent requirements than large batch and mass production, and Blauner (1964) argued that highly automated production led to more autonomy and control for (therefore more dependency on) workers. Other theorists (for example Friedman 1977) have argued that wider economic and political factors, particularly labour market conditions and the strength of trade unions, also have an importance in determining whether a 'responsible autonomy' or a 'direct control' strategy will be followed.

Briefly, the strategy of direct control entails a rigid division of labour with tight supervision, whereas responsible autonomy refers to the delegation of authority down the organization. Clearly, a responsible autonomy strategy is closely related to organizational design based on self-contained tasks (work teams, cells and so on) and also lateral communication and a customer-orientated ethos. This leads to a requirement for more reliable, flexible and probably skilled workers than a direct control strategy. Hence responsible autonomy implies a heightened dependence of the organization on its workers, although a lessened dependence on the agents of direct control such as supervisors and middle management.

On the other hand, a high dependence on suppliers is implied when a policy of single sourcing is involved. Some organizations are willing to heighten their dependence on suppliers, via long-term contracts for instance, in return for the supplier giving priority and loyalty to the organization, and for promises regarding quality, delivery and price. Others prefer to take advantage of the competition between suppliers, constantly playing each off against the others. In the latter case, supplier *characteristics* are not a cause for concern, only the cost of their goods.

Finally, the organization's social, political and economic environment will affect dependency relations in a multitude of ways. As well as labour market conditions, mentioned above, government policies, the political climate, national cultures, and competitive situation are all of importance. Besides affecting the choice of production system, such factors can influence levels of dependency. For instance a slack labour market or a situation of high supplier competition might increase the potential substitutability of constituents. These situations also imply a heightened constituent dependency on the organization. Perhaps more crucially, environmental factors can influence the likelihood of power utilization (conflict). Examples of this might be a strong national culture reducing goal heterogeneity, a government's economic policy which reduces (or increases) the scarcity of organizational resources, or legislation on industrial action which limits the exercise of power capacity by workers. In turning attention to Japanization, such environmental factors will be included in our analysis.

A Theory of Japanization

We argued earlier that high dependency gives the capacity to exert power and influence, while heterogeneity of goals and resource scarcity provide the motivation to exert power and influence. Issues of dependency relations and issues of power in organizations are inextricably intertwined. Thus, as soon as one starts talking about dependency relations, one very quickly enters the realm of influence, control and power relationships, both within and between organizations. When one considers Japanese production methods within the terms of our model, it quickly becomes apparent that they entail high inter-dependencies. This is most apparent in the practice of JIT production, where slack resources are all but removed altogether from the production process. Our model demonstrates that doing this drastically increases the organization's dependency on those involved in the production process.

The implications of the increased dependencies characteristic of Japanese production systems for power relations within the workplace and between the organization and its external constituents will now be outlined. We will then examine how the elements of Japanese industrial practice fit together to cope with these heightened dependencies. Finally, we will comment on the implications of our theory of dependency relations and Japanization for the UK.

Japanization and Dependency Relations

Japanese production methods possess a number of features which self-evidently create greater dependence of the organization on its constituents, the prime example being JIT production. To use Marchington's terms, such a system bestows upon those who work it the capacity to create disruptions which, intentionally or otherwise are likely to be extremely *pervasive*. With little or nothing in the way of buffer stocks, each operation is entirely dependent on the upstream one to deliver; each must meet the requirements of the next just-in-time. Hence the importance of sound plant and machinery and in-process controls — the production disruption caused by a machine breakdown, for example, could be considerable. Equally critical is that the suppliers supply materials on time, and of the right quality. For the same reasons, the effect of production disruption under a JIT system is *immediate*. With low inventories and buffer stocks, the effect of a failure of supply or of the internal system at any one point will quickly ripple through the whole system.

Other total quality principles also heighten the dependency of organizations on their constituents. In particular, if responsibility for quality control, maintenance and so on is largely vested in the suppliers and production workers themselves (thus eliminating the 'slack resource' of quality control inspectors and other specialist groups) then this gives these constituents extra scope to cause disruption, be it by accident or design. The company's dependence on them to perform their functions conscientiously and effectively is hence increased as the safety net of the inspectors is removed. Interestingly, Buchanan and Bessant (1985) describe how some British companies prefer to choose information technologies which invest responsibility for production control in the hands of managers rather than production workers.

Turning attention next to *substitutability*, Japanese production systems entail a difficulty in substituting constituents. Suppliers are likely to be persuaded to deliver high quality goods just-in-time only in return for long-term contracts, and workers who are multiskilled, reliable and flexible are not so easy to replace as those workers who are not. A low level of substitutability, as our model implies, contributes to heightened dependency.

In sum, Japanese systems of production, particularly JIT and total quality control, heighten the dependency of the organization on its agencies or 'constituents', especially employees and supplying companies. This means, as demonstrated by the theories of Pfeffer and Marchington, that the ability of the organization's constituents to exert leverage in their own interests is increased. The obvious implication is that it is imperative that such organizations take steps to counterbalance this by averting the possibility of such power being used.

According to Pfeffer, this requires moves towards goal homogeneity, or resource abundance, or equally profound dependencies on both sides — a logic similar to 'mutually assured destruction'.

Japanization, Power and Dependency

Given that the companies are apparently allowing themselves to be so dependent on their suppliers and their own workers, what mechanisms have evolved to prevent these dependencies being exploited? Close inspection of Japanese practices with respect to personnel strategy and relations with suppliers (described in chapter 1) suggests an answer to this question — the high dependencies of the companies on their constituents appear to be balanced by an equally profound set of dependencies of the constituents on their organizations.

In the light of the vulnerability of Japanese production systems to disruption and in the light of the high dependencies of the organization on its constituents, we suggest that such a system will only work successfully in a situation where organizations have either actively taken the appropriate measures to guard against disruption, or where social, economic and political conditions automatically provide such safeguards. Both this situation and these conditions, we argue, exist in Japan. In other words, Japanese success with JIT and total quality control may be seen as a consequence of an effective fit between their production systems and their strategies for dealing with personnel, supplier relations, and so on, the whole system being supported by an appropriate set of social, political and economic conditions. In Pfeffer's terms, the dependence of the company on its constituents should be balanced by a dependence of the constituents on the company, goal heterogeneity should be minimized, and the problem of resource scarcity should be eliminated. We shall now examine how each of these is achieved.

Beginning with dependency relations, company-based welfare schemes, seniority-based payment systems and lifetime employment (conditional on remaining with the same company) may all function to generate and sustain employees' dependence on their company. For this reason critics such as Briggs (1988) talk of workers 'chained' to their companies, and Kamata (1983) of workers 'tied to the company until the day they retire'. The *mutual* dependencies created by such paternalistic practices reduce the likelihood of the exercise of power by either party.

Japanese companies are also known for heightening the dependencies of their suppliers on the organization. This is achieved, for instance, through creating a situation of monopsony or through a direct stakeholding in the firm, either of which gives the corporation financial leverage over the supplier. Hence the dependency of the organization on its suppliers is balanced by a dependency of the supplier on the organization, and in return for long-term contracts, the organization is in a position to exert control over the supplier. As the case studies in chapter 3 demonstrate, this can mean strong influence over the supplier's cost structure, production process, delivery schedules, and even personnel and industrial relations practices.

Turning attention to goal heterogeneity, it is remarkable how many Japanese practices could be interpreted as contributing to its minimization. An important example is giving employees long time horizons. As one of the present authors has argued elsewhere, differences in the time horizons employed by organizations and those employed by their members can lead to differences of interest that eclipse those attributable to ownership structure. Even under theoretically low conflict conditions of employee ownership, decisions concerning resource allocation frequently 'stick' on the divide between the longer-term interests of the organization as a whole, and the generally shorter-term interests of those who are members of it at any one time (Oliver 1987). The aforementioned practices of lifetime employment and seniority-based payment systems may serve to reduce this difference of interest, essentially by increasing the time horizon of people's association with their company.

Many other practices also plausibly function to reduce goal heterogeneity in Japanese companies. Goal heterogeneity stems primarily from two sources: from an organization's environment, particularly in terms of other groups of which employees are members; examples are professional associations, trade unions, family, friends, political parties and so on. The second source of heterogeneity stems from the structural divisions of the organization itself, which typically lead to the members of different divisions viewing the world in different ways. The typical divide between sales and production, whereby sales desire products as individual as their customers, whilst production seek long, low variety production runs is a classic example of this.

Many Japanese practices function to minimize heterogeneity from both these sources. The practice of recruiting people raw from college, at least for the core workforce, permits people to be more easily socialized into the company philosophy in the course of the intensive training and education programmes through which they are put. In addition, employees' opportunities to encounter goals and values other than those promoted by the company are, as far as possible, minimized. If a core worker marries someone inappropriate or associates with 'unsuitable' groups such as communists or even consumer associations, his lifetime employment is liable to come to an end.

On the other hand, heterogeneity from internal arrangements may be countered by an emphasis on single status (reinforced by everyone wearing the same uniform), internal promotion systems, and rotation between different functional areas. Clegg (1986) reports that experience and promotion in Japan are gained from functional moves, and contrasts the generalist career path of a Japanese manager with that of his more specialist British counterpart:

Japanese man: 'I work for Canon, at present in purchasing.'
British equivalent: 'I'm an engineer, currently with Canon.'

Another example of reducing heterogeneity of goals is the Japanese enterprise union. Being enterprise based and incorporated, rather than craft or occupation based and independent, unions in Japan are far less likely to have goals which are at odds with those of the company; their dependency on the company itself is too great to make that a probability. Moreover, without the same craft or occupational divisions, the scope for conflict between unions themselves due to goal heterogeneity is lessened.

With regard to relations with suppliers, goal homogeneity is essential because of the high dependency of the corporation on its suppliers. Such homogeneity may be achieved through long-term 'relational' contracting, interlocking director-ships and so forth. Dore (1986) suggests that these tactics permit the high degree of subcontracting found in Japan to substitute for vertical integration.

One final contributor to goal homogeneity which finds frequent popular expression could be the nationalism for which the Japanese are renowned. That is, loyalty to the company could be one way of expressing loyalty to the nation. It has been suggested, for example, that one of the reasons why multinational organizations in Singapore, including Japanese organizations, have failed to generate the sort of loyalty found in Japan is that loyalty to the *foreign-owned* companies which predominate in Singapore cannot be equated readily with national loyalty (Wilkinson and Leggett 1985). Whether or not the same might apply to Japanese companies setting up in the UK is an interesting question.

Having considered how Japanese practice functions so as to deal with dependency relations and goal heterogeneity, we can turn attention to resource scarcity. The answer to the problem of resource scarcity is found largely in the wider social, economic and political conditions in Japan, as identified in the preceding chapter.

The dual economy means that the security of the core workers is gained partly at the expense of the insecurity of the many who work on temporary contracts in the major companies, or in the smaller subcontracting companies where condi-tions are very much poorer. Pay and working conditions for women are on average far worse than those for men. As peaks and troughs in demand are borne primarily by those psychologically, if not physically, outside the boundaries of the major corporations, conflict due to resource scarcity may be avoided within these companies. In other words the privilege and protection of core workers is provided by 'rings of defence' in the form of peripheral workers. Of course, at the same time conflict outside the major corporations is also made less likely, because peripheral workers are less likely to be in a position to organize themselves and take action.

Another contribution to resource abundance may be the strategic guidance and support of MITI, coupled with Japanese companies' approach to international marketing. These two factors appear to have created steadily increasing demand for the industrial sectors thus promoted, creating the resources to avoid the condi-tion of resource scarcity which could, in combination with high goal heterogeneity lead to conflict. The relatively long time horizons of Japanese financial institu-tions, which give protection against the vagaries of the market place, further assist in this process. In sum, Japanese organizations, because of the wider political economy, have found themselves in a situation where sustained growth is possible and therefore where scarcity of resources have been less likely. As explained in chapter 1, sustained growth has very recently become problematic for Japanese organizations, and unless this problem can be tackled, the possibility of heightened conflict in the future is raised. In terms of our model of dependency and power, the high dependency of Japanese organizations on their workers means power *capacity* is already there. Slowed growth, to the extent that it creates problems of resource scarcity, could provide the *motivation* to exert power and influence and therefore generate conflict.

Japanization in Britain

Having described our theory of Japanization, the central questions of the book are raised. Is the Japanization of British industry under way? Can companies in Britain — Japanese or otherwise — cope with the dependencies that the new systems force them to have on their constituents — their workers, trade unions and suppliers? And are the wider social, economic and political conditions supportive of such radical changes?

Our basic argument is that Japanization entails the successful management of the conditions generated by 'low waste' production systems, and as we shall see, any consideration of this implicitly includes considerations of power and control. Japanization, we suggest, is a complex but logically coherent process with social and political as well as technical dimensions. We suggest that to consider Japanization as being simply the transferability (or otherwise) of Japanese management practices abroad is insufficient. This down-plays the equally important question of how well the various elements of a company's business strategy fit together — for example how well a personnel strategy fits with an organization's manufacturing and marketing strategies and how appropriate these strategies are given the wider political and economic environment.

Our thesis is that at the heart of the success of the major Japanese corporations lies their ability to manage their internal and external dependencies in a more efficient way than the vast majority of their Western counterparts, and that they have been considerably assisted in this by a supportive set of socio-economic conditions. If there is a 'secret' to Japan's success, we suggest that it lies in the synergy generated by a whole system, and not, as some have suggested, in specific parts of that system.

The remainder of the book attempts to answer the above questions by examining the recent experiences of Western companies operating in Britain in their attempts to emulate Japanese practice, and the experiences of Japanese companies operating in Britain. The evidence for this is provided by a set of case studies, followed by survey and other evidence. After examining the specific implications of, and responses to, Japanization for trade unions, and after consideration of the broad implications for the British political economy, we will then be in a position to draw conclusions.

3

Case Studies in Japanization

In this chapter we present six self-contained case studies designed to give an impression of what the process of Japanization looks like in practice. The first three case studies are British-owned companies attempting to introduce Japanese-style practices, the next two are Japanese companies which have recently made major investments in the UK, and the final one an American-owned organization operating on total quality principles.

The first case study is of Lucas Industries, a major aerospace, automotive and industrial systems and components group. Faced with radical changes in its major markets, Lucas has embarked on a major programme of change in order to transform their 'total approach to achieving and maintaining world-wide competitiveness' (Lucas Chairman's Review 1986). Many of these changes are based on Japanese-style manufacturing practices, and Lucas provides a comprehensive example of the process and nature of Japanization.

The second case study focuses on the Rover Group — formerly Austin Rover, and before that British Leyland — which has similarly, and in line with the UK automotive industry in general, attempted fundamental change of its production and personnel practices in response to heightened international competition, particularly from Japan. In some respects, particularly with regard to flexible work practices and team working, Rover is leading the field of Japanization in the British car industry. However, it seems that although *in-principle* acceptance of new working practices has been achieved from the workforce, the cultural leap necessary for Japanization poses more difficult problems.

With 'Southern Components', the third case study (whose real name is changed at the request of the company), we consider the process of Japanization from the perspective of a subcontracting organization. This company, a subcontractor to the major car manufacturers in the UK, only employs around 100 people. This case illustrates the impact of the Japanization of major corporations on supplying companies. Based on information given to the authors by the company's owner-director, the case provides an insight into the way in which relations between core and peripheral firms are evolving in the automotive industry.

The case studies of two Japanese companies are then presented. First we consider Nissan, who to date have made the largest investment in the UK, and indeed Europe, of any Japanese manufacturing company. We then consider Komatsu, who like Nissan chose the North East as its location. Of course, as recently-investing companies in the process of early growth it is difficult to know exactly how they will evolve, but we have endeavoured to describe their manufacturing systems, supplier relations policies, and personnel practices. Under the banner of the 'Japanese tripod' of 'teamwork, quality consciousness and flexibility', these two companies appear to be successfully implementing many Japanese-style practices.

The final case study is International Business Machines (IBM), the American-owned manufacturer of computer systems. This case study provides an opportunity for readers to compare the practices of one of Peters and Waterman's 'excellent' companies with those of the flagship Japanese corporations. Although there are differences, the similarities are striking – particularly when considered in the light of the theoretical framework outlined in the previous chapter. This qualifies our use of the term 'Japanization', even though IBM is not typical of Western corporations. What we see as being important here is the fact that *some* Western corporations have successfully operated Japanese-style manufacturing and personnel practices for many years. The experiences of these companies are thus of relevance to the issues we are exploring in this book.

Lucas Industries

Lucas Industries is a group of British companies with interests in many countries around the world. Lucas was established in the middle of the nineteenth century and from an initial business manufacturing cycle lamps and accessories moved into products for motor vehicles at the beginning of the twentieth century. Thereafter, the company followed the fortunes of the British motor industry, also developing aerospace and other interests, largely pursuing a policy of growth by acquisition. Overseas interests are represented by subsidiaries and shareholdings in foreign companies. In 1987 Lucas Industries comprised seven companies: Lucas Aerospace, Lucas Industrial Systems, Lucas World Service, CAV, Lucas Electrical, Lucas Girling and Rists. The last four of these all manufacture automotive-type products for applications on cars, trucks and military vehicles. In 1987 Lucas employed 45,565 people in its UK operations in approximately 120 individual business units; UK sales in this year were £714 million. The group employed 18,001 people in its overseas operations, these operations generating sales of £905 million. A reduction in UK assets in favour of international bases is planned, particularly in the case of automotive products for which the most buoyant markets are outside the UK. This is reinforced by the increasing use of just-in-time systems which require suppliers to be reasonably close to the assemblers.

In 1981 Lucas Industries recorded their first ever loss in over 100 years of trading. As Chairman Sir Godfrey Messervy put it Lucas had to face up to the fact that its 'overall performance in most of its major markets had become fundamentally uncompetitive' (Vliet 1986). Lucas Electrical was in particularly deep trouble; a general manager with Lucas Electrical described it thus:

> The business, as a lot of UK businesses currently find themselves, was faced with a decline from profitability. Its volume base had gone down, more or less in line with the UK vehicle industry build. Having destroyed the volume base, clearly the whole economics of the business were put into question. That, coupled with an increase in variety led to pretty massive problems in the factory, and it was quite clear some 12−18 months ago that either some very fundamental changes were necessary or the business would inevitably close. (BBC/OU 1986a)

In order to address this problem, Lucas began a radical programme of change to improve their performance. Individual business units were required to submit 'Competitiveness Achievement Plans' (CAPs), which are plans for the achievement of business performance levels comparable to those of the leading international competitor in the area. Business units were not compelled to submit viable CAPs, but those that did not risked being either closed or sold, and by 1986 40 had been disposed of. CAPs have been described as a combination of a 'policy of vigorous decentralization with an active programme of measuring up' (Vliet 1986).

However, the individual business units were not left totally unaided in realizing their CAPs. In 1983, Professor John Parnaby joined the Group as Manufacturing Director and began spreading the word about Japanese manufacturing strategy and its relevance to Lucas Industries. Initially this took the form of presentations, first at company and then divisional level; later an independent company, Systems Engineering Projects, was set up within the Group to provide advice and assistance to business units which needed to make radical changes in order to achieve their CAPs.

Manufacturing Practices

A substantial amount has been written about the philosophy behind the changes under way at Lucas (Parnaby and Bignell 1986; Parnaby 1986, 1987a, 1987b, 1987c). Central to the philosophy are the principles of systems engineering, centring on a professional, systematic approach to the design and operation of manufacturing systems, which it has been suggested, the Japanese epitomize:

> The Japanese success is not due to luck or accident but rather it is a consequence of a totally professional approach. There is no single skill or technology which is responsible for Japanese success; on the contrary Japanese engineers and managers apply a total systems approach in which

many elements are constantly integrated and applied. They are true manufacturing systems engineers. (Parnaby 1987a)

In this context, the terms 'systems engineering' and 'integration' are used synonymously. The secret of Japan's success is thus ascribed to 'simple, self-adaptive, and well-integrated manufacturing and business systems which make effective use of people and continually respond to market needs' (Parnaby 1986).

Although Lucas are borrowing many techniques from the Japanese, their use of these is best understood as one set of elements in a wider strategy. What Lucas describe as the manufacturing systems engineering approach consists of essentially two phases; a target-setting phase and a target achievement phase. The former consists of deriving competitive benchmarks and formulating appropriate measures of performance in all areas of the business. Such measures include not only financial ones, but also measures of quality, lead times, value-added and so on. In theory, such measures are derived for all areas of the organization. The second phase involves business redesign activities in order to meet the targets set in the first phase. Diagrammatically the process is represented in figure 3.1.

As figure 3.1 demonstrates, the redesign procedure begins with a performance comparison between a Lucas business unit and the leading competitor in the field. Depending on the size of the competitive gap, and based on an extensive analysis of the current state of the business unit's operations, appropriate purchasing, manufacturing and organizational strategies are developed with a view to achieving the aims outlined in the far right hand side of the diagram. Notable is the emphasis given to supplier rationalization and development. Recognizing that success depends on factors external, as well as internal to an organization, a member of Lucas Group Training commented (BBC/OU 1986a): 'Whatever we do inside,

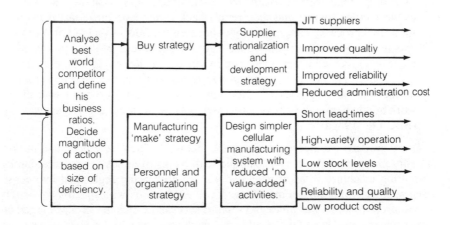

Figure 3.1   Lucas systems strategy
Source: adapted from Parnaby (1987c)

getting our design right, our controls right, getting our house in order, unless our suppliers meet our requirements at the right time, we cannot deliver.'

It is within this wider strategic framework that Lucas are adopting practices which are recognizably Japanese, such as just-in-time production, the grouping of factory machining processes into product families, total quality control and the like. The emphasis has been very much one of matching a business unit's manufacturing strategy to the needs of the market, within the context of a coherent business strategy. In the case of the automotive side of the business this has often meant a switch from systems geared to high volume, low variety production to systems capable of high variety at low cost and short lead-times. The principle focus to date has been very much on the (re)design of manufacturing systems, although attention is now turning to the redesign of supporting structures in the wider organization.

One of the main vehicles for change at Lucas has been the task force. Task forces are typically small, multidisciplinary teams under the control of the local business manager, applying systems engineering principles to develop ways for a business unit to reach the targets in its competitiveness achievement plan. It is task forces who have responsibility for the business redesign activities within the business units.

One of the most visible outcomes from this process has been widespread adoption of cellular manufacturing, sometimes using the Japanese techniques of just-in-time production with Kanban control. The problems of complexity caused by factory layouts organized on a process basis which have developed incrementally (which we discussed in chapter 2) are vividly illustrated by Lucas' experience. A member of a task force looking at ignition equipment manufacture within Lucas Electrical describes the manufacturing processes as they were before the redesign exercise:

> The components start life on the one side of the factory, visit the other side of the factory (twice) and then return back to the side they started from for a final process. This comes about because the floor is laid out on a process basis, so if the components have got to visit several of these processes the travel involved is enormous and in this case is three quarters of a mile ... You've got no control and no ownership of the parts. The inventory on the floor is enormous ... Not only have you got a problem with the work building up, but you don't necessarily know where it is going anyway. (BBC/OU 1986a)

Using systems engineering techniques, factories which have been laid out on a traditional process basis (for example with banks of lathes in one area, banks of milling machines in another and so on) are now being regrouped into cells, each with its own family of machines. A cell is conceived as a specific collection of resources (people, machines and support services) which are grouped together both organizationally and physically and which have clear and precise targets and objectives to meet. The cells are designed to be as self-contained as possible; techniques such as input/output analysis, process flowcharts (to plot information and material flows) and grouping techniques such as Pareto analysis and volume/ variety categories are used. In this way, workflows are dramatically simplified, and much clearer 'ownership' of parts established.

Implications for Work Organization

Turnbull (1986) has characterized the system of cellular production as a series of self-contained mini-factories within a factory. Cell performance is measured against a range of targets − output, quality, lead-time and cash targets. There is a simple structure within the cells; there is a cell leader, 'the father of the team', and below the leader a single level structure comprising manufacturers, manufacturing craftsmen and product assessors. Ultimately the aim is that these roles will be blended together to permit flexibility within the team. This in turn generates a substantial training and development requirement. As a member of a Lucas Electrical task force commented:

> We are aware that this is going to involve a lot of development of our existing labour force. The employees within these areas have to understand the business . . . For this sort of concept to work everyone must be part of the team. (BBC/OU 1986a)

The systems of just-in-time production which Lucas are also implementing place additional requirements both on production workers and the management structures which control and co-ordinate them. A Lucas Electrical task force leader:

> Because of the quality constraints demanded by Kanban, we have to give the right to the operator to shout 'Jidoka!' [Stop the line]. So if we find we have a reject or bad component we don't just keep making it. . . . This means that the management structure has to be able to respond to that − otherwise we'd be stopped for two weeks. (BBC/OU 1986a)

The reorganization of the manufacturing processes into production cells not only affects those directly involved with the production process itself. Personnel who have traditionally been based in centralized functional areas such as production engineering or quality control are placed in the cells under the control of a cell leader − moves that have not always been welcomed by those involved, as people who were once 'promoted' from the shopfloor are now being asked to return to it. Administrative systems are also undergoing the redesign exercise. What is being sought are:

> natural mixed groupings of people around common information flow routes in order to reduce the number of separate fragmented offices and the size of overhead support . . . In principle it should be possible to run a manufacturing product unit with only three mixed discipline office groups. (Parnaby 1987a)

The introduction of cellular production based on just-in-time principles has involved rigorous analyses of the degree of value added to products operation by operation. As far as possible non-value added activities have been eliminated.

In some cases these value-added analyses have revealed that it is more economical to buy in components rather than for them to be manufactured on site. Rationalizing the Group's activities has involved redundancies; the number of people employed in the UK by Lucas fell by approximately 8,000 between 1981 and 1986, a fall of 15 per cent (Lucas Industries Annual Report 1986).

In terms of changes on the shopfloor, there have been experiments with quality circles, though these have met with mixed results. The simplification of workflow and the 'responsible autonomy' which cellular manufacture based on output controls permits will ultimately lead to a flattening of the organizational structure within the business units via a reduction in the number of vertical levels required. Overlaid with these changes, Lucas' 1986 annual report declared the aim:

> To heighten awareness at business unit level of the actions needed to match and beat competitors. This decentralized market awareness and marketing ability has required changes in thinking, attitudes and habits — in other words, moulding a new, dynamic Lucas culture.

As Lucas are still in the process of making these changes it is not possible to make a definitive evaluation of their success, even if one could agree on criteria by which to evaluate such success. This is exacerbated by the highly decentralized nature of the organization — the adoption of Japanese methods appears to have been very successful in certain business units, less so in others. According to business criteria, some of the results obtained are shown in table 3.1.

Whilst accepting that there have been problems with the introduction of some of the new methods, among many people within the company there has been an enthusiastic response. In the view of a Lucas Electrical general manager:

> Most people involved can see the logic in what we're doing ... it's really simple, Japanese methodology is simple, they like it, they can understand it, and there's tremendous co-operation from the workforce. (BBC/OU 1986a)

Writing from a very different perspective, Turnbull (1986) argues that improvements in quality and productivity have been won at a cost to the Lucas workforce,

Table 3.1 Performance improvement at Lucas Industries

Business criteria	Automotive Electronics after 1 year	Automotive Electrical after 2 years
Stock reduction	£3m	80% WIP reduction
Stock turnover ratio	5 (was 4)	13 (was 7)
Manufacturing lead-time	10% of previous	20% of previous
Productivity	up 35%	up 25%
Reject level	20% of previous	50% of previous

Source: adapted from Parnaby (1987a)

and that the new production arrangements face a number of potential problems to overcome *vis à vis* the social relations of production. Turnbull has criticized Lucas' changes on the grounds that the new working methods represent work intensification, with little evidence of skill enhancement:

> The jobs are just the same as before, you just do more of 'em. And there's no big deal to assigning quality inspection to direct operators — you just stick the components under a feeler gauge several times a day to check things are going OK. (Senior shop steward, Lucas Electrical, quoted in Turnbull 1988, p. 12)

For Turnbull, one of the most significant elements of the shift to cellular manufacture is the implication for the social relations of production:

> The success of module production is dependent on a social organization of the production process intended to make workers feel 'obliged' to contribute to the economic performance of the enterprise and to identify with its competitive success. (Turnbull 1986)

Conclusions

At the time of writing (late 1987) Lucas are still very much in the middle of their programme of change. Consequently, it is difficult to untangle events at the company which are essentially 'management of change' issues from those which are indicative of the success or failure of Japanese techniques *per se* in the West. Three aspects of what Lucas are doing are of particular relevance to the question of Japanization. The first point is the way the company is utilizing specific aspects of Japanese practice as appropriate elements in a total business strategy. Secondly, as figure 3.1 illustrated, there are clear signs that Lucas are increasingly considering the 'fit' between manufacturing strategy and other aspects of corporate strategy, such as personnel practices and organizational design, supporting our 'strategic fit' argument presented in chapter 2. Thirdly, the changes at Lucas are attracting a great deal of attention from academics and practitioners alike, and the accounts of these changes demonstrate sharp divisions in views of Japanization. From a managerial or business-efficiency perspective, Japanese techniques are seen as welcome means of restoring competitiveness and hence ensuring business survival and success. On the other hand, writers such as Turnbull (1986, 1988) view these changes in a highly critical way, on the grounds that they lead to an intensification of work and a greater concentration of power in the hands of capital. This division runs through the whole Japanization debate and we shall return to it many times in the course of the book.

The Rover Group

Rover (prior to 1986 Austin Rover and before that British Leyland) began collaboration with Japanese car manufacturer Honda in the late 1970s, and between then and now has attempted to make fundamental changes to its production and personnel practices. While most of the changes would have been sought regardless of the collaboration — certainly Rover's major competitors in the UK have attempted the establishment of similar practices — Rover have doubtless benefited from ideas from Honda. Many of the new practices, certainly, are very similar to those already existing in Japan, and the whole British car industry has been attempting to emulate certain Japanese practices with varying degrees of success. The changes have been sought in response to damaging competition from car manufacturers, both at home and abroad. In 1981 for example, the company's output was 347,500 vehicles, scarcely half its 1976 figure of 688,000 vehicles (*Financial Times* 31 March 1982). This drop in output, incidentally, was largely responsible for the trouble that Lucas Industries' automotive operations found themselves in in the early 1980s.

This case study draws heavily on the detailed work of Smith (1988) and Marsden et al. (1985), and describes changes in supplier relations, the production process and working practices, and personnel management and industrial relations. The role of wider contextual factors in the process of change at Rover is also explored.

Production and Working Practices

During the 1980s Vauxhall, Talbot, Ford and British Leyland all attempted to introduce flexible working practices as part of attempts to improve efficiency of operations. On the production line this meant an attempt to blur distinctions between craft and assembly workers, and in particular to give assemblers responsibilities for machine maintenance and inspection. Marsden et al. claim British Leyland went further than the others in breaking down demarcations. This was associated with the implementation of the *Blue Newspaper* in April 1980, which stated that:

> Any employee may be called upon to work in any part of his employing plant and/or to carry out any grade or category of work within the limits of his abilities and experience, with training if necessary.

This replaced 'a mass of restrictive provisions on individual and gang mobility contained in plant level direct and indirect agreements' (Marsden et al. 1985, p. 100), and was associated with a job evaluation scheme condensing around 500 job classifications into five company-wide grades for hourly paid employees. Despite some union resistance, and indeed a refusal to accept the status of the *Blue Newspaper*, implementation of new working practices was achieved in most British Leyland plants by 1983. Marsden et al. report further that by 1985 all operators at all British Leyland plants were accepting some responsibility for quality by 'signing off' their work after self-inspection, a practice which was rejected by the unions at Ford around the same time during their *After Japan* campaign.

Most significantly, the changes at British Leyland involved the creation of a team organization, in which the foreman became the 'linchpin' with responsibility for output within his 'zone', and all resources necessary for production within the zone came under the foreman. With little demarcation between the jobs of individual members, rotation of some tasks, and the delegation of some responsibilities for maintenance and quality control to the teams, this was a significant break from past production practices characterized by task fragmentation and specialization of 'support' functions. Further, within the teams progression from materials handler to operator to quality controller to maintenance would be possible. Figure 3.2 shows the composition of production teams at British Leyland.

Similar changes have been attempted by other car companies. For example, Ford has recently renewed its own attempts to introduce new working practices, announcing at the end of 1987 its intention to implement an 'area foreman' plan (*Financial Times* 6 November 1987). The area foreman, as at Rover, is to be a shopfloor 'mini-manager' with wide responsibilities for different aspects of production, including assembly, maintenance, inspection, materials handling and janitorial functions. Many of these have traditionally been controlled by specialist foremen, who are likely to find their authority, if not jobs, under threat. Beneath the area foremen will be group leaders who manage multiskilled semi-autonomous production teams.

If successful, the changes will represent a radical shift away from classic Ford production line principles. At the same time, Ford have asked their unions to commit themselves to a 'quality improvement manifesto', backed up by 'quality

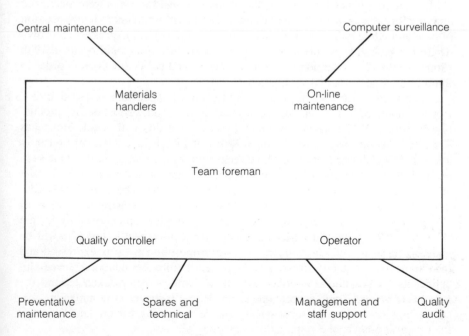

Figure 3.2   Composition of production teams at British Leyland
Source: Willman and Winch (1985)

discussion groups', and are looking to harmonize blue and white collar employment conditions and the introduction of a training programme aimed at 'enhancing job security'.

Personnel Management and Industrial Relations

The introduction of new working practices was achieved after the end of a period of 'participation' under Sir Don Ryder and the reassertion of managerial prerogatives under Sir Michael Edwardes. Interestingly, team working had been discussed in various joint committees in the Ryder years (1975–7), but was implemented only after the removal of 'mutuality' (where managers had to agree changes in advance of implementation of new practices with shop stewards) in 1980 (Marsden et al. 1985). The 1980s initiatives in work organization appear to have been related unambiguously to an attempt to break down restrictive practices and improve efficiency – they involved neither the participation nor the concern with quality of working life and job design characteristic of the Ryder years, although in some respects the results were similar.

Having reasserted managerial prerogatives and lessened the strength of shop steward organization in its plants, partly by reducing the number of full-time shop stewards from twenty to six in the first few years of the 1980s, the company took various steps in a Japanese direction which might be seen to support the changes in production and working practices.

Moves to harmonize pay and conditions of hourly-paid workers were mentioned above. More recently, the company announced its commitment to harmonization of blue and white collar workers, and Rover's unions have expressed their own desire for such change. It seems likely that harmonization could occur in 1988 (Smith 1988). The intention is to remove 'them and us' distinctions in order to improve co-operation and motivation.

In line with flexible work practices and enhanced shopfloor responsibilities, Rover announced in 1987 an intention to recruit more educated labour for production line jobs. While we do not know exactly what this will entail, Smith has described the various means by which Rover at Longbridge have very recently attempted to change the culture of the factory in a Japanese direction. One such means is the introduction of an induction programme for new recruits, and about 700 new recruits passed through the course in early 1987. The induction foundation course lasts one week, consisting of a series of demonstrations, practical exercises, videos, tours and so on. As well as providing an opportunity for the new recruit to be introduced by his supervisor to the specific tasks he will be undertaking at Rover, the company's history and philosophy is expressed and the importance of quality stressed. Immediately before the induction, successful applicants have spent a Saturday with their families being taken around the Longbridge plant. Smith reports one senior Rover manager as commenting that 'we are not just looking for manual skills and dexterity. We want to know whether their aspirations are the same as the company's'.

Of course, in itself the induction programme is unlikely to be sufficient to create the shared aspirations sought by Rover, but from early 1986 Rover introduced 'zone briefings' and 'zone circles', to encourage employee involvement and to establish direct communication channels. These developments are in line with the increased use of consultation and direct communication in all the major car firms in Britain in the 1980s.

Zone briefings are a mechanism for direct communication with the workforce, and involve stopping the production line whilst the team foreman provides information on targets, output, performance and related matters. The briefings include plant and company-wide matters as well as matters specific to the zone. Smith reports that within a year enthusiasm for zone briefings had considerably waned, many operators, and indeed foremen, seeing them as a waste of time, and welcoming them only insofar as they provided a break from production. The most common complaint related to Smith appeared to be that senior managers tended not to respond, or respond negatively, to questions and suggestions from workers.

Lack of enthusiasm for zone circles − Rover's version of quality circles − is similarly related by Smith. This is despite serious efforts at success including the training of around 100 supervisors in a three-day leaders' training course. Twenty-seven circles, each made up of small numbers of volunteers within production zones and headed by zone supervisors, had been established between February 1986 and May 1987, but these are small numbers out of around 10,000 shopfloor workers at Longbridge. In 1987 management at Rover continued to push zone circles and to train supervisors in circle leadership skills. The main reason for the failure of zone circles according to supervisors interviewed by Smith is the opposition of the unions to an institution which could threaten the role of the shop steward — stewards were reported as 'getting at' potentially successful circles. Other supervisors reported simple apathy and mistrust, and at least one suggested a lack of commitment from management.

Marsden et al. reported that formal union responses to quality circles and other briefing methods have been negative in the other automobile manufacturers in the early 1980s − the successes with quality circles at Jaguar (which are discussed in the next chapter) being an exception. As at Rover, the opposition of manual unions has been based on the assumption that the schemes are deliberate attempts to bypass established trade union channels and thereby weaken union strength.

Supplier Relations

At the same time as changes were made to the production system and working practices, as part of the pursuit of 'right first time' and total quality philosophies, British Leyland attempted to tighten control over suppliers − including influence over their industrial relations. British Leyland insisted that any wage rises in supplier companies should not be passed on to British Leyland in the form of higher component prices (Marsden et al. 1985). By the mid-1980s Austin Rover, in common with their competitors, were seeking to move towards just-in-time supplies, having announced intentions to reduce supplies-in-hand from ten days to two days and to take deliveries of high value components up to four times a day (Smith 1988).

In order to achieve such aims, Rover announced in 1987 its intention to give 'preferred supplier status' to a small number of component suppliers on long-term contracts. Suppliers expressed concern about the future of business with the Rover—Honda ventures, but Rover replied that short-term contracts would be replaced by 'business in perpetuity' to selected companies (*Financial Times* 30 March 1987).

Contextual Factors

Rover have in some respects been at the forefront of the introduction of the 'Japanization' of the car industry, at least as far as work organization is concerned. However, while they appear to have had success in introducing new work practices and production methods, and certainly in making improvements in quality and efficiency, they still have a long way to go. This is the case with regard to the creation of a stable and reliable supplier network necessary for the operation of a fully functioning just-in-time system of production, though important measures are currently under way in this regard. Perhaps more problematic for Rover is the creation of a new company culture accepting of change and willing to give commitment to the institutions aimed at worker involvement. The fact that unions — despite the removal of 'mutuality' in 1980 — have been able to impede the zone circle initiative indicates their continuing independent influence and a failure on the part of the company to bond workers to the company above all else and to give them aspirations identical to those of the company.

Smith comments that the changes introduced by Rover have been accepted by the workforce not because of the security they are given by the company, as may be the case in Japanese companies, but because of the *insecurity* they faced under recent political and economic circumstances. This might indicate a compliance rather than a commitment on the part of the workforce. Today, Rover's future hangs in the balance, there being considerable uncertainty as to how much more deeply Honda might become involved in the venture, whether Rover might be privatized, and indeed whether Rover will continue to exist in its present form.

In these circumstances workers are less likely to give their long-term loyalty to the company, a loyalty which is sought by Rover as part of its package of change. And it seems that Rover is not alone among Britain's car companies in this regard — what one Ford spokesman called 'the real breakthrough in attitudes' (quoted in Marsden et al. 1985, p. 112) has not yet occurred. Under present circumstances Rover is not in a position to offer long-term employment and premium pay and conditions to a core workforce — the 'political and cultural supports' for loyalty are simply not there. Smith relates the comment of one worker during Rover's induction programme, which brought murmurs of assent, which captures the essence of the limitations to cultural change at Rover: 'my mortgage is with the Halifax, not the Rover group'.

Southern Components

Southern Components is a small specialist light engineering company, based in Southern England. The company manufactures a range of components for the motor industry. Established in the mid 1970s, by 1987 Southern Components employed approximately 100 people. The company's major customers are vehicle manufacturers and other component manufacturers who in turn supply the vehicle manufacturers; output goes to both these sets of customers in approximately equal proportions. The company does not recognize a union, although about 20 per cent of the workforce are members of the Transport and General Workers Union. There are no restrictions on working practices — skill levels are the only constraint on flexible working. There is a Works Committee, elected by compulsory voting. The majority of jobs in the factory are semiskilled; turnover is about £2 million per annum.

The pressures for change which Southern Components are experiencing originate primarily from the changing demands placed on them by their major customers, particularly the vehicle assemblers. The most significant changes are reductions in the number of suppliers to the major vehicle manufacturers; preferred supplier status; improved quality of supplies and just-in-time deliveries.

Reductions in Numbers of Suppliers

All the vehicle assemblers are in the process of reducing the number of their suppliers. There are two main motives behind this: to reduce the amount of administration generated by purchasing activities and to enable closer relationships to develop between suppliers and purchasers. Part of this drive comes from a wish on the part of the major assemblers to push more responsibility for components out to the subcontractors; in the words of Southern Components' managing director:

> In many cases customers encourage — demand — major changes in suppliers' procedures and major investment in new techniques and hardware, an example being electronic data communication. If the volume of business they place with you isn't large then as a supplier you are not likely to wish to tailor your operations to their needs unless the ideas make sense in their own right . . . and many of them do *not* make sense other than for a specific customer.

Preferred Supplier Status

'Preferred supplier status' is a term given to a special relationship between a customer and a supplier, bestowed on the latter by the former. A supplier who is granted preferred supplier status receives a commitment for a particular volume of output or for a particular period of time from their customer. This status also involves customer—supplier co-operation on issues concerning quality systems and product development, and confers a degree of stability on the relationship. In return for this stability, the supplier has to make a commitment to maintain price, which is generally negotiated annually. In practice there is little movement between suppliers on the grounds of price; quality or delivery problems are more likely to lead an assembler to change suppliers. For companies such as Southern Components, preferred supplier status has changed the rules of the game in terms of winning contracts. Prior to preferred supplier status contracts were awarded on the basis of price, after which product development, tooling and so on would take place. This often involved substantial investment by the customer in equipment and tooling to be used on the supplier's premises. Such investment then constrained the customer's ability to withdraw, giving the supplier scope to bump up the price without losing the business. As a supplier's books are open to the assembler under preferred supplier status, the assembler is substantially protected against the supplier taking advantage of this situation. Under this arrangement the supplier is protected against externally generated increases in costs — for example increases in material costs — but not internally generated increases in costs.

There are also advantages in this arrangement for the suppliers. For Southern Components the benefits of involvement in product development were particularly marked. As suppliers typically better understand their own manufacturing processes than do the designers employed by their customers, participation in the design and development process can create substantial savings in the manufacturing costs of the component — Southern Components estimate that it is not unusual for components designed with supplier participation to cost 75 per cent of equivalents designed without supplier participation.

Quality Systems

It is in matters concerning quality assurance and especially quality systems that Southern Components are experiencing some of the most marked and dramatic changes. The company's major customers are demanding practices such as self-certification of product quality and stringent quality systems, including the use of practices such as statistical process control. A standard definition of a quality system is those 'organized procedures and methods of implementation to ensure the capability of the organization to meet quality requirements' (BS 5750, 1979). For Southern Components, it is quality systems:

> where they (the assemblers) most penetrate. In many ways this has been positive and constructive but sometimes it leads to quite bizarre situations where the quality assurance systems of, say Ford and Rover are at variance, and therefore any attempt to incorporate the preferences of one leads to the immediate rejection of the system by the other.

The demand that the company guarantees its products to be defect free may have been easy for its customers to make, but it was less straightforward to implement. In the words of the managing director, Southern Components was suddenly required to be 'brilliant and accept no failures'. However, the existing products and designs made this difficult to accomplish:

> Faced with a zero defect quality goal and trying hard to achieve it, we found we were trying to squeeze excellence out of poorly designed products. The only way to protect ourselves from being squeezed between the customers' poor designs and their demands for a perfect product was to deliberately attack the design processes and inform the customers that better design could be achieved if suppliers were more involved.

One element in the changes in quality systems which the car companies —

particularly Ford — pushed through at Southern Components was
process control, the principles of which were described in chapter 1. The
has enjoyed substantial benefits from the use of statistical process control,
ing it as 'the best Japanese import'. The use of these techniques led to a co
decision to upgrade the company's recruitment standards in order to ensure that
personnel were capable of using them. According to the managing director, the
new requirements, which cannot always be met because of the tight labour market
in the region in which the company is based, rule out about 60 per cent of school-
leavers, the company's main recruits. There was some resistance on the part of
the existing staff to the new techniques, 'mainly due to a lack of confidence with
sums'.

Just-in-time Supply

The final major change which Southern Components has undergone concerns just-
in-time manufacture and delivery of products to its customers, and it is this
development that has caused the company the most difficulty. Ford was the first
company to push for just-in-time deliveries; 'their demands became more
demanding' in 1984. Other assemblers do not have such a deliberate policy of
just-in-time delivery, but as they have pursued policies of stock reduction and
now do not hold more than two or three days worth of stock, just-in-time happens
by default. Although this idea may be satisfactory in principle, in practice it is
not without its problems:

> JIT call off from customers is a fine concept but as a supplier it means that
> your lead time in response to changes in demand has got to be quicker
> than that required by the customer. This is very difficult to achieve.
> Customers are demanding almost immediate changes in supply —
> component to component and quantity to quantity.

In line with the traditional approach in British mechanical engineering, past
policy has been to make maximum use of machinery and to let work in progress
stocks take up variations in manufacturing efficiency. As JIT requires the creation
of a surplus stock of machinery with perfectly flexible labour and very low set-
up times (so that manufacturing can be turned on at a moment's notice), a radical
re-orientation from the traditional approach has been required:

> If you read the literature appearing in the management magazines there is
> a gradual recognition that JIT often works by swapping the 'waste' of excess
> stocks for the 'waste' of excess machine capacity.

Successful JIT production is obviously dependent on having the raw material
available. However, Southern Components have found that it can be very difficult to pass JIT up the line to its own suppliers. The company has a weak supply
base, with few suppliers and long lead-times for changes in orders — typically
8–10 weeks, sometimes as long as 14 weeks. Thus it is only when demand is
sufficiently stable for it to be predictable that JIT can be passed on successfully.
In the automotive industry the ultimate supplier is often the British Steel
Corporation which does not, or cannot, apply JIT principles:

A supplier like Southern Components is therefore piggy-in-the-middle, squeezed between giant customers at one end and monopoly suppliers at the other.

Because of this situation, many suppliers are finding that their optimum response is to increase the quantities of stock that they themselves are holding. Where this is occurring, JIT is essentially achieved by the transference of stockholding from customer to supplier. One manifestation of this is the fact that Rover and Jaguar have set up warehouses near their factories at Oxford and Coventry respectively, into which suppliers are required to ship goods. The warehousing costs are met entirely by suppliers and the customers can call off supplies on a just-in-time basis, whilst ensuring stability of supply. Southern Components again:

> JIT has been used as a myth on which to hang the transfer of the responsibility for stockholding to another point in the supply chain — anywhere so long as it does not cost the assemblers money.

Summarizing recent events and trends, Southern Components' view of contemporary changes in manufacturing was of a wave of innovation in the last few years, a wave which had risen quickly, and had not yet broken: 'Everything is coming suddenly: JIT, quality requirements. Electronic data communication will be next.'

Nissan Motor Manufacturing (UK)

Nissan's new plant in Sunderland is especially important in our discussion of Japanization as it represents the biggest commitment of a Japanese company in the UK to date. It is also of interest because unlike Rover (also described in this chapter) and other car manufacturers already established in Britain, Nissan have started from scratch, with no traditions of trade union organization or established shopfloor custom and practice, and have hence been able to experiment with a system of their choosing from the beginning. Nissan may, then, represent a pointer for the future.

With extensive media coverage Mrs Thatcher opened the Nissan plant formally in September 1986. The £350 million investment in an area of industrial decay and high unemployment was welcomed with few murmurs of dissent: around 3,000 manufacturing jobs in a prestige company with a long-term commitment were to be created by 1991. The Washington New Town Development Corporation had attracted the company to the North East in the face of competition from many other local authorities across Britain. In December 1987 Nissan announced plans to produce, on the same site, a high volume small hatchback car in addition to the Bluebird which was already being produced. The output target was doubled to 200,000 cars per year by 1992, with an additional 1,400 jobs to be created. The total investment in Sunderland, now to be the largest of any Japanese company in Europe, will be over £600 million (*Financial Times* 15 December 1987).

This case study draws heavily on an article by Crowther and Garrahan (1988) who refer to Nissan as 'the most complete example of Japanization in Britain' and on *The Road to Nissan* (1987) by Peter Wickens, Nissan's Director of Personnel. The case study examines developments at the Nissan plant under three categories: production and working practices; personnel practices and industrial relations, and supplier relations. It then comments on the wider implications of Nissan setting up production in the UK.

Production and Working Practices

Wickens (1985, 1987) identifies a Japanese 'tripod' of working practices which Nissan intended to introduce to the UK — teamwork, quality consciousness and flexibility. Supervisors, as work team leaders, are central in the production process having, according to Wickens, 'responsibility for everything that happens in their area', almost, he goes on, 'a return to the old-style foreman before the specialists took away and diminished many of his tasks'. Job flexibility and the delegation of responsibility for inspection and minor maintenance are made feasible with only two job titles for manual workers, with no grade numbers and no job specifications. Manual workers are classified simply as 'manufacturing staff' or 'manufacturing technicians'. There are daily work area meetings at the beginning of each shift. The content of these meetings frequently concerns quality issues, but matters such as schedules, work distribution, training and social events are also raised. Wickens (1987) reports that most of the discussion concerns matters of relevance to the team's daily work, and only occasionally is there 'a great message from on high'.

Work at Nissan is intense. On its application forms the company states:

All applicants should carefully consider the following points:
The pace of work will be dictated by a moving production line and will be very demanding.
Work assignments will be carefully defined and will be repetitive.
Protective clothing will be necessary for some jobs.
You may be moved on to a new operation or transferred into a different department at very short notice.
(Wickens 1987, p. 176)

The flexibility demanded by the company extends to working hours — Crowther and Garrahan (1988) report that in 1987 Nissan was working a 47 hour production week, of which eight hours was compulsory overtime. The intensity appears to have been too much for some of Nissan's recruits, who were given widespread media attention in May 1987. *The Daily Telegraph* (6 May 1987), for instance, listed the following shopfloor complaints, some of them made anonymously for 'fear of victimization': production lines move so fast men have to work unpaid before shifts begin and during breaks to fulfil targets; pay is stopped when men are off sick because supervisors do not believe them; overtime is imposed with minimal notice. The divisional organizer of the single union, the AEU, described a 'certain disillusion' among some of the workforce and said he hoped the reports would drive workers to join his union. A Nissan spokesman said 'In my own experience I have never seen anything but people who are dedicated to their work.'

Nissan responded quickly to such reports, which included workers being interviewed on TV. The local *Evening Chronicle* (6 May 1987), for instance, reported a Nissan spokesman as saying that work in the car industry can be 'fast, competitive and tough', but that Nissan's lines moved slower than in other car factories because of quality considerations. It was further argued that the company's working practices, including overtime at short notice, were made plain to all potential employees during the selection process. In subsequent comments Nissan stated that it had cut absenteeism to 3 per cent and labour turnover stood at around 4 per cent — both remarkably low figures for the UK motor industry (*Financial Times* 8 May 1987; 18 June 1987). And at the time of the 1987 TUC conference where the AEU—Nissan single union deal was on the agenda, Nissan made a lengthy statement claiming it had used the best of Japanese and British strengths to create a 'harmonious and productive working environment' (*Guardian* 8 September 1987).

Personnel Practices and Industrial Relations

Wickens (1985) argues that Nissan's success depends on recruiting, training and motivating people at all levels in the company with a commitment to quality. The selection process is described as 'tough', and Nissan seek employees willing to be flexible, capable of teamwork, and committed to quality. Bassett (1986, p. 151) states that 'Nissan could winnow out those applicants who possessed the quality it wanted — a positive, constructive attitude towards the company, reducing the risk of conflict from selection onwards'. Certainly Nissan can be choosy: male unemployment in the area is around 30 per cent. The application forms for the first manual jobs were distributed through job centres — approximately 20,000 of them were requested in response to the company's advertising. These application forms totalled seven sides; the fact that this would probably put off the less enthusiastic was seen as an advantage. About 11,500 application forms were returned completed, a response rate of 57.5 per cent. The applicants were initially narrowed down to 1,900, largely on the basis of their answers to a simple questionnaire included in the application form. This number was further reduced through a series of aptitude, numerical, fluency and mechanical comprehension tests, reducing the number of candidates to 1,100. The next stage consisted of a series of tests of practical skills.

> At all times we were looking for their attitude and approach to problems, and this was further reinforced by a general discussion involving candidates and supervisors. (Wickens 1987, p. 178)

At this stage a total of 500 jobs were on offer (*Guardian* 8 September 1987).

The company takes on some workers on five month fixed term contracts to enable the company to meet peak demands. The contract includes one month's training, and temporaries are paid at the same rate as full-timers. The best performers are selected to join the full-time workforce. The use of temporary workers at Nissan for the assembly of cars, which gives more security for the core workforce and contributes further to flexibility, is the first time this practice has been used in the UK motor industry since the 1940s (*Financial Times* 16 February 1987).

As already indicated, the work team is an important mechanism of motivation, and by implication control, at Nissan. Without detailed evidence it is difficult to assess its success though Nissan's personnel director has described how some work sections, at the initiative of workers, make public displays of attendance lists — absent workers find their names on the list. He further comments:

> Sometimes they come up with things like that, but we don't go around saying everybody has got to do it. . . . The whole philosophy is to try to create the atmosphere where that sort of thing is possible, but not to insist on it. (*Financial Times* 19 August 1987)

An equally important communication channel at Nissan is the Company Council. Representatives of all groups of employees — manual and non-manual — sit on this body, which has three main roles. These roles are a consultative forum, as the final decision-making body in the in-house grievance procedure, and in sessions entirely separate from its usual (quarterly) meetings, the negotiation of pay and conditions. Such agreements are ratified by the full-time AEU official overseeing the negotiations (Wickens 1987). The council's chairman and secretary are appointed managers, and workforce representatives are elected from different sections of the plant. The company has a veto over who can stand as representative on the Company Council (Crowther and Garrahan 1988).

McFadden and Towler (1987) have criticized the Nissan consultation system on the grounds that it weakens trade union power and influence: daily work area meetings led by the team foreman eliminate the traditional role of the shop steward as conveyer of information to the locality; and the company council, made up of members who do not have to belong to a trade union, 'has the effect of portraying the trade unions as trouble makers when they raise valid and legitimate issues with the company'. Figures ranging from 10 per cent to 25 per cent have been cited regarding union membership at Nissan.

The single union agreement signed between Nissan and the AEU in 1985 — prior to production beginning — does not forbid strikes, but it does make them unlikely and is in most respects similar to other single union deals signed by Japanese and Japanizing companies in the 1980s, discussed in detail in chapters 5 and 6. Specifically, a company council is the primary forum for collective bargaining — the union only becomes involved at later stages in the case of failure to reach agreement — and the agreement stipulates union support of productivity goals and flexible working practices (Crowther and Garrahan 1988). Wickens (1985) argues that the agreement 'owes more to the work of British and American companies than to agreements reached between Nissan and the Japan Auto Workers' Union'. Its effect, nonetheless, is to reduce the likelihood of industrial action and therefore provide the industrial relations stability necessary for a just-in-time system of production. Further, the company council does have similarities with Japanese company unions.

Crowther and Garrahan (1988, p. 56) make the following comments on the Nissan—AEU agreement:

> There are a number of reasons why Nissan decided upon this option; the prospect of creating a company union was not seen as being realistic in a region dominated by national unions; to be non-union would have the effect of uniting all unions against Nissan. . . . By offering the carrot of exclusive recruitment rights to a single union, but not stipulating in advance which union, Nissan split them through competition and ensured agreement on its own terms.

Nissan's view of the union situation is rather different from the one expressed above. The personnel director describes the process of union recognition as follows:

> The Nissan decision to recognize the AEU came not from any assessment of the political tendencies of the unions, their numerical strength in the region or who would give us the best deal, but from our judgement as to which union our employees were likely to join . . . A number of commentators have suggested other motives, laying particular evidence on the supposed national moderation of the AEU as opposed to the TGWU. But all such tendencies are transitory and to base a decision on such a factor would lead us down the wrong path. There simply was no ulterior motive in the Nissan decision. (Wickens 1987, p. 137)

Industrial relations at Nissan and other Japanese and Japanizing companies will be taken up again in a later chapter. However, in discussing supplier relations we shall see how Nissan's influence over industrial relations may go beyond the confines of its own plant.

Supplier Relations

Sunderland Borough Council parcelled off an area of land three times the size needed for Nissan's own factory, giving Nissan 'unfettered control over its immediate production environment'. Nissan has since began to attract to this site subcontractors who are entering long-term trading relationships with the company — Ikeda Hoover being one of the first to be attracted to supply seat and head liners. Being in close physical proximity, of course, means deliveries can be made 'just-in-time' for Nissan's production needs. This is one sign that Nissan intends to develop its supplier relations in a similar manner to those it enjoys in Japan. Another is that Nissan has taken an 80 per cent equity shareholding in a newly-formed joint company with Yamatu Kogyo Ltd. The company will locate in Sunderland and supply small body pressings. This shareholding of 80 per cent is, of course, an extreme case — Nissan's policy is reported as being to gain 20 per cent holdings in its supply companies, this being considered sufficient to gain some financial leverage. Crowther and Garrahan (1988) describe this as a 'spatially concentrated production process', and suggest that such spatial concentration is a key element of Japanization. This idea is consistent with our argument in chapter 2, as it represents one aspect of heightened dependency relations between organizations and their suppliers.

According to McFadden and Towler (1987) Nissan's policy is to keep stock levels to seven hours of production needs, and to attract 'trading partners' capable of delivering components every two hours. Further, a heavy reliance on Nissan is preferred, as is a 20 per cent Nissan stake in the supplying company. The deputy managing director of Nissan UK has added that British suppliers should adopt the policy of 'negative pricing' — reducing sale prices by continually raising productivity by double digit figures every year; he added that such a culture may take several years to take root (*Financial Times* 8 May 1987).

Gaining a long-term trading partnership with Nissan is not easy. Nissan looks in detail at the supplier's cost structure, quality control procedures, material stocks and purchasing policies. In addition, industrial relations, work practices, trade union structure and strike record are examined. McFadden and Towler comment that this means many workers in supplier companies could be subject to the same type of industrial practices as exist at the Nissan plant itself.

Wider Considerations

As well as having a 'knock-on' effect through the British components sector, Nissan are clearly providing a lead for the rest of the British car industry, which is rapidly attempting to adopt many of the above practices and often justifying them on the grounds of competition from Nissan. As we described in the case of Rover, British manufacturers have been attempting changes along the same lines for the past several years, but the pressures for change are now more explicit and more immediate. Occasionally existing car manufacturers have voiced fears of Nissan swamping the UK market, but overall Nissan have received wide public support, particularly insofar as they are generating jobs in an unemployment blackspot. Crowther and Garrahan (1988) point out, however, that Nissan has been a recipient as well as provider of public goods — they have received free media exposure (mostly good news) and free public relations ('Far East Rescues North East' was a typical headline) as well as around £120 million of regional aid and selective financial assistance.

As readers may have observed both in this case and in the case of Lucas Industries, two distinct and sharply contrasting perspectives on Japanization are apparent — one which is generally positive about the process, the other which is critical. The premises from which this divergence of views arises raise important issues about the adoption of Japanese-style practices in the UK, and we shall return to these later in the book.

Komatsu (UK)

The Japanese firm of Komatsu was founded in 1921 as a manufacturer of machine tools and mining equipment. Today it is the second largest manufacturer of earth moving and construction equipment in the world, the largest being Caterpillar. Komatsu (UK) was set up in Birtley, North East England in 1986, the fifth Komatsu manufacturing operation to be set up outside Japan. The company has set up other operations in Brazil (in 1975), Mexico (1976), Indonesia (1982) and the USA (1985). The forces behind this offshore investment have been a desire to be closer to markets, and hence more responsive to them. In the case of the European investment a further advantage is the avoidance of trade friction and the competitive disadvantages conferred by a strong yen (*Industrial Relations Review and Report* 5 May 1987).

Komatsu UK's operations were established in a factory which had been vacated by their major competitor, Caterpillar, in 1984. The company received a grant of 15 per cent of approved capital expenditure (*Industrial Relations Review and Report* 5 May 1987), conditional on the company undertaking to ensure 60 per cent local content in the final product. At the time of writing, in late 1987, the company employed 200 people; it is anticipated that this will rise to about 270. The company plans to produce 2,400 earthmoving vehicles per year at Birtley, for a sales area comprising Europe and North Africa. This case will consider Komatsu's activities and experiences in three distinct areas: the production process, personnel practices and industrial relations and supplier relations.

The Production Process
The average skill level of shopfloor workers is between semiskilled and skilled. Manufacturing practices include total quality control; voluntary quality circles are encouraged. There is a 'U' shaped manufacturing and assembly line, and an above average degree of automation (Gleave 1987).

Loyalty and commitment to the company were put to the test in the task of getting the production process under way and running smoothly. In the early days production workers were working seven days a week and the strain began to tell. A number voiced concerns that the company was asking too much of them – particularly in terms of expecting the company to come before family life. (Interestingly, in Japan the term 'My Homeism' is sometimes used to describe a weak orientation to the company.) Of course any company in a start-up situation is likely to make substantial demands on its workforce – hence the effect of Komatsu being Japanese is confounded with Komatsu also being a company setting up operations in a new location. One production worker commented:

> We realize that the company has got to succeed for everybody's good, but to what extent do you take it? Speaking for myself, my family comes first. Obviously without the company I wouldn't have a job, so I'll do my best, but I'll draw the line in certain areas. (BBC 1987)

One issue which caused problems was that of teabreaks. Initially, the company insisted that there be 'bell-to-bell' working, which for the production workers meant a four hour stint in the morning without a break until lunchtime. The afternoon also comprised a four hour block, again without a break. Workers are expected to come in early (and unpaid) for a team briefing before production commences. The emphasis on bell-to-bell working is regarded by some as the secret of Japan's success. As a production supervisor commented:

All that the British worker has got to do to work to the Japanese system is to work during the time he is paid . . . once the British worker has done that he has fulfilled the Japanese system. (BBC 1987)

The issue of teabreaks was raised at the Advisory Council, and was resolved by the installation of beverage machines adjacent to the production lines. However, an initially uncompromising position by the company caused some cynicism about the allegedly consensual nature of the Advisory Council's decision-making processes.

By mid-1987 one quality circle had been set up voluntarily by personnel in the paint shop. The circle met regularly for approximately an hour after production had finished for the day. The members were not paid extra for the time spent at these meetings.

Personnel Practices and Industrial Relations
Recruitment was handled largely by local job centres and the Professional and Executive Register. There were 3,000 applications for the first 70 production line jobs. An initial screening reduced these to 200, all of whom were under 35; few had any history of trade union activism. The applicants were put through a rigorous selection procedure, involving pencil and paper psychological tests. The company selected for the appropriate attitudes — particularly those supportive of teamwork and flexibility — more than for the basic skills or experience necessary for the production process.

The induction period for new recruits spans ten weeks, and begins with an initial half day programme. Thereafter, new recruits undergo five formal and five informal induction sessions. Some supervisors were sent to Japan for four weeks of specialist training. Everyone receives a copy of the company handbook on joining. This is a glossy ring-bound folder which is built up with professionally produced handouts as the employees move through their induction procedure. When complete, the handbook is over 75 pages long, and contains items such as background information on the company, company philosophy (particularly with respect to quality control), terms and conditions, details of the agreement with the recognized trade union and so on.

There is a comprehensive performance review and appraisal system, which covers everyone within the company. The Komatsu handbook states that:

The company's policy is to match individual development with that of the company . . . Komatsu UK's policy is to help staff develop their own careers in order to help the company grow.

The methods of performance analysis were devised by managers and supervisors in workshop sessions during February and March 1987. There are two elements to this system. Performance review is recorded on a standard 18 item form; the superior of the person being appraised makes a rating on each item. The breadth of the characteristics covered by this system is striking. Items include not only the more conventional ones such as job knowledge, quality of work, work rate and reliability, but also others such as flexibility, adaptability to change, determination, teamwork, personal contact skills and activities 'beyond the contract'. The second element in the system, that of appraisal, is completed jointly by the person being assessed and the reviewer and considers the former's strengths, weaknesses, future work preferences and development needs.

Initially, it was planned that the performance appraisals would be carried out quarterly, with merit pay adjustments twice a year — however six monthly reviews and annual merit pay adjustments were considered to be more realistic, and this system is currently operating, although the reviews may be reduced to once a year (*Industrial Relations Review and Report* 5 May 1987).

The AEU has sole negotiating rights at the site. Single union recognition was agreed before the set-up decision was announced officially at the end of December 1985. The company chose the AEU on the grounds that it was the most appropriate given the combination of engineering, technical and supervisory staff in the plant. The union represents all full-time staff up to and including supervisors. The fact that the AEU divisional organizer had experience in negotiating start-up deals in the North East — in particular with Nissan — is said to have given the AEU an advantage over the rival GMB union. Under the terms of the agreement all employees enjoy conditions of employment of the same status. This includes a common pension scheme, sick pay from the first day of illness, free medical cover and uniform. All employees are required to wear the same uniform (and perform morning exercises) to emphasize the single status nature of the company, a situation which sits uneasily for some of the managerial staff:

> I spent 20–30 years of people telling me that when you get promoted and when you move on you take the overalls off and put a white coat or a suit on. And for 20 years I dreamed about the day I would go to work with a tie on and polished shoes and a suit . . . that had to go out of the window here. (BBC 1987)

In the event of an industrial dispute which cannot be resolved internally, the agreement with the AEU permits reference to ACAS for conciliation; if the issue is still unresolved:

> Both parties may agree to refer the dispute to an independent arbitrator who will determine positively in favour of one side or the other . . . Both parties agree to accept the decision of the arbitrator. There will be no industrial action of any kind while an issue is in procedure or the subject of conciliation and arbitration. In the unlikely event of total exhaustion of the above procedure without resolution, no industrial action will be taken without a full, secret, audited ballot of all affected employees. (Komatsu/AEU agreement)

There is a comprehensive clause in the agreement concerning the use of manpower. The union accepts 'complete flexibility and mobility of employees' and that 'Changes in processes and practices will be introduced to increase competitiveness and that these will improve productivity and affect manning levels', and that 'Manning levels will be determined by the Company using appropriate industrial engineering and manpower planning techniques'. Union membership (which Komatsu agreed to encourage) stands at about 50 per cent of all those eligible for membership and at 70 per cent of those from the production areas.

Although the AEU has a presence at Komatsu and membership is encouraged by the company, the main institution for collective representation is the Advisory Council. This body consists of elected representatives from each area of the company (an area typically consisting of about 30 people), a president (normally the managing director), a secretary (appointed by and a member of management) and the union divisional organizer. The Komatsu handbook describes the role of the Advisory Council as follows:

> The Advisory Council is not a 'talking shop' without muscle, neither is it a traditional 'Works Council' where managers and employee representatives sit and glare at each other from entrenched positions. It exists to share information, pool ideas, represent staff and company interests and come to agreed conclusions. It cannot dictate to Komatsu UK what policy will be, but it can and will influence the company's future direction in the mutual interest of Komatsu UK and Komatsu UK employees.

An example of the operation of the Council is provided by the first annual pay review, which took place in March 1987. The council was presented with information on the company's performance in its first year, on movements in the cost of living and in earnings in comparable industries and on the basis of this information made a recommendation of a 5 per cent increase in basic pay to management. This was granted and so no real negotiations over pay took place (Gleave 1987).

Relations with Suppliers
In Japan, Komatsu sends its engineers into its suppliers to improve their production methods in order to get their costs (and hence prices) down. The detailed approach of the Japanese to negotiations with would-be suppliers led to some hard bargaining, as suppliers disagreed with Komatsu's estimates of appropriate costs. In the words of one potential supplier to Komatsu:

> We have to disagree with their estimates of how long it will take us to produce in our own factory, based on their experiences of how long it takes them in their factories in Japan. . . . It is making us turn our thinking inside out and upside down — we're looking at everything from new angles — trying to think in Japanese terms, really. (BBC 1987)

The process of the negotiations over contracts was also unfamiliar to Komatsu's would-be suppliers. One commented on the 'Japanese ability to go into minute detail and not make a decision until everything has been gone through in detail'. The manager of Curl Engineering, a medium size engineering company pursuing a contract to supply cab doors to Komatsu commented, 'Komatsu first turned up in February. It was six months before we got an indication that there might be an order. We had three or four meetings a week during that period.' With the contract awarded, this pattern continued. 'The Japanese tend to camp out on your doorstep. We've got English firms that we see once or twice a year . . . it's nothing for the Japanese to turn up two, three or four times a day' (BBC 1987).

Supplied parts are an obvious pressure point in this situation, as Komatsu have an obligation to meet the 60 per cent local content ruling. To achieve this whilst maintaining cost and quality targets has not been easy, and early production was dogged with problems with supplied parts being delivered late and not up to scratch in terms of quality.

Conclusions

From his study of Komatsu, Gleave (1987) concludes that in general Komatsu appear to have been quite successful in their first two years of UK operations. Labour turnover and absenteeism are low, and all major deadlines (such as reaching the 60 per cent local content level) have been met. Describing Komatsu's personnel practices Gleave notes the latitude which has been given to the UK personnel director in this area, and summarizes the system which has emerged as a 'unionized human resources system'. A comment from the personnel director himself provides a thought-provoking conclusion to the Komatsu story so far:

> This is not a case of just going and working for a foreign company. This is a case of assisting a foreign company to have a base in the UK which will in fact revolutionize the attitudes in British industry. If it doesn't then I don't believe we [the British] have an industrial future.

International Business Machines (IBM)

Although manufacturing methods based on total quality and just-in-time methods, and personnel systems which encourage company loyalty are characteristic of large Japanese corporations, we have already commented that many of the practices they use have their roots in Western ideas and experiments. In fact some Western organizations, atypical as they may be, are remarkably similar in many respects to their Japanese counterparts. One such company is IBM, the subject of this section.

IBM manufacture computer systems for a wide range of applications. In 1986 turnover was $150 billion, and the company employed 400,000 people throughout the world. Drawing largely on data collected by ourselves and Spiridion (1987) from IBM's Havant plant, this case will focus on IBM's personnel and industrial relations practices which support its total quality philosophy, just-in-time production systems and customer orientation. In order to facilitate comparison between IBM and large Japanese corporations their practices will be considered under the categories of manufacturing methods; employment contracts; selection, induction and training; payment and reward systems; consultation and communications; and industrial relations.

Manufacturing Methods

Ward (1987) reports that the IBM corporation set itself the goal of becoming *the* low cost producer in its sector in the 1980s. Continuous flow manufacture (CFM) was identified as a key means of achieving this goal. CFM is, to all intents and purposes, identical to just-in-time production. Although the basic strategy was formulated at corporate level, each plant had discretion to develop methods of implementing it to suit their particular circumstances. The Havant plant developed a set of ten techniques, revolving around eliminating waste, improving manufacturing flexibility (reducing lead-times) and more effective asset utilization. On the manufacturing side the techniques used to achieve this were reductions in work-in-progress, group technology (self-contained tasks), mixed-mode assembly and Kanban control. Related to these was a drive towards zero defects and a philosophy of management by sight − the latter assisted by the simpler workflow conferred by group technology and the reduction in inventories. To support these strategies greater multiskilling was demanded to contribute to line balancing, as was 'teamwork through co-operation' across the functional areas of the organization (Ward 1987). Finally, the development of closer supplier integration was embarked upon. Suppliers were viewed as extensions to the whole manufacturing process.

Employment Contracts

IBM has a full employment policy, and can boast that it has never had to lay off any worker from its UK plants which currently employ around 18,000 people. According to Mercer (1987, p. 22) this is achieved through a tight manning policy: '(IBM) largely resources, in manpower terms, to meet the troughs. The peaks are met by its employees working that much harder; sometimes very much harder'. The flexibility gained through devoting huge resources to training and multiskilling also contributes in this regard: 'Employment security is not . . . the same as job security. Jobs are constantly disappearing in IBM, and their holders are moved on, retrained, to new positions' (Mercer 1987, p. 192). Around 5 per cent of IBM's manpower is permanently committed to internal education, costing IBM around $600 million in direct costs in 1984 alone. Peach (1983) describes the beneficial outcome to IBM as follows:

> The result of this 'full employment' practice is to engender a feeling of security which in turn generates an acceptance of change. If one's livelihood is not threatened one is more likely to recognize the need for, and so speed, the acceptance of change which in a high technology industry is essential to survival and prosperity.

As in Japanese companies, the full employment policy is a moral rather than legal or contractual obligation. That IBM has met these obligations to date in the UK is made all the more remarkable by the fact that temporary workers are not employed, though some 'rings of defence' may be created by IBM's practice of subcontracting non-core operations wherever possible. In addition to providing lifetime employment, IBM pays favourable rates compared with other leading companies in the UK, and carefully monitors rates in other companies to ensure IBM stays ahead of the competition. This pay survey results in salary ranges and pay boundaries; pay for specific individuals is an individual matter, to be described shortly.

Selection, Induction and Training

IBM's policy is to select candidates of the highest intellectual calibre. IBM's wages and reputation allow it to be selective: in 1984 there were 1.3 million applicants worldwide for jobs with IBM. Perhaps overstating the case a little, Mercer (1987, p. 104) claims that 'IBM is able to, and often does, employ as "workers" people who would qualify as directors in many other organizations; and can afford to pay them as such'. Intellectual calibre is judged by educational performance, and also by IBM's own rigorous intelligence tests.

IBM also seek, according to an IBM personnel development manager, candidates likely to 'fit in' and work as a member of a team; their 'acceptability' to existing employees is an important consideration − candidates who will accept IBM's values are sought. Commenting on American 'excellent' companies, including IBM, Pascale (1984, p. 62) comments:

> The company subjects candidates for employment to a selection process so rigorous that it often seems designed to discourage individuals rather than encourage them to take the job. By grilling the applicant, telling him or her the bad side as well as the good, and making sure not to oversell, [excellent] companies prod the job applicant to take himself out of contention if he, who presumbly knows more about himself than any recruiter, thinks the organization won't fit his style and values.

In 1987 IBM was reported as using the Economic League − an organization which investigates political and trade union activities of individuals on behalf of companies for a fee − to screen potential employees, paying them £5,000 in October 1986. IBM admitted its relationship with the Economic League but said that it had brought it to an end. *The Financial Times* (7 July 1987) reported IBM as stating that the vetting procedure was dropped because its own pre-employment procedures were adequate, *not* because of adverse publicity. Another IBM spokesperson commented that 'I think it embarrassed us in the sense that the average employee was not aware that this sort of investigation was being carried out' (*Labour Research* August 1987, p. 18). (A recent (1988) World in Action programme reported Komatsu and the Rover group as also making use of the services of the Economic League.)

Once recruited, IBM employees all go through an induction process, the responsibility for which falls with the new employee's immediate superior, but which is guided by a formal induction checklist from central personnel. Within four weeks, superior and subordinate must sign and return the form which covers social introductions to colleagues, and so on, as well as activities relevant to job duties and company policies and practices. Socialization continues with initial training, when new recruits are introduced to the philosophies, traditions and history of the company.

Training continues throughout an employee's career due to IBM's emphasis on flexibility, multiskilling and internal promotion. Promotion to managerial status normally requires a minimum of four years' service, and typically can take up to ten years. This usually involves job rotation so that generalists rather than specialists are created, and a comprehensive training in interpersonal skills such as awareness, sensitivity, and appraisal and interview techniques. According to Spiridion (1987, p. 67):

> every manager must have absorbed IBM's strong corporate culture in order
> to put it to practical use in his dealings with his subordinates, and in order
> to communicate to his subordinates the values which it embodies.

Interpersonal skills are reinforced with special managerial training every year – in the case of the Havant plant this is for at least five days per year. In common with many Japanese companies, IBM has single status terms and conditions.

Payment and Reward Systems

Payment and rewards at IBM are not based on seniority considerations, and nor are they a collective matter. Rather, rewards are an individual affair geared to the one-to-one relationship between manager and subordinate. Pay and grading reviews occur every year in the Appraisal and Counselling (A&C) interview. This is a detailed, participatory review of the employee's performance against mutually agreed objectives, undertaken by the immediate superior and overseen by the superior's superior. Fierce competition for promotion occurs in IBM, but this is tempered by the need to display good interpersonal skills and an ability to work in teams. Any problems in these regards would be raised at the A&C. Good performance is also reinforced with symbolic rewards in the form of awards, plaques and trophies which are awarded to departments and work groups for public display.

Motivation is also encouraged by regular and often public feedback of performance. At IBM Havant for instance canteens and work areas have performance displays regarding output, quality, and so on in the form of graphs and charts. According to one manager, a reading of some of the displays in the work areas could lead to the ready identification of high (and low) performing individuals. Their use was spontaneously suggested by the workforce. As well as motivating individuals to perform better, public feedback encourages collective effort in the solution of problems. As Spiridion (1987, p. 26) puts it:

> Commitment is measured by one's willingness to contribute to a solution.
> . . . The fact that the problem originates in (say) another department absolves
> no-one of responsibility for contributing to the solution, provided they are
> aware of the requirement to do so. Since problems are likely to come to
> light anyway, because of the public way in which performance measures
> are communicated, it is probably in the best interest of those who are
> experiencing difficulties to request assistance 'spontaneously'.

A final comment worth making is that although Japanese organizations appear at first sight to be the opposite of IBM in terms of payment and reward because of the seniority element, many are now attempting to place more emphasis on merit and appraisal in pay determination. Public displays of performance are also commonly found in Japanese organizations.

Consultation and Communication

Informal and extensive face-to-face communication at IBM is encouraged with open plan offices and an 'open door' policy as well as the frequent use of team-work. As indicated already, the primary mechanism for direct communication with employees is the immediate manager of the work area, and this is backed up with a company newspaper, financial updates, notice boards, management information letters and monthly departmental meetings. In addition, a two yearly internal opinion survey, which has a response rate approaching 100 per cent, covers a whole range of matters with about 100 questions (Bassett 1986).

Upward communication is achieved, apart from the survey, through the immediate superior, who is expected always to be receptive to expressions of subordinate dissatisfaction and to solve the problem at that level. Managers failing to solve specific grievances are soon discovered, because of IBM's Open Door procedure. According to Tom Watson Junior, the previous chief executive of IBM, Open Door 'acts as a deterrent to the possible abuse of managerial power' (quoted in Mercer 1987, p. 197). Under the procedure employees may take their grievance, failing its satisfactory solution by the immediate superior, to as high a level as they feel necessary. Typically employees go to the superior's superior. The manager approached must document the complaint formally and investigate and respond quickly. If a decision is to take longer than two weeks the manager must tell the appellant why. The appellant, if still not satisfied with the outcome, may go higher and higher, theoretically to the chairman of IBM UK or even worldwide.

IBM has a second formal upward communication programme called Speak Up, whereby employees can submit written complaints and suggestions, this time anonymously if required, to the appropriate senior person. Anonymity is built in by the complaint going through the Communications Department which redirects the enquiry to the appropriate manager minus the name of the complainant. The Communications Co-ordinator then forwards the reply, which must be given in writing within ten days, to the complainant.

Spiridion (1987, p. 60) sums up the effect of these communication systems on management style as follows:

> They impose a considerable pressure upon managers to resolve their subordinates' dissatisfactions *before* they are formally expressed as griev-ances. In particular Open Door appeals against a manager can potentially reflect adversely on his performance record. Thus, it is in a manager's interest to act sufficiently flexibly to preserve harmonious relationships with his subordinates.

Industrial Relations

Open Door deals with many of the sorts of grievances handled by shop stewards in other companies. However, whereas the anonymous Speak Up procedure produces over 1,000 'speak ups' each year, Open Door produces far fewer — only 19 in IBM UK in 1984 for instance. Bassett (1986, p. 169) comments that: 'From the evidence of its opinion surveys, the company acknowledges that some employees neither understand, nor believe in, the system. In particular, they feel that its use may damage their career prospects.' Nonetheless, communication channels, together with careful selection procedures, a consultative management style, premium wage rates and individually negotiated pay, probably account in large part for the difficulties trade unions have had in attempting to recruit at IBM — gaining recognition at IBM has been described as the trade union equivalent of putting a man on the moon. In 1977 ACAS was asked by several unions to consider a claim for recognition at IBM's Greenock plant in Scotland: ACAS found that 99.2 per cent of respondents to their survey of IBM employees across the UK (95.2 per cent response rate) were not in unions, and that only 4.9 per cent (8.9 per cent at Greenock) wanted a union to bargain for them (Bassett 1986).

Unions have continued to be frustrated by IBM in the 1980s, seeing the company as a threat to trade unions not just in itself but also with regard to the example it sets to its suppliers and 'hi-tech' industry in general. Senior officials of the EETPU, for instance, claim IBM in Scotland has persuaded electronics companies there to become or remain non-union, establishing a virtual anti-union cartel.

IBM and its Environment

As we mentioned earlier, the Havant plant included supplier integration as part of its improvement programme. Relations between IBM and its suppliers do in many ways equate with the Japanese model, in that they are characterized by being generally long-term and high-trust in nature, as one would expect given a use of just-in-time supply, and the emphasis IBM places on the quality of its products. A couple of features are worthy of note; IBM has a policy of not taking more than 15 per cent of the total output of its suppliers in order to avoid any company having such a dependency on IBM that the cancellation of a contract would put them out of business. Perhaps to offset any casualness that this might encourage, IBM tends to offer good prices to its suppliers, and settles its accounts promptly — within 30 days.

A further aspect of IBM's relationships with its environment concerns its orientation to its customers. Certainly there is a strong customer-driven ethos about the company (described in Peters and Waterman 1982), but anecdotal evidence suggests that the picture is less clear cut than this. Because of its sheer size IBM traditionally enjoyed market dominance; perhaps, it could be argued, to the extent of exerting some control over its customers. One example of this is in the personal computer market. Although IBM entered the market relatively late, with a product that was regarded by many as not technically the most superior, its sheer muscle made the IBM machine the industry standard. This was exacerbated by IBM's special relationship with industrial and business computer users, many of which had an 'IBM only' policy. (IBM's advertising reflected this; one advertisement carried the caption 'No-one ever got fired for buying IBM'.) Certainly anecdotes collected whilst carrying out this research cast doubt on the image of IBM as simply the servant of its customers. Comments ranged from a damning 'Up-market bovver boys' (from a competitor in the office systems market), to intimations that breaking the IBM-only policy had permitted substantial improvements in computer-assisted production control (in a large British engineering company).

Although we do not wish to make any claims as to how far one can extrapolate from such anecdotes, they do suggest an added dimension to how organizations can manage their dependencies — by reaching out and influencing the market itself. In the USA IBM has been the target of a number of anti-trust (monopoly) actions, none of which have been successful.

IBM and Japanization

Philip Bassett (1986, p. 164) describes 'the IBM way' as 'exactly opposite to the Japanese method' on the grounds that their basic philosophy of 'respect for the individual' runs counter to the Japanese practice — including Japanese companies in the UK — of 'forging a corporate whole through collectivism'. Yet a comparison of IBM with Japanese companies in Japan (see chapter 1) or with Japanese companies in the UK (for example the cases of Nissan and Komatsu) reveal some remarkable similarities. There is not space in this book to explore the full implications of this coincidence, but it is worth remarking that IBM is a Western organization — albeit an exceptional one — which has for many years done many of the things for which the Japanese have become famous recently. Clearly then, Japanese management practices, or at least many of them, are not culturally-specific. The IBM case also qualifies, of course, our use of the concept of 'Japanization'.

Conclusions

The above case studies are intended to provide insights into and a 'feel' for the process of Japanization. They are, however, brief descriptions, and we recognize the limitations of case study evidence when arguing that a broad change is taking place — the companies described could be exceptional. The next two chapters, however, provide broader evidence of the adoption of Japanese-style practices. These are based on our own and other survey evidence, supported by case study and other material where appropriate. Chapter 4 presents a broad picture of what is happening in the 'emulators' — Western companies operating in Britain who are emulating Japanese-style practice. Chapter 5 examines the practices, policies and experiences of Japanese-owned manufacturing companies which have set up operations in Britain.

Chapter 4 on the 'emulators' is obviously of crucial importance to our thesis that a fundamental transformation is being attempted — after all if it is only Japanese companies investing in Britain who are using Japanese-style methods, then change could hardly be considered fundamental or widespread. That said, we suggest that the activities of Japanese companies are of serious import. This is in part because Japanese investment in the UK is growing rapidly in importance, and also because their activities heighten the visibility of Japanese practice to British companies, many of which point to investing Japanese companies as a direct threat to competitiveness and a model to be followed. It was not by accident that Ford's major initiative to improve their competitiveness was called their 'After Japan' campaign.

Turning attention to the emulators, in the introduction we argued that a crucial aspect of Japanization is the attempts of British companies to borrow from Japanese practices, albeit in some cases the received, rather than actual wisdom about such practices. There is plenty of anecdotal evidence to suggest that British companies are attempting to copy aspects of Japanese-style practice, and in this chapter we have presented three case studies which support this view. However, accounts such as these could be misleading and imply a breadth of change which simply does not exist. For this reason it was decided to conduct a simple survey of leading manufacturing companies in order to gain an impression of the scale of (in Ackroyd et al.'s terms) mediated Japanization.

All the companies in the 1986 *Times 1,000* index which were known to have manufacturing operations were approached and asked to complete a short questionnaire. The questionnaire covered background information on the companies, such as number of employees, date of establishment, number of sites in the UK and so on. In total, 375 companies were approached, of which 66 completed questionnaires. The operations of the participating companies are shown in table 3.2.

The companies varied in size from 300 employees up to 52,000, and from one manufacturing site up to 78 different sites. The majority (72 per cent) were unionized; of this 72 per cent, 6 per cent had single unions; the rest (66 per cent) had multiple unions. Approximately half the sample companies (48 per cent) were British owned, with a substantial proportion of the others (38 per cent) being American owned.

In the following chapter we explore the results of this survey and other evidence, much of it illustrative, in order to measure both the depth and breadth of the transformation in British manufacturing industry.

Table 3.2 Operations of survey companies

Operations	Number in sample	% of sample
Vehicles and automotive	5	8
Electronics, electrical	10	15
Engineering	9	13
Food, drink, tobacco	8	12
General manufacturing	16	24
Petrochemicals	11	17
Pharmaceuticals	7	11
	(66)	(100)

4

The Emulators

In this chapter we examine the experiences of British companies attempting to emulate aspects of Japanese practice. Unlike the previous chapter which sought to give a picture of contemporary changes for entire organizations, this chapter looks at the experiences of a number of companies with specific elements of Japanese practice; the chapter is thus *practice* based rather than company based. Throughout, our analysis is guided by the theoretical conclusion of chapter 2; namely, that Japanese-style industrial organization is characterized by high dependency relationships, and therefore requires effective strategies for handling such dependency.

One important problem should be borne in mind regarding this chapter. As we describe the often problematic experiences of companies implementing Japanese-style practices in Britain, we risk confounding the feasibility and likely impact of importing Japanese methods with 'resistance to change' or alternatively 'honeymoon' problems. The latter, of course, might be expected in *any* change process.

As we argued in the conclusion to chapter 2, there are good theoretical reasons for viewing the new manufacturing and personnel practices as a 'package' or 'socio-technical system'. Thus we reject totally any suggestion that the success of the major Japanese corporations can be simply assigned to any one set of practices, such as manufacturing methods, personnel practices or strategic marketing. What is critical is a good fit between the different elements of a business strategy and a set of wider supporting conditions. It is with this in mind that our analysis of the application of these practices in the UK considers both the relative successes and failures, and the effects that they have had throughout the organizations in which they have been implemented.

The results of our survey of manufacturing companies from the *Times 1,000* index (introduced at the end of chapter 3) form the basis of this chapter. A range of further material is introduced to support (or qualify) our evidence at appropriate points. We discuss the experiences of the emulators under the categories of manufacturing and working practices, personnel and industrial relations practices, and buyer–supplier relations.

Manufacturing and Working Practices

Six sets of production arrangements for which the Japanese are renowned were explored in our survey. We include work organization in this discussion – specifically the use of work teams, flexible working and quality circles – due to their important roles in relation to the production process itself. The information on these elements is presented in table 4.1 in descending order according to degree of current usage.

Group working and the use of work teams are the most widely used of these practices, although as we shall see there is considerable variation in nature of group working schemes. In the 'purest' instances group working means multi-skilled workers operating their own 'mini-factories', with their own financial, output and quality targets to meet. The system of cellular production which Lucas are adopting (described in chapter 3) constitutes an example of this. In other cases, team-working may mean little more than briefings by supervisors and perhaps some job rotation.

After group working, flexible working is the practice next most widely used, with 80 per cent of companies claiming some degree of flexibility in working practices. It is noteworthy that virtually all those companies not currently using flexible working are implementing or planning its use.

Quality circles are the next most widely used practice, with 68 per cent of companies indicating some usage of circles, closely followed by statistical process control (67 per cent). There is, however, a striking difference in the status of the two practices. Although about a third of companies were not currently using

Table 4.1   Production methods and practices

Practices	Never used (%)	In use (%)	Planned or implementing (%)
Group working/work teams	10	85	5
Flexible working	2	80	18
Quality circles	27	68	5
Statistical process control	9	67	24
Total quality control	5	60	35
Just-in-time production	36	34	30

Number in sample   64

either practice, 24 per cent were implementing or planning to implement statistical process control as against 5 per cent in the case of quality circles. This suggests that the feverish interest in quality circles which gripped the management world in the late 1970s and early 1980s has eased off, and that the primary focus is now on production techniques, a picture confirmed by the proportion of companies planning or implementing the final three items in table 4.1, namely statistical process control, total quality control and JIT production.

The pattern for statistical process control is repeated for the other production methods and practices, namely total quality control and JIT production. In the case of these practices, a high proportion of those companies which were not using them at the time of the survey were in the process of planning or implementing them. Total quality control stands out markedly here; of the companies not already applying total quality principles, 87 per cent were involved in planning or implementing them. It looks as though in the future these techniques will become more and more prominent in the major companies operating in Britain.

The Wave of Change

A second important factor to consider, implied by the picture above, is the timescale of the development of these practices in the West. It could be argued that some of the so-called Japanese techniques have in fact been around for years, but are simply now carrying different labels, for a variety of reasons. To explore this, we asked companies to indicate the date of introduction of each practice in order to test the perception of a 'wave of change' sweeping through British industry. The results of this analysis are presented in tabular form in table 4.2.

As may be seen there has been a massive surge in the usage of these methods, particularly in the five years between 1982 and 1987, although some stand out as being particularly recent arrivals. Most noteworthy in this respect is JIT production with 92 per cent of the companies which use this method having adopted it in the period 1983–7, the median date of introduction being as recent as 1986. There are a few companies who introduced some of these practices many years ago — for example four companies adopted total quality control before 1942. The table indicates a flurry of interest in flexible working, group technology and work teams in the 1960s and 1970s; we suspect this to be a reflection of the interest in quality of working life issues shown by many progressive companies during this period. The recently pronounced development of these practices, we will argue, appears to be driven by considerations of responsibility and accountability rather than concern for the quality of working life *per se*. Experiments at Rover (see chapter 3) are consistent with this interpretation.

Evaluation of Production Methods

The survey companies were asked to evaluate their experiences with each practice using a simple four point rating scale. The responses this generated are presented in descending order of success in table 4.3. Scores for each item can range from a minimum of one (unsuccessful) to four (highly successful).

As the mean scores in the table indicate, there are no practices which appear

Table 4.2 Dates of introduction of Japanese manufacturing methods

Practices	Pre-1942	1943–1947	1948–1952	1953–1957	1958–1962	1963–1967	1968–1972	1973–1977	1978–1982	1983–1987	Median date	Number in sample
Just-in-time production	—	—	—	—	—	—	—	1 (4%)	1 (4%)	26 (92%)	1986	28
Total quality control	4 (9%)	—	—	3 (7%)	2 (4%)	3 (7%)	3 (7%)	2 (4%)	5 (11%)	23 (50%)	1983	45
Statistical process control	—	—	1 (3%)	—	2 (5%)	1 (3%)	2 (5%)	3 (8%)	4 (10%)	26 (67%)	1983	39
Quality circles	—	—	—	—	—	—	—	2 (6%)	14 (39%)	20 (56%)	1983	36
Group working/ work teams	—	—	—	—	1 (3%)	2 (5%)	1 (3%)	5 (13%)	8 (22%)	20 (54%)	1983	37
Flexible working	—	—	—	—	2 (5%)	1 (3%)	7 (19%)	4 (11%)	6 (16%)	17 (46%)	1981	37

Table 4.3   Evaluation of production methods

Practices	Not successful (%)	Quite-very successful (%)	Highly successful (%)	Mean
Total quality control	2	65	33	2.98
Flexible working	6	69	25	2.91
Group working/work teams	2	68	17	2.78
Statistical process control	2	82	16	2.60
Just-in-time production	7	87	6	2.50
Quality circles	17	78	5	2.12

Number in sample   45

to have been unsuccessful across a very substantial proportion of companies. Total quality control is evaluated most favourably, followed by flexible working and work teams. When we get to quality circles and JIT there is a marked increase in the 'unsuccessful' rating: only 5 per cent of companies rated their experiences with circles as highly successful; with JIT only 6 per cent of companies reported a high degree of success.

Having considered some of the overall patterns and trends in the use of these methods by British companies, we shall now consider each one in rather more depth, with the exception of total quality. We omit a discussion of total quality in its own right for two reasons. First, in our experience the label 'total quality control' is often used as a blanket term to cover the more specific practices such as SPC, JIT, self-certification for quality and so on. Secondly the term is rather nebulous, and two programmes both carrying the total quality banner may differ widely in practice.

JIT Production
Just-in-time production is discussed in this section with reference only to production within a particular plant, and as such concentrates on companies' attempts to reduce batch sizes by reducing set-up time and improving material control. JIT *supply* is discussed separately later in this chapter.

Our survey findings concerning the adoption of JIT broadly concur with those of Voss and Robinson's (1987b) survey. From a sample of 132 companies, they found 57 per cent to be implementing or planning to implement some aspects of JIT, a figure close to the 64 per cent recorded by our survey. Voss and Robinson proceeded to explore the nature and extent of the changes taking place under the general title of JIT. Only a minority of the companies implementing or planning JIT (17 per cent) claimed a major JIT programme; 20 per cent reported that they were using JIT on an experimental basis; 46 per cent described their use of JIT as essentially consisting of *ad hoc* modifications to existing systems. The remainder had not taken any concrete action at the time the survey was conducted.

Moving on to consider the use of specific elements of JIT, a considerable variation in degree of usage of the elements of JIT may be seen. This is shown in table 4.4.

A number of items which Voss and Robinson included as aspects of JIT were considered as separate items in their own right in our survey (for example flexible working, SPC, and work teams) on the grounds that these techniques may be implemented independently of any moves towards JIT-proper. However, they do constitute important elements in a JIT system. It is striking that the proportion of companies who have implemented the 'core' techniques of JIT − Kanban, U-shaped lines, cellular manufacturing and so on − are in a minority. On the basis of this data Voss and Robinson conclude that 'many companies are implementing individual aspects of JIT rather than the whole concept'. Moreover, they argue that it is the easy-to-implement techniques which are being applied, not necessarily the most useful ones. Despite this partial or piecemeal approach, many companies reported benefits from their use of JIT. Work-in-progress reduction was ranked as the greatest benefit, followed by increased flexibility, reduction in the use of raw materials and improved quality.

Our evidence points to the need for radical shifts in philosophy − at all levels − in organizations adopting JIT. For example, the system of measuring work in standard hours − the number of hours of output at a given (standard) rate of production − creates a pressure for long production runs. If one is frequently performing machine set-ups, then performance according to standard hours will go down. In a number of companies we visited the 'standard hours culture' constituted an obstacle to the implementation of JIT.

A further source of adjustment problems surround the fact that one does not just work for the sake of it under a Kanban system, but only when the containers,

Table 4.4   Aspects of JIT implemented
or planned

Aspects	%
Flexible workforce	80.0
Work in progress reduction	67.1
Statistical process control	58.6
Set-up reduction	54.3
Work team quality control	50.0
Modules or cells	44.3
Smoothed build rate	25.7
U-shaped lines	22.9
Kanban	11.4
Number in sample 70	

Source: adapted from Voss and Robinson (1987b)

with Kanban attached, are there to be filled. A team leader from a company using Kanban remarked:

> If a guy's been working the old system for 25 years you can't change it in 25 minutes. People want to work. It's difficult to say to a guy: 'Stop. Don't fill up any more. Stop, Stop.' Because he's used to working. And I know everybody says that workers don't want to work, but we've found the reverse. People get very jumpy when there's no work so they try to create work. Now I don't mind them creating work as long as they're sweeping the floor or emptying the bins. What we don't like is creating work when there's an on-cost on the material when it gets shunted down the line. And it's very difficult. Sometimes you have to handcuff some people.

A factory manager from Lucas Electrical provides an impression of how widespread the old philosophy was in his company, indicating that the problem stretched far beyond the shopfloor:

> We've introduced an animal called the material controller whose sole job is to ensure that we don't make stuff that is not required . . . and let's be honest, it wasn't just the foremen. Factory managers, everyone served the god of output. And we didn't really understand the implications of that. (BBC/OU 1986a)

As we described in chapter 2, one of the essential elements in creating a successful JIT system is to attack the premises on which economic order quantities are calculated, and hence to reduce economic batch size to a theoretical figure of one. In an established manufacturing operation this typically involves major changes in procedure in order to get machine set-up time down. Evidence from British companies suggests wide variation in the ease with which this can be accomplished.

One of the success stories, recounted by Lee (1986), concerns set-up time reduction in the production of engine blocks at the Cummins Engine Company. Here the programme of set-up time reduction was embarked on as part of a wider drive towards JIT manufacture. The programme comprised three key elements: a training programme for all production operators, immediate support staff on the engine block line, and the establishment of Set-Up Reduction (SUR) action teams. The training programme consisted of about 10 hours of training in JIT concepts and practices, the business environment in which the plant was operating, and methods of recording and analysis. The attendees were then formed into *action* (not simply *study*) teams, with the target of a 50 per cent reduction in set-up time within six months, and a further 25 per cent within twelve months from the start of the programme. The core membership of the teams were the two or three operators who were regularly involved in setting up the machine under study, supported by a process engineer, the tool room supervisor and a maintenance operator. Set-ups were video-recorded and later analysed by each team.

Lee stresses that care was taken to ensure that the recording was carried out openly and became 'the property of the team'. He comments: 'There needs to be an environment that ensures that the team (particularly the shopfloor members) can trust beyond doubt that the video will not be misused in any way'. At Cummins, ideas for improvement in set-up times 'flowed like water' at the early team meetings. These ideas were recorded and documented, organized into a prioritized action plan, and particular individuals were assigned responsibility for its execution. Meetings continued on a weekly basis until the teams were happy, whereupon another video was made of the set-up. This was done for a number of reasons; to recognize the team's success, to serve as a training aid, and to ensure that the new method became the standard method of working. According to Lee most of the SUR teams at Cummins met their targets of 75 per cent reductions in set-up times within a few weeks of the team activity commencing.

In contrast to Cummins' experience, an engineering company visited by one of the authors encountered considerable difficulty in attacking set-up times. The company was seeking to reduce set-up times in order to bring batch size down and reduce lead-times and inventories. Resistance to this stemmed from the fact that the machine setters felt threatened by what they perceived to be an intrusion into their territory. At the time of the visit the company had been trying to get set-up times down for about six months, and the trade unions had withdrawn their support from joint groups overseeing the change process over the issue. Two issues appeared to lie at the heart of the problem. First, the observation and timing demanded by a programme of set-up time reduction carried work-study connotations and was therefore resisted. Secondly, the machine setters saw their skills, and indeed the set-up operation, as *their* property; outside interference was not seen as legitimate.

At the time of the visit agreement had just been reached on a pilot scheme, but after a lengthy process of negotiation. Management had appealed to 'motherhood' considerations such as waste reduction in persuading those involved to accept the pilot scheme. As one manager said:

> This appeals to the idea that most people recognize that waste is a pretty wicked thing ... 'We're just trying to reduce waste here lads' ... there aren't many people who'll say 'No, no I *want* to waste my time, I believe it's right I waste my time.' So we hit those sort of things.

The distinction between 'personal' and 'company' property which this company encountered in attempting to reduce set-up times may reflect an important difference in the way Japanese and British workers typically view their relations with their companies. An executive of Sony's Bridgend plant recounted a story with a similar theme. A senior Japanese manager walking round the plant noticed how a group of workers had developed a system which enabled them to do their jobs a little quicker, and hence make up some time for a rest. Whilst admiring the ingenuity of the system the workers had developed, he expressed his regret that the workers were keeping the benefits of the system to themselves − in the form of free time − and not sharing the benefits with the company.

To summarize, successful JIT production necessarily entails social and cultural change, and its threat to the 'property' of skilled workers may be resisted.

Concomitant changes in personnel and industrial relations practice may therefore be necessary, a point to which we return later.

Statistical Process Control
One could be forgiven for imagining that the introduction of statistical techniques to assist in-process controls would be relatively untraumatic. Certainly, SPC carries fewer political implications than does, for example, the flexible working demanded by JIT but technically its effects are considerable, and in many cases a dramatic re-think in production management philosophy has been called for. An instructive example comes from Ketlon, an engineering company who supply components to the Ford Motor Company. Ketlon first heard of SPC in 1980 during a presentation by Ford to their major suppliers. Typical comments from Ketlon managers were:

> We were told quite clearly that to survive − the expression Ford used was that they were going to be best of the rest after Japan − we had to meet these requirements [SPC] head on. (BBC/OU 1986b)

> We were pushed into it, we certainly didn't discover it on our own. (BBC/OU 1986b)

As we described in chapter 1, SPC requires studies to be carried out into the 'natural' variation which machines generate in their output. These capability studies turned out to be a shock for many companies. A task force member from Lucas Electrical commented:

> We carried out process capability studies which measure the capability of the plant to meet drawing specifications and found that 75 per cent of the plant was incapable of providing components to the drawing. (BBC/OU 1986a)

The factory manager from Ketlon describes a similar reaction:

> SPC highlighted a lot more problems than we knew we had. Every job we looked at we said 'We're not capable, we can't run it, what can we do?'. We were all running round in circles and panicking. As the dust settled, we realized that we couldn't put it in overnight. (BBC/OU 1986b)

Ketlon started introducing SPC on its finishing processes, and gradually worked back up the factory, systematically overhauling and rebuilding its machines so that they were capable of consistently producing components to the required specification. The resources required to do this were of course considerable, but Ketlon were fortunate in having the skilled personnel to enable them to carry out this operation in-house. Rebuilding its machines was only part of the process; also essential was a comprehensive training programme to introduce operators to the principles and philosophy behind SPC. The company are pleased with the results, and say of the pre-SPC days:

> Back in 1978/79, we, like many suppliers thought we were in control but in fact we weren't, because quite honestly, we didn't know that we weren't. We were surviving by 100 per cent inspection. (BBC/OU 1986b)

Positive changes for Ketlon include the extra confidence that they (and hence their customers) have in their components, but also a change in attitudes as well. In particular, the traditional rift between the quality department with their emphasis on conformance to specification, and production with their emphasis on output, has closed as production now have the means to control their own processes. In common with Southern Components, whose case study was reported in chapter 3, Ketlon appear to have whole-heartedly embraced SPC, and extol its virtues. Notable, however, is the fundamental change in philosophy in the production areas which SPC has generated.

Relating this back to our theory of Japanization, the introduction of SPC highlights the importance of tackling sources of uncertainty at source, rather than evolving strategies to cope with the consequences of an inability to control a process. What is particularly striking is how the disciplined performance measurement demanded by SPC revealed the extent to which Ketlon and Lucas were simply not in control of their manufacturing processes. The effect of this may be less traumatic than that of simply stripping away the protection of slack resources because introducing SPC does not generally precipitate crises. However, its effect in terms of exposing problems that companies did not even know existed is similar.

Cellular Manufacture and Team Organization
Work organization at shopfloor level is a difficult topic to discuss in general terms, as different organizations are emulating different aspects of Japanese practice; moreover, the organizations with which we have had direct or indirect contact are all at different stages in the change process. However, most of the emulators appear to be following the well publicized example of the Toyota production system and some clear patterns of factory organization are emerging. We would argue that these practices centre around accountability for (and hence control of) the production process, in order to gain the advantages of reductions in slack resources and/or improvements in performance with respect to costs, quality and lead-time. Actions to achieve these aims are taking a variety of forms, but central to these actions are the creation of accountable units by organizing production on the basis of cells, modules or work teams. In addition to creating greater accountability (and hence we shall argue, permitting greater control) these arrangements also provide the simplified work flow necessary for JIT with Kanban control to work successfully.

Arguably, one of the most important conditions in a total quality organization is for their sub-units − and ultimately the individuals within those sub-units − to be accountable and responsible for what they do. One mechanism for achieving this is to organize production in such a way that each group has clearly recognizable inputs and outputs. These may be physical such as raw material as an input and finished product as an output, or non-physical, for example an administrative task involving information-processing. Each unit should be able to define their outputs, the recipients of those outputs and measures of performance to gauge the standard of these outputs. Describing IBM's policy in this area Harrington (1982) writes:

Everyone has a customer for their output, from the janitor who sweeps my

office to Mr Opel [then president of IBM] who directs the business of the
corporation in such a way that the IBM customer receives superior products
and services, and the stockholders receive a fair return on their investment.
If you find someone who does not have a customer for his output, you have
to question if there is a need for him in the organization.

For many UK manufacturing companies, achieving this has meant a radical
reorganization of plant configuration. In the case of older plants in which production processes have developed incrementally over many years — a line being
added here, a new wing there and so on — what Schonberger (1986) has described
as a 'clustered, jumbled' type of factory organization has resulted. This type of
organization is characterized by clusters of generic work stations, little organization
along product flows, and no easily identifiable flow paths.

Our evidence suggests that a change to cellular manufacture, particularly if
carried out as part of a JIT programme, represents a major upheaval of existing
practices, both on the shopfloor and in the wider organization. Part of this trauma
undoubtedly stems from the fact that such a dramatic reorganization essentially
re-draws the organizational map — with all that that implies for territory, resources
and power relations. As previously centralized departments such as maintenance
and production engineering are dismantled and their staff are dispersed amongst
teams or cells, empires disappear — to the understandable chagrin of their
emperors. In a company visited by one of the authors which was adopting cellular
manufacture, production engineers were being dispersed from a centralized
production engineering department which 'serviced' the whole production area
into cells, and placed under the control of the cell leaders. Many saw this return
to the shopfloor from their office-based positions in a centralized function as a
demotion.

Other potential 'losers' from this form of organization are factory supervisors
and managers. As we argued in chapter 2, organizations with substantial vertical
structures comprising many levels of supervisors and managers have adopted a
strategy for co-ordination and control which the Japanese would regard as wasteful.
A switch to forms of organization based around the concept of 'responsible
autonomy' largely removes the *raison d'être* for such groups. The whole philosophy on which factory middle management has been based in many British
companies is antithetical to the responsible autonomy concept. Commenting on
the suitability of his existing foremen and supervisors for a factory being designed
on a cellular basis, an engineering company manager made the following remark
(at that time the company employed 70—80 people in factory management roles):

> We probably don't need 70—80 and we certainly don't need the 70—80
> we've got . . . we've appointed seven or eight team leaders and to be quite
> honest we don't like those that are left very much . . . the type of people
> we employ as foremen just aren't team leader material. . . . They are a
> mix of progress chasers and backside kickers in their current jobs and they
> just won't have a role.

Cellular manufacture carries implications over and above the simplification of workflow necessitated by JIT techniques. We illustrated, above, the implications for managements and specialist groups of skilled and professional employees. Another major impact relates to the sense of ownership of a product which cellular production makes possible. This is illustrated in table 4.5, which compares product ownership load under cellular organization compared with that of the same product when production is organized on a process basis. The figures in this table were calculated during a shift to cellular production in a large British engineering company.

Arranging production in this way can have dramatic effects on the climate within a company. As a manager in a company which had recently adopted cellular manufacture commented to one of the authors:

> [What cellular manufacture] gives you is a fantastic vehicle on which to float other things − continuous improvement, ownership, training − all those things. You *could* just go out and do them now, but it would be bloody hard work and they probably wouldn't work . . . but the cells give the guys the ownership, and get the commitment . . . You can do your training plan, you can do your continuous improvement, you can do your local control . . . anything you want you can do more easily in a cellular environment; but it doesn't achieve very much on its own, other than the simplified workflow . . . We're doing things in cells that we would *never* have negotiated with the whole factory in 20 years.

This quotation demonstrates how organizing production on a team basis can make control of a factory so much easier. It encourages an ethos of 'serving the customer' − whether internal or external − and accountability is greatly heightened. Combined with a low-stock policy, problems are clearly and quickly pinned down to a particular work team − they cannot be hidden. The use of public displays of team performances − frequently used by total quality organizations − intensifies this visibility and accountability. The whole system, then, creates an imperative

Table 4.5 Product ownership load before and after cell manufacture

Operations	% Before	% After
Turning	29	—
Milling, drilling, grinding	38	4
Assembly	12	—
Processes	13	10
Inspection and test	6	—
Other	2	—
Production cell	—	86
	(100%)	(100%)

to meet output and quality objectives which would be far more difficult to achieve with more direct control methods.

Shop stewards from the same (multi-union) plant also recognized that the move towards cellular production would significantly affect their position. As one AEU steward commented:

> Let's be honest, all this cellular manufacture is destroying trade unions, that's what it's all about. [In the future] we won't be talking as parochial trade unionists around the table, we'll be speaking solely for the people on this site. I would think our jurisdiction over people in that environment would be of a lesser nature than it is at this point in time ... without a shadow of a doubt.

There is the danger to managements, of course, that autonomous teams or cells become loyal unto themselves at the expense of the company, perhaps deliberately restricting output or 'covering' for members behaving deviantly in the eyes of the company. Such a situation was observed in an American-owned total quality organization operating a production system based on semi-autonomous work groups. In this case the reponse by management was to reassert more direct supervision for those cells considered problematic (Wilkinson and Smith 1983).

A third major impact of team organization, intimated above, is on the number of levels in the management hierarchy. At Ford, Marsden et al. (1985) reported a devolution of responsiblity downwards. At plant level this involved the division of activities into four areas: stamping, body construction, paint and trim, and final assembly. The managers of these areas are now responsible for all the activities within them, including quality control and maintenance as well as production itself. Small teams of specialists work under each area manager; formerly these staff were located in central functions to which production managers had no direct access. This permitted the number of layers in the management hierarchy to be reduced from eight to five. More recently, Ford has also announced an 'area foreman' plan, which we described in chapter 3. The idea is for there to be 'mini-managers', responsible for semi-autonomous groups. Area foremen are to take responsibility for production, skilled maintenance, inspection, materials handling and janitorial functions. Beneath area foremen there are to be group leaders, managing production teams including both skilled and semiskilled workers, and encompassing some maintenance functions.

This pattern is emerging in many companies; the changes at Lucas and Rover, which we also described in the previous chapter are in many respects similar to those occurring at Ford. At many of Lucas' factories a drop in the number of management levels from six to three is taking place; Jaguar have reduced their levels of management from eight to six. Consistent with our theory of Japanization, the move towards self-contained teams, and the related simplification of workflow, are obviating the need for complex management structures to control the production process.

In summary, the shift towards teamwork and cellular manufacture is associated with, and often made problematic by, the dispersal of specialist departments, visibility and accountability in the production process, and a 'flatter' organization structure. In terms of the theoretical concepts of chapter 2, self-contained tasks lead to a simpler workflow, eliminating the need for elaborate vertical structures.

Flexible Working
The 'elimination of waste' philosophy has an obvious corollary with flexible working, in that it means human resources should be deployed as required by production demands, reducing another source of inefficiency in resource utilization. Such a change implies a reassertion of managerial prerogatives over labour deployment, and hence may carry a cost to trade unions. This is because the ability to control the deployment of labour represents control over a resource essential to the production process, and is therefore a bargaining counter.

Examples of moves towards greater flexiblity may be discerned in three basic areas: temporal flexibility, numerical flexibility and functional flexibility. Temporal flexibility refers to flexibility in the use of working time; an example is the six day working scheme which British Coal are currently trying to push through. Another scheme which is increasingly emerging is the system of annual hours, whereby personnel are contracted to work so many hours per year, rather than per day or week, thus permitting slack or busy times to be accommodated without overtime or lay-offs. Numerical flexibility refers to the ability of organizations to vary the number of workers they employ according to demand. There is little that is new in this — many organizations which experience fluctuations in the demands made upon them have developed a range of labour strategies to cope. Obvious examples are the hotel, catering and retail industries, all of which make substantial use of temporary and part-time workers. As we have seen, Japan's dual economy provides the conditions for numerical flexibility. Functional flexibility, on the other hand, refers to an organization's ability to move its people around between different jobs, according to when and where they are needed.

Different sectors of industry appear to favour different forms of flexibility. A report by NEDO (1986) showed numerical flexibility to be used most widely in the service sector, reflected in an increasing number of part-time staff in low skill jobs to meet fluctuations in customer flows. Obvious examples of these strategies are to be found in the aforementioned retail and catering industries. In manufacturing industry, flexibility was in the main achieved via the use of overtime, and most significantly through functional flexibility. The NEDO report also identified a number of constraints on moves towards greater functional flexibility, the most significant being first, inadequate skill levels and training resources, and second, divisions relating to differences in status and union membership.

Clutterbuck (1985) argues that different types of flexibility may be mutually exclusive, in that the more firms achieve numerical flexibility through the use of supplementary workers of peripheral status, the lower the functional flexibility they can expect from those workers. This is because companies are less willing to train for functional flexibility in their peripheral workers, and that the workers themselves have little motive to supply it, concluding that where pools of deskilled peripheral workers exist, 'they confer a one-way flexibility only, and inhibit versatility in response to change'. Because of this, companies are tending to segment their labour markets, thus locking groups such as part-time or temporary workers into peripheral status, and achieving functional flexibility among the core group.

It is the development of functional flexibility which is of the most immediate significance to the organization of production along 'Japanese' lines, and it is this aspect of flexibility on which the following section focuses. What have companies been doing in this area and how have they fared?

As we saw from the survey findings, about a quarter of the responding companies considered flexible working to be highly successful; only 5 per cent went so far as to indicate a failure in flexible working. Our anecdotal evidence suggests that it is not flexible working *per se* which is the problem area for companies, but rather managing the transition from traditional working practices to more flexible systems. In situations where companies are setting up on green-field sites, flexible working is generally implemented fairly painlessly, as the evidence from Japanese companies described in chapter 5 illustrates. The insistence of many inwardly investing companies on single union agreements – if any union is recognized at all – is one way in which the demarcation disputes which can impede functional flexibility are avoided. Established multi-union companies have looked to other strategies, although some (for example, Ford for their planned new site at Dundee or Hitachi at Hirwaun in South Wales) have also gone for single union deals. This issue is further explored in chapter 6 on trade unions and industrial relations.

A number of companies which have been relatively successful in implementing flexible working are those which have recognized a need to 're-tune' their reward systems to encourage functional flexibility. For example Pirelli, at their Aberdare plant, have introduced a system whereby there are only two grades of direct labour. Production operators begin at a basic (though relatively high) salary. People receive increments according to the skills which they develop. Skills are grouped into 'skill modules' which operators work through. At the time of writing, attaining the skill level in each module adds £250 to an operator's annual salary.

Birds Eye Walls, part of the Unilever Group, successfully negotiated the introduction of a multiskilling programme for their 500 craftsmen, represented by the AEU and the EETPU. As in the case of Pirelli, payment was linked to multiskilling, although the Birds Eye Walls' system is less individualistic than that of Pirelli. Essentially craftsmen were paid an extra £7 a week (an increase of 5 per cent) for agreeing to flexibility in principle, and for participating in a multiskilling training programme. In return they were expected to be 'willing to apply both electrical and mechanical skills to the limit of their capability, unhindered by artificial demarcation and with due regard for safety' (*Incomes Data Services Report*, no. 502, August 1987). On satisfactory completion of the training programme individual craftsmen receive an extra £15.80 a week, a further 10 per cent increase.

However, our evidence suggests that for some companies effecting the change to flexible working has been problematic. Some increases in flexibility have been achieved by linking flexibility improvements to pay increases, although such moves have met resistance in other companies, among them Ford, who in early 1988 were facing the prospect of national strike action (for the first time in over ten years) over a combined pay increase and flexibility plan. One of the major sticking points in this case was the resistance of skilled workers fearing that flexibility would bring skill dilution, and hence a weakening of their bargaining position. The Birds Eye Walls experience suggests that flexibility within or between the craft unions may be less of a problem than flexibility which crosses the skilled/unskilled divide.

One company visited by one of the authors encountered both political and economic constraints on the introduction of flexible working. As part of the drive to reduce non value-added operations, skilled machinists were required to sweep up around their own machines and generally engage in more 'housekeeping' tasks, as well as learning to operate a wider range of machines. At the time of the visit, no modification to reward systems had been made; consequently flexible working came to be equated with an increased work load and status reduction for no compensation. This particular company had suffered a severe decline in its major markets, and so was in a poor position to make cash offers to smooth the change.

In another company visited, skills constraints provided an obstacle to flexible working, in addition to the reluctance of some workers to take on extra tasks. As with the case described above, the company lacked a reward system which encouraged multiskilling. The moves towards multiskilling were taking place in tandem with a gradual reorganization of production from a process basis to a product form, based on work teams. The leaders of the teams had addressed the 'reluctance problem' largely by selecting workers in their early thirties, who were young enough to be flexible, but old enough to have plenty of experience. The fact that people in this age group are also likely to have young families and large mortgages (and hence a high dependency on the company) was seen as a further advantage by at least one team leader interviewed. Indeed, with many of these practices, but flexible working in particular, the importance of people's 'attitudes' is continually stressed. This is very marked in the selection and recruitment practices of Japanese companies operating in Britain, which are analysed in the next chapter, but the point also holds for the Japanizing companies.

A quotation from a team leader from a company setting up work teams, and charged with the task of recruiting operators into his team, described the features he was seeking as follows:

> I personally wasn't interested in what they'd done before. Obviously that came into it, but that wasn't what I was after. What I was after was people with the right attitudes ... as I said to [the assistant personnel manager] 'You could almost forget the job spec and write attitude'. ... A guy came in for interview and sat down and said 'I've been with the company for 38 years. I'm not the fastest guy in the world and I'm not the best operator in the factory and I never will be the best operator in the factory. But I

tell you what — I'll do whatever you want me to do. I'll help you in every way that I can. I'm always here. And I'm never late.' I said 'You've got yourself a job.'

A second constraint on flexible working in the same company concerns the ability of the existing workforce. Historically the strategy of employing unskilled people (at unskilled wage rates) for unskilled work may have made sense financially, but it had left a troublesome legacy, in that the company had large numbers of employees who could not be moved around. A senior manager commented: 'rationalizing has generally meant rationalizing upwards; we need fewer people, but of higher quality'. The company now includes trainability as a criterion for selection. The account of a team leader bears out this picture; he perceived people to be scared of performing jobs that were unfamiliar to them, which he combated by getting people to double up on jobs until the person unfamiliar with the job gained some confidence. Even so, the team leader estimated that only about 50 per cent of his (selected) staff were capable of performing a range of jobs satisfactorily. This meant that even within the team, which consisted of 15 to 20 people, there was an elite who moved between jobs, and the rest who were restricted to relatively simple operations.

The managing director of the AB Electronics group, describing the company's struggle for survival from 1980 onwards also places a heavy emphasis on the role of attitudes supportive of flexibility:

> It was obvious that if the company was to survive let alone move ahead a radical change of attitude on the part of both management and employees was going to be necessary. One of the key problems was perceived to be an almost complete lack of trust between the workforce and management. One of the ways that this manifested itself was an almost total lack of flexibility ... To my mind the greatest obstacle to remove was the 'them and us' syndrome. We had to get across the message that we were all in the same lifeboat and we'd all better bail. (Merrette 1987)

To get this message across AB adopted a number of tactics: an open communications system, improvements in the working environment — the toilets, canteen and so on — and a single status policy. Hours of work, holiday entitlements, pensions, sick pay and canteen facilities were all harmonized. In addition, a commitment to training to furnish people with the *ability* to work flexibly was adopted. Each of AB's operating units is compelled to spend the equivalent of 2 per cent of its payroll on training.

In 1980 AB's main site was at Abercynon in South Wales, where some 3,000 people were employed. The management view was that the site was unprofitable, suffered from poor industrial relations and productivity was 'abysmal'. It was here that the company began its programme of change, part of which involved 400 redundancies. The managing director regarded AB's initiative at Abercynon as a failure:

We attempted to improve communications, but the shop stewards did every-thing they could to prevent it. We tried to encourage training schemes to enable people to extend their range of skills, maximize their potential. Again almost total lack of co-operation. We offered profit-sharing schemes, incentive bonuses, harmonization. We failed, we were not able to overcome the entrenched attitudes. (Merrette 1987)

In the light of their lack of success, instead of placing new investment at Abercynon, AB began spinning off new businesses on greenfield sites. These businesses were started from scratch with modern, single status facilities and only one union in each case. The sites were deliberately kept small (AB regard about 500 employees as optimal) in order to 'foster the family concept' and maintain 'a sense of ownership on the part of the workforce and the management'. The managing director continued:

We will never willingly start up another venture with a multiplicity of unions and I would make the recommendation to any inward investor that he should always seek to reach agreement on representation with one union. (Merrette 1987)

In the company's view this strategy has been a success, and via its new ventures it has grown substantially. Some change at the Abercynon site has occurred, albeit slowly. In 1987 employment at Abercynon was down to 900.

A factor which frequently appears to obstruct flexible work practices is the lack of harmonization of terms and conditions. Indeed it could be argued that single status provisions are a prerequisite for total flexibility of deployment of labour — at a stroke it eliminates problems of comparability of terms and conditions associated with different jobs and removes the possibility of union resistance on these grounds. Typically a greatly simplified pay structure is associated with the introduction of single status arrangements for the same reasons (Linn 1986). For instance at the Bedford van plant 100 job classifications and 30 pay grades were abolished to be replaced with nine grades covering both blue and white collar workers, allowing complete flexibility within grades (*Financial Times* 26 June 1987). Rover (see chapter 3) undertook a similar simplification.

The links between flexible working practices, appropriate reward systems, harmonization of employment conditions, and single unions appear, then, to be strong. Attempts to introduce flexible work practices are likely to meet serious problems unless account is taken of the other factors.

Quality Circles

Of all the Japanese-style practices included in our survey, quality circles are the least favourably rated, with 17 per cent of companies rating their quality circle programmes as unsuccessful, and only 5 per cent describing quality circles as highly successful. A number of explanations for this are plausible. The pattern may partly reflect the fact that quality circles were one of the first elements of

Japanese practice to be emulated by British companies, and hence there has been more chance for the 'honeymoon effect' to wear off. In addition, it may be that as a relatively low investment innovation, quality circles failed in many cases to attract the necessary commitment, being treated merely as 'bolt-on' accessories. However, unlike some of the more recent practices such as JIT, quality circles have received a fair amount of research attention, and it is useful to consider some of the documented successes and failures here. We shall consider two aspects of quality circles: the motivation of Western companies in setting them up, and the reasons for the apparent successes and failures of circle programmes.

A handbook on quality circles produced by the Department of Trade and Industry's National Quality Campaign outlines three main reasons for introducing quality circles: to bring about improvements in quality and in so doing increase job satisfaction and pride in one's work; to improve management–shopfloor communications; and to improve communications between departments via systematic analysis revealing problems in other areas. Consistent with this, a reading of the burgeoning literature on quality circles demonstrates companies to have a wide range of aims and objectives in their introduction. Typically improvements in quality feature most highly in these objectives, but issues concerning motivation, morale and industrial relations come a very close second.

Some early experiments with quality circles were claimed to produce spectacular results, and many of these were widely publicized in the management literature. Two such cases are Rolls-Royce (aero engines) and Wedgwood Potteries, both of which initiated circle programmes in 1979–80, the results of which began to be publicized in the early 1980s. Rolls-Royce claimed savings of hundreds of thousands of pounds from its circle programme. Wedgwood suggested a payback to investment ratio of 3:1, in addition to less tangible benefits such as changes in people's enthusiasm and attitudes towards work (Fletcher 1984). More recently, quality circles at Jaguar Cars caught the popular imagination, and there have been a string of publications on Jaguar's success with the technique (*Industrial Relations Review and Report*, no. 277, 1982; Isaac 1984; Egan 1985). It is not our intention to review the extensive literature on quality circles here. Rather, we focus on examples of success and failure, concentrating especially on Jaguar (apparent success) and Ford (failure).

Jaguar has one of the more successful programmes of quality circles. The account which follows is based on research carried out by one of the authors at Jaguar's Radford and Brown's Lane plants in 1984, and backed up by other published accounts.

In 1980 Jaguar was losing £2 million a month on sales of just 14,000 vehicles a year – half the sales volume of 1978. A high proportion of the workforce were on short-time working. The company was beset by problems of quality and delivery – in the USA, its major market, '1979' cars were a year late in reaching the market place (Isaac 1984). The newly appointed Chairman, John Egan, attacked the problem on two main fronts: Jaguar's internal quality management and the quality of their bought-in components. As approximately 65 per cent of a Jaguar is composed of components made by other manufacturers, the performance of the finished vehicle will obviously be heavily influenced by the quality of these products. Jaguar addressed this problem by substantially tightening up its contracts with suppliers:

> One of the first facts to become obvious was that 60 per cent of the faults were the responsibility of our supplier body. . . . In order to have common purpose with our suppliers, we made them bear the financial pain for replacement parts and the dealer labour costs of faults in the field. . . . This seems to have concentrated minds remarkably! Faults which have existed for decades have mysteriously been cured. (Egan 1985)

The second major assault on Jaguar's quality problems entailed a close look at what could be learned from their major competitors BMW and Mercedes, and the Japanese vehicle producers. In the light of this, the company began adopting a number of Japanese-style practices, under the banner of their 'Pursuit of Perfection' campaign which began in mid-1980. The key working objectives of this programme were to improve in-company communications and involve employees at all levels in problem-solving, to improve product quality and reliability in a measurable way in comparison to the competition, and to reduce operating costs in all areas, but particularly production. Jaguar's manufacturing director commented: 'We were utterly dedicated to the fact that our number one priority was to improve quality and reliability' (Beasley 1984).

The company took a number of actions. The quality problems afflicting the cars were documented − there were over 150 of them − and multi-disciplinary task forces were set up to tackle them. The board of directors took on responsibility for the 12 most serious quality problems. Other steps included the aforementioned actions with the supply of bought-in parts, a reduction in non value-added activities such as inspection (the inspection department was cut by 50 per cent) and reductions in inventory. By 1984 inventory turnaround had been lifted from 2−2.5 times to 12 times per year. A comprehensive communications programme was initiated, and a bonus scheme for both hourly paid and staff employees was introduced, 'rewarding employees for their efforts as part of a team' (Beasley 1984, p. 20).

All these initiatives are worthy of attention in themselves, but it is in Jaguar's adoption of the quality circle that is of particular interest to us here. What is striking about Jaguar's quality circles is how they took root so well − which begs the question of why they worked so well at Jaguar but failed in other contexts.

One important element in the background to Jaguar's remarkable turnaround from near-bankruptcy to solvency and success may lie in the company's links with British Leyland. Management and workforce alike both resented being part of British Leyland − Isaac reports that the company's subordination to British Leyland had 'stifled local pride and taken away workers' sense of their "Jaguariness"', a view reinforced during visits to the company by one of the authors. Certainly interviews suggested that many of Jaguar's workers saw themselves as craftsmen, and different from other car workers. The fact they were put on the same pay grades as workers in other British Leyland plants was thus a further source of resentment. Jaguar's trim makers, who were largely leather workers, were put onto the same grades as trim workers on British Leyland's Mini line. This situation, coupled with the desperate financial circumstances in which the company found itself, appeared to generate a degree of common-purpose, partly by British Leyland being seen as a 'common enemy' (on which many of the company's problems were blamed) and partly because of the perception that their backs were against the wall and 'everyone had to pull together to save the ship from sinking'. Thus the combination of a product in which there was scope to take pride, a common enemy and a situation of high dependency — to use our terminology from chapter 2 — we would suggest were important in creating the right environment for the changes which were subsequently made.

Prior to its full-blown efforts to transform its product quality Jaguar had made some attempts to improve its situation. In 1977 for example, they had had a programme entitled 'Quality 77', which had a budget to produce posters, run competitions and so on. In 1984, the Radford plant manager described it thus, 'We came to the end of 1977, having considered we had done a fair amount of repair to the quality problem . . . so then we said "What's next?" — and quality circles had just come up on the horizon.' Approximately two years of discussion about the introduction of quality circles took place between management and senior shop stewards, but very little progress was made. The first major break was a decision to begin making videos for communications purposes. The Radford plant manager again:

> We started the first film ourselves called *The Price of Quality* and it shocked even me to see what was going on. We took some pictures in our repair yards up in Leeds of (faulty) engines lying on the floor — engines out of cars not more than 12 months old, and that really shook me, because I always had a good opinion of the quality of our engines.

This film was shown to the shopfloor in groups of about 200 at a time. After each showing a management team would go in and answer questions about the video and the issues it raised. There were some ribald comments during question time at some of the showings of this video. However, with subsequent videos questions became more serious, and ribald remarks less and less frequent. Other communications were also introduced, including a plant directors' briefing which is circulated weekly and gives information about the company's performance, especially with respect to quality levels. Since then communications videos have been shown three times a year, each followed by a question and answer session. By the middle of 1983, the videos were beginning to lose some of their impact. In the words of the manufacturing director: 'They became slightly repetitious, always droning on about quality. It got to the stage where people were saying "Oh, here we go again, more quality."' (Isaac 1984, p. 42). In order to combat this the videos began to talk about company affairs more generally: where the money came into Jaguar, and how it was used. The company also tried to link quality to matters of immediate concern to the shopfloor by pointing out that every lost customer 'cost' the company 21 jobs, which helped make the videos meaningful again (Fortune and Oliver 1986). Substantial resources, both financial and in terms of management time, were put into the programme. In 1984 the in-house videos cost £6,000 each to produce. Professionally produced communications videos typically cost Jaguar £20,000 each.

Thus there was a high awareness of the quality problems facing the company, and deep concern about Jaguar's future. It was into this environment that the quality circle idea was introduced in 1980. By 1984 there were 60 circles operating, encompassing some 10 per cent of the workforce. All circles have followed a few basic ground rules. Membership is voluntary; circles have been allowed to grow and develop naturally, with little 'forcing' by management. Trade unions agreed to keep a watching brief over the operations of the circles and industrial relations issues are excluded from the agenda of circle meetings. An issue which soon arose was the risk of redundancies if circles came up with ideas which meant that processes could be run with fewer staff. In response Jaguar provided a 'cast-iron' guarantee that there would be no redundancies as a consequence of circle suggestions. Any workers displaced as a consequence of circle suggestions would be redeployed within the company.

Within the circles, efforts are made to promote democratic operation. On the minutes, for example, names are in alphabetic order and no job titles or other indicators of status are used. Circle members receive training in problem-solving techniques. Generally foremen or superintendents lead circles, but at the Radford plant there have been instances of hourly paid employees acting as circle leaders. 'Deficiency action reports' are kept on each issue raised; these are carried forward from meeting to meeting until the issue is resolved to the circle's satisfaction. A group of senior managers allocate an hour a week to review progress with one or two of the circle chairmen, partly to offer assistance if necessary, partly to demonstrate their commitment to what the circles are doing. If circles come up against a block to solving a problem, they are empowered to approach the plant manager about it directly. They also have the power to visit suppliers themselves if there is a persistent problem due to a bought-in part, and this has happened. The Radford plant manager described the effect of this on suppliers as follows:

> In the beginning it started to frighten them to death ... bung four circle members in a car and go off for the day and get into the factory where they make the parts. Tell them you're the quality circle and you've come to talk about their rubbish. It doesn't half make a difference. A managing director of a firm gets a load of people knocking on his door: 'Who are you?' 'We are from the quality circle, we fit these parts, and what a load of rubbish they are ...'. Confronted, attacked on their own doorstep they find difficulty in wriggling out of it.

The results of Jaguar's quality improvement have been impressive; in 1983 sales were up to 29,000 (more than double the 1980 figure), although this was undoubtedly helped by a strong dollar and weak pound — America is Jaguar's major market. Warranty claims declined by 40 per cent by 1984, and performance according to Jaguar's own quality index improved substantially. The quality index is calculated by taking completed cars off the production line and stripping them down. Cars start with 100 points, and points are deducted for each fault found — the number of points varies according to the nature and severity of the fault. In 1980 the average score was 30 — by 1984 it was 70. For engines, by 1984 the score was in the 90s. In the longer term designing for manufacture is being used as a strategy for quality improvement. For example, the body of the XJ6 was made up of over 560 pieces; the new XJ40 body comprises only 330 pieces (Isaac 1984).

Jaguar's transformation has not been effected totally painlessly. There were about 3,500 redundancies, although by 1985 about 2,500 new jobs had been created. Half the quality department were made redundant when responsibility was handed over to the operators, some of whom felt they were now earning 'blood money' by filling the roles of their redundant mates. In addition there were some cases of operators simply not checking the quality of their own work. After due warnings have been given, this is a sackable offence.

The introduction of quality circles and other total quality techniques has affected the roles of other personnel in the factory. Process engineers voiced complaints about quality circles constantly bringing problems to them — greater shopfloor involvement brought more work for them. Managers and supervisors have had no choice but to develop more open styles of management in the face of an opening up of communications within the company more generally, although some appeared to be unhappy with the new order. A factor which may have been significant here is the proportion of Jaguar management who have risen through internal promotion. Jaguar has never had a graduate recruitment programme of anything like the magnitude of that of, for example, British Leyland. The commitment of senior management to the changes seems to have helped in this respect. In the early days, shortly after his arrival, John Egan was insisting on involving everyone in quality control. A couple of managers voiced their disagreement with this — to which the message went out that any dissenters should make an appointment with Egan to discuss their future with the company. There were no takers.

In contrast to Jaguar's success with quality circles, Ford, who introduced them at about the same time as part of their 'After Japan' campaign, met with rather less success. The account which follows draws heavily on an analysis of the 'After Japan' programme by Guthrie (1987).

The 'After Japan' campaign was a programme of productivity and quality improvements, a major part of which was the introduction of quality circles to the shopfloor of Ford's European car plants. The company invested substantial sums of money in the programme, including training circle leaders and members in techniques of problem-solving and analysis. Three people were appointed to co-ordinate the programme at company level, and plant managers were responsible for circle activities in their plants. There was a short pilot project after which quality circles were launched across all the plants in the UK. Guthrie suggests that there was little consultation with unions or lower levels of management, as senior management considered quality circles to be 'a minor change for the better'. In the six months or so following their introduction, some successes are documented (for example a 2.5 per cent saving in scrap at the Bridgend engine plant). However, union resistance was mounting and in 1981 the trade unions withdrew their support from the programme. According to Guthrie's analysis the programme was a 'resounding failure' in terms of its aims of improving work attitudes and generating net cost savings.

Why did the programme come so badly unstuck? The management's view was that the programme failed largely due to union bloody-mindedness. Guthrie's analysis however identifies a number of reasons for the failure, many of which contrast interestingly with the conditions we have just described at Jaguar. A major reason for trade union resistance was the way in which the programme was pushed through without consultation. Moss Evans, then the leader of the TGWU is quoted as saying 'We would co-operate to the maximum with efforts to improve the quality of products. But we believe this should be done in the normal way − through trade unions' (*Financial Times* 25 April 1981). As well as resenting the lack of consultation by management, the unions were concerned that circles, by creating direct communication links with management, would bypass union channels − a fear for which there was some basis, as it is alleged that workers were encouraged to take their grievances to management via their supervisors, rather than through their shop stewards.

Trade unions were not the only groups to be concerned about the introduction of quality circles. Middle and lower management were also concerned by having these developments imposed on them. With their 'bottom up' implications, circles do not sit easily with the culture of hierarchy and authoritarianism which has traditionally characterized Ford. According to Guthrie, 'Many were sceptical of a new "vogue" management technique, or even felt threatened by their lack of control over quality circles and vulnerable to criticism of the quality and legitimacy of their decisions.' Unsurprisingly, sentiments such as these found expression in a dislike of the programme and an unwillingness to implement circle proposals, exacerbating shopfloor disillusionment. Moreover, some supervisors and middle managers doubted the capacity of their subordinates to behave responsibly, and felt that circles would be used simply to waste time. Although training was provided to shopfloor workers, the largely immigrant and generally poorly educated workforce were not well equipped to conduct group discussions or use the problem-solving techniques taught as part of the training.

In 1984 the company began an attempt to introduce employee involvement amongst its 13,000 white collar workers in Britain, but this too ran into trouble. At Dagenham ASTMS demanded the disclosure of the five and ten year business plans for the plant, a written guarantee of no redundancies, a pledge that staff would not be redeployed elsewhere, and agreement that only union members could be staff representatives on steering committees in the involvement scheme (*Financial Times* 23 February 1985).

In 1987, an ASTMS national report expressed concern about quality circles on similar grounds to their resistance to them at Ford. In a paper distributed to senior negotiators, ASTMS objected to quality circles on the grounds that they contained only self-appointed or management-selected members, that they narrowed discussion to a worker's immediate environment, promoted an often false identification with management aims, failed to provide a means for distributing productivity gains due to circle suggestions, and jumped over the hierarchy of supervision and management through which commands normally flow — obviously a concern to ASTMS as many of their members perform such jobs (*Guardian* 10 January 1987).

Many of the features which distinguish between conditions at Jaguar and Ford map on to much of the published survey evidence about quality circle success and failure. Dale and Hayward (1984) found that 42 companies out of 67 had experienced failure of parts of their quality circle programmes, and suggested that the failure rate is likely to increase as the programmes grow older; 18 of the 67 companies had suspended their programmes completely. In analysing the problems companies face in running circle programmes, Hill (1986) distinguished between logistical reasons for quality circle failure — such as labour turnover, company restructuring and/or redundancies — and behavioural ones such as hostility from key groups or lack of commitment. In practice, of course, so-called logistical problems may simply be manifestations of more deep rooted behavioural problems. To illustrate this Dale and Hayward's results are considered in tandem with Hill's in table 4.6. It should be noted that the Dale and Hayward figures refer to quality circle *failures*, whilst the Hill figures refer to *problems* faced by circles.

In terms of 'behavioural' rather than 'logistical' problems, it is interesting to note that resistance from middle management and supervisors is seen as a greater problem than trade union resistance. In another study of circles in 22 companies Dale and Barlow (1984) noted that managerial resistance centred around fears that circles would show up their shortcomings as work organizers, and that their control and authority might be encroached upon. Drawing on accounts from the facilitators of quality circle programmes, Dale and Barlow identified the three most important conditions for quality circle success as: the 'unswerving support and commitment of senior, middle and supervisory management'; sustained management recognition and uncompromising support of circles; and the integration of circle activities with broader policies of employee involvement, training and development.

Table 4.6 Problems faced by quality circles

Problems	Dale and Hayward (1984)	Hill (1986)
Redundancies/restructuring	21.7% (54)	8.0% (3)
Turnover/loss of QC staff	19.3% (48)	5.0% (2)
Lack of QC leader/manager time	18.1% (45)	13.5% (5)
Lack of co-operation from middle management	18.1% (45)	13.5% (5)
Lack of co-operation from first line supervisors	13.7% (34)	5.0% (2)
Trade union hostility	2.0% (5)	13.5% (5)

Sources: adapted from Dale and Hayward (1984), Hill (1986)

When we began our analysis of Japanese-style practices, our feeling was that quality circles, not being central to the production process were unlikely to have major ramifications when implemented — unlike JIT which carries obvious implications for power relations. In the light of the evidence two conclusions emerge, which are in a sense, different sides of the same coin. The first concerns the conditions necessary for successful circle implementation and operation, the second concerns the effects that a circle programme, once implemented, can have on the wider organization. Considering the facilitative conditions first, the contrast between Ford and Jaguar is informative. Partly by circumstance, partly by design, Jaguar was successful in creating the conditions for circles to flourish. The company had a strong identity, and a product in which the workforce had traditionally taken pride. The combination of financial crisis and dislike of being part of British Leyland probably functioned to unite groups usually antagonistic to each other. (An indicator of this is how privatization was welcomed by management and workers alike as a means of freeing Jaguar from British Leyland.) The fact that many of the managers had worked up the company via internal promotion, rather than through graduate entry, may also have assisted in this — note the similarity here to Japanese practice. Of course, this is not to say that the community of interests is such that there is no conflict — indeed, there were a number of strikes in 1984 in the first round of pay talks following privatization.

The manner in which Jaguar introduced circles is also significant in their success. The comprehensive communications programme ensured that quality was seen as an issue of genuine importance, and not just the slogan of the week. The obvious commitment of top management and a preparedness to give the circles a genuine capacity to attack problems provide further support. Trade union concerns were largely allayed by ensuring that industrial relations issues were excluded from circle affairs; the no-redundancy promise shows an interesting parallel to elements of the Japanese system, and helped overcome concerns about job losses as a consequence of efficiency gains.

This contrasts markedly with the case of Ford. Circles were introduced into an environment of highly adversarial relations, and with little or no consultation of the key interest groups concerned. Given that circles were introduced into that environment, in that manner, their failure is unsurprising. Guthrie (1987, p. 31) concludes:

> Quality circles are a feature of a very different management technique to that practiced by Ford. They can and do lead to improved quality of work, if that is what the company is really aiming for. They do not allow an autocratic management to get more for less out of an unwilling workforce. The unions saw the programme for what, at least in part, it was: manipulation.

The evidence from companies' experiences with quality circles thus seems to bear out our argument from chapter 2; that many Japanese-style techniques depend on an appropriate set of supporting conditions if they are to operate successfully. In many ways the nature of quality circles renders them particularly sensitive to this. Because participation in them is voluntary, and hence seen as something beyond the employment contract, companies using them are particularly dependent on the goodwill and co-operation of their workforces. Given this heightened dependency, we would expect to find successful circle programmes in companies where such co-operation exists, whether by accident or design. The cases of Ford and Jaguar seem to bear this out.

Personnel Practices

At a number of points in our analysis of British companies' attempts to emulate Japanese manufacturing practice, we have touched on the critical role of appropriate workforce attitudes and industrial relations climate in the successful operation of these practices. In some cases the link is very explicit, AB Electronics being one such instance in the case of flexible working. The experiences from Jaguar and Ford also illustrate the importance of the right climate within an organization if quality circles are to take root and operate successfully.

Our argument is therefore that Japanese-style manufacturing practices require particular worker attitudes and behaviour, obvious examples being a willingness to perform a range of tasks, the commitment to engage in activities of continuous improvement and a preparedness to do what is required to satisfy one's customers – be they internal or external. This implies that a good fit is required between a company's manufacturing strategy and its personnel and industrial relations strategies. Many companies are implementing practices in this area, which if not Japanese-inspired, certainly bear some resemblance to Japanese practice. With this in mind, our survey also explored the nature and extent to which such practices were being adopted by companies operating in Britain.

Patterns of Change

This analysis reveals a less dramatic, though nonetheless interesting, picture to that found in the case of manufacturing practices. Table 4.7 shows the status of six Japanese-style personnel practices.

Table 4.7   Personnel practices

Practices	Never used (%)	In use (%)	Planned or implementing (%)
In-company communications	3	89	8
Employee involvement	3	88	9
Single status facilities	12	80	8
'Staff' benefits at all levels	9	74	14
High job security for core workers	32	68	—
10%+ temporary workers	44	56	—

Number in sample   64

A very high proportion of companies (over 70 per cent) reported the use of comprehensive in-company communication, employee involvement schemes, single status facilities and 'staff' benefits at all levels. Approximately two-thirds claimed to offer high job security to their core workers, and about half reported a substantial use (defined as 10 per cent plus) of staff on temporary contracts.

When these practices are considered according to their dates of introduction, marked differences from the production methods are apparent. Although the incidence of these practices shows a marked upward trend over time, this trend is both less recent and increasing less sharply than is the case for manufacturing methods, as table 4.8 demonstrates.

The most recent of these practices by median date of introduction is the use of temporary workers, a pattern consistent with national trends. Although table 4.8 indicates a sharp upward trend, it should be noted from table 4.7 that no companies reported that they were in the process of planning or implementing policies based on substantial use of temporary workers. (The pattern for part-time staff revealed an even lower incidence of usage, and less of an upward trend.) This may be attributable to the fact that our sample companies were large, 'core' manufacturing companies. The NEDO report on flexibility which we quoted earlier in this chapter suggested that it was primarily the service sector who were adopting strategies based on numerical flexibility, such as the use of part-time or temporary staff, whereas manufacturing was relying more on overtime and functional flexibility, and our results are consistent with this.

Employee involvement schemes such as team briefings also have a median date of introduction of 1983, and display a marked upward trend in the mid-1980s, probably in line with the increasing interest in teamwork and perhaps quality circles. In-company communications appear to have a longer pedigree with a steady increase apparent from the mid-1960s onwards, albeit with a slight dip in the mid-1970s. Similar patterns are discernible in the case of single status facilities and staff-type benefits for blue collar workers, although the median date of introduction of these practices is 1977. Of the six practices described here the provision of staff benefits at all levels in the organization looks set to show the sharpest increase in the next few years, with 14 per cent of companies at the stage of planning or implementation.

High security of employment for core workers, one of the best known characteristics of the major Japanese corporations, does not appear to be a new development in these companies, suggesting that those companies who claim to offer it have not linked its introduction to the new production methods. Indeed, the pattern is of a decline in the incidence of promises about job security in the period 1983–7.

Our interpretation of the data on personnel practices is that many of the sample companies introduced them for different reasons and under different pressures to those influencing their adoption of Japanese manufacturing practices. The earlier dates of introduction — particularly the slight 'humps' around the late 1960s and early 1970s suggest changes probably driven by personnel departments at a time when progressive employment policies were in vogue based on 'quality of working life' considerations.

Table 4.8 Dates of introduction of Japanese-style personnel practices

Practices	Pre-1942	1943–1947	1948–1952	1953–1957	1958–1962	1963–1967	1968–1972	1973–1977	1978–1982	1983–1987	Median date	Number in sample
10%+ temporary workers	—	—	—	—	—	1 (5%)	—	—	6 (32%)	12 (63%)	1983	19
Employee involvement	1 (2%)	—	—	—	1 (2%)	3 (7%)	5 (12%)	4 (10%)	6 (14%)	21 (52%)	1983	41
In-company communications	3 (7%)	—	1 (2%)	—	1 (2%)	3 (7%)	6 (14%)	4 (10%)	11 (26%)	13 (31%)	1980	42
Single status	1 (3%)	—	1 (3%)	2 (5%)	2 (5%)	3 (8%)	5 (13%)	6 (15%)	9 (23%)	10 (26%)	1977	39
'Staff' benefits	1 (3%)	—	—	—	1 (3%)	4 (12%)	4 (12%)	3 (9%)	10 (29%)	11 (32%)	1977	34
High job security	3 (18%)	—	—	—	1 (6%)	1 (6%)	3 (18%)	3 (18%)	5 (29%)	1 (6%)	1973	17

Evaluation of Personnel Practices

On the whole, these personnel practices were evaluated slightly more favourably than manufacturing practices (see table 4.9). Policies concerning the harmonization of employment conditions, such as single status facilities and staff-type benefits for other grades of workers are most favourably rated. This may not be surprising given that harmonization is likely to be welcomed by most blue collar unions. In some cases (for example at Ford) in-company communications were viewed as attempts to bypass shop stewards; this may explain their relatively low rating in the table. We will return to these issues later.

Just how 'Japanese' these practices are is debatable. Personnel practices such as the harmonization of employment conditions generally have a longer history in our survey companies than do the production methods we explored. This suggests that their introduction is not necessarily part of a package — a total business strategy — of production methods and employment practices.

In order to test this idea, simple statistical (correlational) analyses were performed to explore how far manufacturing practices were supported by appropriate personnel practices. This was done in two ways. First correlations (measures of association) were computed between the various degrees of usage for each practice. This was done in order to establish whether those companies which made extensive use of, for example, quality circles also tended to be the ones who offered high security of employment. We report only the chief conclusions.

The most striking point about the results of this analysis was the lack of association between the use of Japanese-style manufacturing practices and the use of Japanese-style personnel practices. Although there was some evidence of certain practices coming in 'clusters', this was almost entirely confined to clusters of *manufacturing* practices or clusters of *personnel* practices, but rarely a mix of both. For example, only 10 companies who reported an extensive use of Japanese-style manufacturing practices also reported extensive use of the commensurate personnel practices. Strikingly, in general these companies reported much greater success with the manufacturing practices, particularly with respect to flexible

Table 4.9 Evaluation of personnel/industrial relations practices

Practices	Not successful (%)	Quite–very successful (%)	Highly successful (%)	Mean
Single status facilities	—	64	46	3.15
'Staff' benefits for all	—	62	38	3.09
High job security	—	64	36	2.97
Employee involvement	5	76	19	2.76
10% + temporary workers	6	80	14	2.69
In-company communications	3	78	19	2.66

working and total quality control. There were significant correlations between the use of JIT and the use of total quality control, quality circles and group technology or work teams. In general, however, those companies most extensively using JIT did not appear to be those who were using the personnel practices which our theory in chapter 2 suggested it would be prudent to do (in order to ensure levels of stability and dependability given the system's vulnerability to disruption). Unsurprisingly, however, those companies which use substantial in-company communication also tended to exhibit greater employee involvement, and also reported greater use of single status facilities.

To add a slightly different perspective to the issue, the same analysis was performed to see if practices grouped together by *date of introduction* rather than by degree of usage. Again, broadly the same pattern emerged; certain restricted sets of practices did tend to bunch together, but relationships between the introduction of JIT and practices likely to be supportive of harmonious industrial relations were conspicuous primarily by their absence. Those practices which did cluster together in this analysis were quality circles, work teams, flexible working and practices concerning involvement, communication, single status and the provision of staff benefits to blue collar workers. Further, and consistent with the findings from the NEDO report on flexible working, those companies which reported extensive *functional* flexibility made significantly less use of the numerically flexible labour strategy of temporary workers.

The picture presented from our survey, then, suggests that the personnel practices which we argue are supportive of Japanization are not synchronized with the introduction of manufacturing practices. This contrasts with the picture at Japanese companies recently locating in the UK, as is seen in the following chapter. The explanations for this lack of synchronization, and the problems it gives rise to, will now be summarized by further examination of the experiences of Japanizing companies in the UK.

Direct Communication and Single Status

The introduction of extensive communication systems, employee involvement schemes, and the harmonization of terms and conditions all have relatively long histories in the UK. Our theory suggests that where they do not exist, or where they are inadequate, they make problematic the introduction of Japanese-style working practices. This was demonstrated vividly earlier in the chapter in relation to Ford's failure with quality circles. In contrast, Jaguar was successful in part because of strong communication and a more genuine involvement on the part of employees. As we saw, middle managers can perceive the introduction of employee involvement (through quality circles, for instance) as a threat, and this can lead to their subversion and ultimately failure. Similarly, AB Electronics achieved flexible working practices in part by introducing an open communication system, and at the same time a harmonization policy; in addition this company compelled its operating units to devote substantial resources to training to ensure a workforce capacity for flexible working.

Judging from our discussion of case study and anecdotal evidence in chapter

3 and earlier in this chapter, it appears that many of the emulating companies face problems in introducing Japanese-style manufacturing and work practices partly because of the inadequacies of their existing communication and involvement schemes and partly (and relatedly) because existing company cultures sit uneasily with the new practices. This suggests that many emulators may find successful Japanization problematical — as is indicated in the frequent reportage of 'them and us' attitude problems.

Selection, Recruitment and Socialization

Unlike newly-investing Japanese companies, the emulators are mostly attempting to impose Japanese-style practices on managers and workforces already acculturated in different ways. Hence the 'raw recruit' option available to Japanese companies is not so readily available, and established attitudes, values and patterns of behaviour have to be addressed. This is particularly the case where, as in most British manufacturers, the changes are sought in the absence of rapid growth. Rover's expansion at Longbridge was a minor exception, and here (as we saw in chapter 3) attitudes and characteristics in line with the company's ends were sought. These were considered at least as important as technical skills and abilities. The focus on attitudes rather than technical skills is by no means unusual in Japanizing companies which are in the process of recruitment. In the words of a team leader quoted earlier, 'you could almost forget the job spec and write attitude'.

In the main the emulators are faced with a major problem of re-socialization, because as we have demonstrated, reluctance and cynicism from both middle managers and workers is often the response to attempts to Japanize. Hence at Rover zone briefings often degenerated into what team leaders saw as 'time wasting sessions' and production workers as nothing more than a 'welcome break'. Our description of the failure of Ford's quality circles suggests the same problem.

Again Jaguar may be exceptional in this regard. Here, a shift to total quality principles was achieved through serious attention to the re-socialization of workers and managers. In particular, resources were poured into the communications programme. Of course, Jaguar was also fortunate insofar as it was commonly agreed that the alternative to new working practices was almost certain bankruptcy, and to the extent that there already was a degree of pride in and identification with the company's product. Ford on the other hand would obviously have difficulty in convincing its employees that 'all our backs are against the wall'.

Management—Union Relations

A final constraining factor on the introduction of Japanese-style manufacturing and working practices in the emulating companies is the existing state of management—union relations. Unions may be on the defensive in the 1980s, but as chapter 2 clearly demonstrated, the high dependencies which Japanese manufacturing systems create mean high degrees of co-operation are demanded from all parties. A simple lack of goodwill on the part of a trade union can be sufficient to pose major problems. We have already illustrated this by describing the scuppering of zone circles at Rover and quality circles at Ford.

Basically, any independent and potentially adversarial party is antithetical to the Japanese-style organization, and most emulating companies are faced with several independent trade unions whose rationale is the protection and advancement of the interests of particular occupational groups. Japanization demands a transformation from this situation to one where the union, if a union exists at all, is responsible for the whole of the company's workforce, and where the union identifies a common interest between company success and worker welfare. Because unions in the emulating companies are typically on the defensive in the 1980s, their resistance to Japanization appears to have been at a local, 'covert' level. This subversion is, however, as we have seen, a major impediment in many cases. In addition, as long as the emulating companies take refuge in the apparently weak position of power of trade unions, they risk the possibility of overt resistance and conflict at some point in the future. Indeed, at the time of writing, Ford's plans for teamwork (described above) were facing overt resistance by its manual workers' unions which were demanding that the company drop plans for skilled workers to be available to man production lines, despite the fact that Ford had already given in on the introduction of Nissan-style temporary workers.

Buyer—Supplier Relations

As we saw in chapter 1, buyer—supplier relationships in Japan are characterized by being of higher trust, longer term and obligational in nature. We shall look at three elements of 'Japanese' buyer—supplier relations in the British context: the use of subcontracting, quality assured supplies and JIT supply.

As the table illustrates, the most widely used practice of this collection appears to be the contracting out of non-core activities, with 87 per cent of companies replying that they subcontract. Rather less use is currently being made of quality assured and just-in-time supplies. These two practices go very much hand in hand, as it is not feasible to operate the latter in the absence of the former. About a quarter of the sample reported that they were implementing or planning to implement these practices. In their survey Voss and Robinson (1987b) found that about 50 per cent of companies with JIT programmes had implemented, or were

Table 4.10   Status of buyer—supplier practices

Practices	Never used (%)	In use (%)	Planned or implementing (%)
Subcontracting non-core activities	8	87	5
Quality assured supplies	16	61	23
Just-in-time supplies	31	42	27
Number in sample 64			

planning to implement JIT purchasing. The dates of introduction of these practices as found in our survey are given in table 4.11.

Buyer—supplier relationships present a similar picture to manufacturing methods in terms of the recency of their introduction. Just-in-time supply systems are recent arrivals with 1986 as their median date of introduction. Quality assured supplies come next with a median introduction date of 1985, followed by subcontracting of non-core activities with a median of 1980 as its date of introduction.

Our visits to companies suggest some problems with these figures. First, to some companies 'non-core' activities refer to little more than catering, security and cleaning operations; many organizations have contracted out such activities for years. More significant is the increase in subcontracting out parts of the production process according to a value-added analysis of their operations. This is manifesting itself as the question of 'Make or buy?' Figure 3.1 in the preceding chapter illustrates the approach which Lucas are adopting in this area. Our impression of the subcontracting amongst this sample is that it is subcontracting of the former rather than the latter type which is most predominant at present.

The most troublesome practice has been just-in-time supplies (13 per cent unsuccessful). In the case of JIT supply two conditions have to be met if the system is to work effectively. First, the quality must be right, as there is little or no slack in the system if products are unusable. Secondly, and self-evidently, the goods must arrive on time; with little stock in the system a late delivery can mean disaster. As the level of complaints about quality assured supplies (5 per cent unsuccessful) are low, it is probably delivery rather than quality which has been the problem area. This can change the demands made on the purchasing function. The case of one company which had both moved over to internal JIT production and had contracted out production previously performed in-house is instructive. The company had run into trouble in doing so; buyers had not yet adapted to the new situation, and this was reflected in numerous problems on the shopfloor. Many of the subcontracts were felt to be unsatisfactory, and much of the blame for this was put on the purchasing department:

> Everyone is twitching about stuff coming in from outside . . . unfortunately we've gone off half-cocked − on the supply side especially . . . In the buying office you need people who not only have an input into what they're buying, but also into what we're producing as well.

Product Quality and Buyer—Supplier Relations

One company which has led the way in terms of changing the nature of its relationships with its suppliers is the Ford Motor Company. In the company's words:

> To improve the quality of bought out parts, Ford is reducing its supply base, changing the emphasis on quality assurances and encouraging a greater supplier involvement in the product . . . which helps build a long-term relationship with Ford. (Ford Motor Company 1984)

Table 4.11 Dates of introduction of buyer–supplier practices

Practices	Pre-1942	1943–1947	1948–1952	1953–1957	1958–1962	1963–1967	1968–1972	1973–1977	1978–1982	1983–1987	Median date	Number in sample
Just-in-time supplies	1 (4%)	—	1 (4%)	1 (4%)	1 (4%)	1 (4%)	1 (4%)	—	1 (4%)	16 (66%)	1986	23
Quality assured supplies	1 (4%)	—	—	—	—	1 (4%)	1 (4%)	2 (7%)	2 (7%)	20 (74%)	1985	27
Subcontracting non-core activities	1 (3%)	—	—	—	—	3 (8%)	2 (6%)	2 (6%)	15 (42%)	13 (36%)	1980	36

Table 4.12   Evaluation of buyer—supplier practices

Practices	Not successful (%)	Quite—very successful (%)	Highly successful (%)	Mean
Subcontracting non-core activities	—	83	17	2.69
Quality assured supplies	5	84	11	2.41
Just-in-time supplies	13	74	13	2.29
Number in sample 64				

As about 50 per cent of the parts which go into a Ford car are manufactured by outside suppliers, the quality of these finished parts will obviously have a crucial bearing on the performance of the finished product. In its 1984 'Durability, Quality and Reliability' report Ford declared the objective of reducing the number of its suppliers by 33 per cent, and its intention to source:

> . . . only from those with a proven quality track record who can show they have the necessary control systems in existence consistently to produce components to specification. As the number of suppliers is reduced, it is only those prepared to make the effort *and honour the trust placed in them* who will obtain an increasing share of the Ford business. [Emphasis added]

Prior to recent changes, Ford operated a scheme of supplier quality assurance for many years. This scheme was used to survey and check the adequacy of the control systems which the suppliers were using. The emphasis recently has shifted much more to *self-certification* by the supplier, in which suppliers are held totally responsible for the quality of their products: they become more involved in their design, and are held accountable for their performance once fitted to completed vehicles. In order to achieve this Ford appear to have been the UK leaders in supplier development, with their famous Q101 quality manual (of which 40,000 were printed) clearly spelling out the expectations they have of their suppliers. Ford have laid on substantial training programmes for their suppliers in techniques such as SPC, although in 1987 suppliers were charged £250 a day for such training. Many other companies have copied Ford's Q101 programme; some have even simply photocopied pages from it, removed the Ford logos, and included it in their quality documentation to suppliers.

Clearly Ford's behaviour towards its suppliers bears some resemblance to elements of Japanese buyer—supplier relationships. From the suppliers' point of view, though, the marriage with Ford has been entered into under some pressure. The fact that all the motor manufacturers are reducing their numbers of suppliers is creating a degree of competition among them that is certainly assisting the major vehicle assemblers in getting their requirements accepted and implemented by their suppliers. This applies not only to the relatively smaller suppliers, but also to suppliers who may themselves be large multinational companies. For example, in 1984 Pirelli (who supply tyres and seat suspension to the motor industry) invested heavily in sophisticated computerized quality information systems, partly because of pressure from Ford to do so (Oliver 1986). We have no evidence that Ford, or indeed any of the other vehicle or automotive manufacturers who have copied Q101, have interfered in any other areas of the running of their suppliers' businesses, such as personnel management, although the fact that preferred supplier status gives the buyer to right to examine a supplier's books confers some degree of monitoring and hence control.

The suppliers to whom we have talked certainly seem to see the changes as having been more or less forced on them, although once implemented the advantages of practices such as SPC have not gone unnoticed by the suppliers themselves. Southern Components regard SPC as the 'best Japanese import', a sentiment echoed by managers at Ketlon Ltd.

How far these changes represent a genuine mirroring of Japanese buyer—supplier relationships is difficult to ascertain. As far as quality assurance is concerned, a case could be made for signs of closer, more co-operative relationships emerging. When we turn to JIT supply, a slightly different picture emerges.

JIT Supply

As we saw in chapter 1, just-in-time supply is widely used between customers and suppliers in Japan, and, as the case of Southern Components illustrates, is a feature which is becoming increasingly sought by many UK based companies. However, our theoretical framework outlined in chapter 2 suggests that simply removing the 'safety-nets' of buffer stocks and goods inward inspection carries a price in terms of increased dependency of the buyer on the supplier, particularly when combined with purchasing policies based on a restricted set of suppliers. This has led some commentators to question the wisdom of adopting these techniques in the UK. For example Ramsey (1985) has argued that:

> The combination of minimal safety stocks and single-sourcing is perfectly rational and desirable for Japanese purchasing departments, but highly risky for their UK counterparts. Adopting Japanese purchasing techniques without first creating conditions in the UK economy comparable to those in Japan appears foolhardy . . . single-sourcing plus a just-in-time stockholding policy looks suspiciously like a recipe for disaster.

In support of this Ramsey compares the number of working days lost through industrial stoppages in Japan and the UK in the period 1978—82. In the UK 532 working days were lost per thousand employees. The equivalent figure for the same period in Japan was 23. The results from our survey certainly provide some support for Ramsey's view, with JIT supply being rated as one of the relatively less successful Japanese imports. Consistent with this, quality assured supplies also come well down the list. Other evidence also suggests that JIT supply has aggravated the effects of disruption in the motor industry. In October 1986, for example, 12,000 people were laid off at Austin Rover due to industrial action at Lucas Electrical's Cannock plant. According to newspaper reports part of the reason for the speed and severity of the disruption was attributable to Rover's adoption of JIT supply arrangements. When the staff at Lucas went on strike Rover only had a few days worth of components in stock, and so production was swiftly halted (*Guardian* 9 October 1986). As we argued in chapter 2, if companies are to run high dependency systems successfully, appropriate strategies must be adopted if the system as a whole is not to be vulnerable to disruption — disruption due to late deliveries, inadequate quality and so on. The motor industry is probably furthest down this road so far, and so it is useful to consider developments in this sector.

One of the first features when considering buyer—supplier relationships in the motor industry is that of the unequal balance of power within the industry — more specifically the economic muscle of the major assemblers over their suppliers gives them an ability to push through changes in supplier practices. Discussing JIT supply in the American car industry, Main (1984) comments:

> . . . the auto companies are forcing suppliers to 'eat inventory' — in other words much of the inventory still exists, but instead of being in the manufacturers' warehouses it has been pushed out to suppliers. A mere shifting of inventory, of course, will largely defeat the goals of just-in-time. Over the long run the suppliers will find a way to get manufacturers to pay for it.

This situation contrasts with the high trust, long-term nature of relational contracting as practised in Japan. The question which this raises is whether UK companies are enacting strategies which will in the longer term enable them to genuinely emulate Japanese buyer—supplier relationships, or whether they are removing the slack from the system (or forcing it on to someone else) without taking steps to live with the increased dependency which results. Our evidence suggests that it is a mix of both.

As far as JIT supply is concerned, it appears that the larger motor manufacturers are indeed forcing their suppliers to 'eat inventory'. To recount a comment from the managing director of a subcontracting company in the automotive industry:

> JIT has been used as a myth on which to hang the transfer of the responsibility for stockholding to another point in the supply chain as long as it ain't the blooming car companies . . . Basically most people who have achieved it have done it by switching it to some other poor sod.

One factor which seems to be often overlooked is that to work effectively JIT requires a certain stability of demand; if suppliers know some time in advance the types and quantities of products required, then these can be made to order. In the face of uncertain customer demand for the final product, and a determination on the part of the car companies not to build for stock, JIT looks a potentially precarious undertaking. In chapter 1, we showed how Toyota's JIT system is in fact dependent on some predictability of demand, and the 'smoothing' of production over a monthly period.

In terms of the UK experience thus far, our evidence suggests that this 'smoothing' is not occurring, at least as far as certain manufacturers in the motor industry are concerned. This may be because certain companies — Rover being the prime example — face a much more uncertain market than do companies such as Toyota.

Without a position of dominance, there are real problems in creating the conditions of relative stability and certainly for a JIT system of supply to work effectively.

A second problem which many British companies face when implementing JIT supply is one of geographical dispersion. This has obvious disadvantages when JIT supply is in use as transport time is yet another source of lag — and sometimes uncertainty — in a production system. As was described in chapter 3, the spread of JIT supply is one of the factors causing Lucas to locate an increasing proportion of their production abroad, close to those areas where car production is most concentrated.

Again, the motor industry in the UK provides instructive examples of adaptive strategies. Given a geographical dispersion of component suppliers, a desire to minimize stockholding and at the same time a need for high security of supplies, both Rover and Jaguar have built warehouses close to their factories, to which their suppliers deliver components, and from which they withdraw supplies as and when required. The advantage of this system to the vehicle assemblers is that the stock remains the property of the supplier (and hence is held at the supplier's expense) until it is withdrawn. Moreover, whilst it is in the warehouse, the supplier is charged rent for the warehouse space it is occupying. In the case of Rover this operation is subcontracted out to British Road Services. BRS has a storage depot a mile from Rover's Cowley plant and the firm takes responsibility for storage, selection and delivery of components. Twenty BRS employees are based at Cowley itself, moving components right to the assembly lines (Turnbull 1988).

Conclusions

Many British and established foreign-owned companies in the UK are now committed to major programmes of Japanization. However, they face major obstacles — problems which often relate to either an unawareness of the importance of the management of the heightened dependency relations which arise, or perhaps more often to an inability or incapacity to cope with the heightened dependencies. We have focused on the consequences of the heightened dependencies of companies on their employees and suppliers, and the importance of attending to the potential problems to which this gives rise. With regard to employees, new communication, pay grading and selection systems are examples of means by which workers may be made more likely to identify with the company; the breaking down of independent employee representation is another step necessary to prevent workers taking advantage of their enhanced power capacity. With regard to suppliers, the importance and difficulty of achieving long-term 'obligational' relationships has been demonstrated.

If the emulators face problems, how do newly-investing Japanese companies fare? This question is addressed in the next chapter. Then in the final chapter we will draw together our conclusions and explore the broad policy implications of the Japanization of British industry.

5

Japanese Companies in Britain

This chapter explores the nature and extent of Japanese direct investment in the UK — 'direct Japanization' in Ackroyd et al.'s terms — and examines the practices which these companies are employing. The chapter is based largely on survey work undertaken by ourselves, and surveys and case studies by other members of the Cardiff Business School — Morris (1988b), Gleave (1987) and Pang (1987).

The Extent of Japanese Direct Investment

The establishment of Japanese manufacturers in the UK has recently received a great deal of media attention. As well as frequent news items, *Sayonara Pet* and *Chopsticks, Bulldozers and Newcastle Brown* — TV documentaries on Nissan and Komatsu respectively — were screened nationally in 1986 and 1987. The attention is warranted, for although Japanese direct investment is still very small compared with, say, American investment, the figures suggest that Japan is indeed becoming a significant investor in the UK.

Morris (1988a) demonstrates that Japanese investment in the UK began on a significant scale only in the mid-1970s, and the most recent figures show a sharp acceleration of investment in the mid-1980s. The rapid growth is part of a trend on the part of Japanese investors to increase overseas investment worldwide, reflecting the effects of trade frictions and the strong yen. The Japanese Ministry of Finance calculated direct investment overseas (cumulative total since 1951) to have increased from US$4.7 billion at the end of 1973 to US$22.3 billion by 1979. By the end of 1986 the figure stood at almost US$106 billion, of which US$28.2 billion was accounted for by manufacturing industry. US$34.5 billion of the total at the end of 1986 was committed during the previous two years alone, and 1986 saw an 82.7 per cent rise in overseas spending over 1985 (Anglo-Japan Economic Institute 1987).

The Finance Ministry further calculated that in the UK direct investment from Japan reached a cumulative total (since 1951) of US$4.1 billion at the end of

1986, almost US$1 billion of which was committed in 1986 alone. US$4.1 billion represents around 4 per cent of the total invested overseas by the Japanese. The UK, up to now, has been the recipient of almost a quarter of the total Japanese investment commitment in the EEC. *The Financial Times* (24 April 1987) reported that Japanese investment in the UK was worth £3.2 billion, and involved the direct employment of over 17,500 people. During 1987, of course, further investment decisions were made, and many Japanese companies already established announced expansion plans which would increase investment commitments and employment levels. Nissan alone announced a plan to add £250 million to its present commitment of £350 million, creating an additional 1,400 jobs by 1992, and during 1987 Japanese companies invested £560 million in the UK (*Western Mail* 22 January 1988).

Japanese manufacturers accounted for 13,557 of the total employed by Japanese companies in the UK at the beginning of 1987 (Morris 1988a), which means that although manufacturing investment is still a small proportion of total Japanese investment, it accounted for around 75 per cent in employment terms. This contrasts with the situation at the end of 1983 (just over three years earlier) when Japanese manufacturers accounted for less than 6,000 employees – around 38 per cent of the total employed in Japanese companies (Dunning 1986).

In addition to the figures cited above, there are at least two more reasons to expect an increase in the significance of Japanese direct investment. One is the expected inflow of suppliers to the major Japanese corporations – 'follow my leader'. A second is that (at least until Nissan arrived) manufacturing investment commitment was heavily concentrated in the electronics sector – it is possible that other sectors could follow. Indeed the big Japanese construction companies, already well-established overseas in the Far East and Australia, are now looking further afield – including to Europe (*Financial Times* 18 May 1987).

It must be emphasized that Japanese direct investment and employment in Japanese companies in the UK are still low in comparison to US companies, and how long the situation which is leading to substantial Japanese commitments – the strong yen, political pressure and so on – will continue is debatable. Nonetheless the long-term commitment of those companies which have invested appears to be there, as is shown in the following quotation which indicates an intent to increase both the quantity and the quality of investment. The quotation is part of a speech made by Takao Negishi, European director of Japan's Electronic Industries Association, speaking at the launch of a pamphlet celebrating the Japanese contribution to Britain to be sent to all 633 British MPs:

> We are in a transition period, at the infant stage, and we need time and understanding . . . in the second stage we will be picking up the best brains in the country.

The Research

The practices of Japanese companies with manufacturing operations in the UK were explored using a similar survey questionnaire to that used to explore the practices of the 'emulators' described in the previous chapter. (Of course, because most companies had set up within the last few years there was little point in examining the dates of introduction of practices.) Questionnaires were sent to all 49 Japanese manufacturing companies whose addresses were given in the 1986 Anglo-Japanese Economic Institute's Japanese company directory. 14 were returned completed, a response rate of 28 per cent. The companies varied in size from three employees up to 2,550. Two of the companies were established ones which had been taken over by Japanese companies in the two years prior to the survey in 1987. Although this sample size is small, three other studies into Japanese companies in the UK were carried out at the Cardiff Business School in 1987: Gleave (1987), Morris (1988b) and Pang (1987). In combination the four studies cover a total of 31 companies (about 60 per cent of the total number of Japanese manufacturers in Britain in 1987), providing us with complementary data on many Japanese practices. The mean size of the companies in our survey was 469, though many expected rapid growth over the next few years. This chapter explores the activities and experiences of Japanese companies in four areas: their location, operations and markets; their manufacturing practices; their personnel and industrial relations practices; and their relations with suppliers.

Operations and Geographical Location

The operations of the 31 Japanese companies on which we have full or partial data are shown in table 5.1. As this table shows, manufacturers of electrical and electronic products were dominant in our sample, as indeed they are in the total population of Japanese companies operating in Britain. The companies falling into the category of miscellaneous represent a diverse array of operations, from sports gear to PVC sheeting. Notable are the number of companies in the vehicle and automotive category; this is likely to increase as Japanese subcontractors follow the major vehicle assemblers overseas. In terms of the markets the companies served, the focus was on Europe. Out of the fourteen companies who responded

Table 5.1 Operations of the sample of Japanese companies

Operations	Number in sample	% of sample
Vehicles and automotive	4	13
Electronics, electrical	16	52
Engineering	1	3
Food, drink, tobacco	1	3
General manufacturing	9	29
Petrochemicals	—	—
Pharmaceuticals	—	—
	(31)	(100%)

to this question six described their main markets as 'European', five as 'British', and three as 'Global'.

In the authors' own survey, Japanese companies were asked to indicate the nationalities of up to four of their major competitors. The responses to this question are given in table 5.2. Interestingly, other Japanese companies were most often seen as the major competitors by our sample firms, which makes questionable the popular stereotype of 'Japan Inc.'. Notable also is the presence of the Pacific Basin countries as competitors, a trend which is likely to continue as these countries become more highly developed.

The location of Japanese manufacturers in Britain is most marked in the depressed regions of the North East and South Wales, though many appear to have preferred new towns such as Livingston in Scotland, Milton Keynes and Telford. According to Morris (1988b) *all* decisions to locate have been met with local and national government aid.

Manufacturing and Working Practices

Manufacturing practices are presented in descending order of usage in table 5.3. Because of the recent establishment of these companies, current usage was combined with the 'planned and implementing' category, on the grounds that a number of companies had simply not had time to implement these practices at the time they completed the survey.

Table 5.2 Nationalities of main competitors

Japan	10
USA	7
Britain	5
Pacific Basin (Taiwan, Korea, etc.)	5
Other European countries	11

Table 5.3 Status of manufacturing practices in Japanese firms

Practices	Never used (%)	In use, planned or implementing (%)	Number in sample
Total quality control	0	100	19
Flexible working	5	95	19
Group working/work teams	7	93	14
Statistical process control	21	79	14
Quality circles	27	73	30
Just-in-time production	36	64	22

Sources: authors' survey; Morris (1988b); Gleave (1987); Pang (1987)

The first feature to note about the table is that all companies were either using or implementing total quality control, although of the 14 companies in our own survey over a third (36 per cent) reported that they were still in the process of planning or implementing total quality control (TQC). This implies that TQC is taking the Japanese companies some time to develop in the UK environment (or that it is something that they themselves are still learning about). Flexibility and the use of work teams also showed extensive usage. The incidence of usage of other techniques is less marked: only two-thirds of companies report the use of JIT. In our own sample 42 per cent of companies reported they were currently using JIT, although half of the non-users were planning or implementing it. Of the companies in our own sample not already using statistical process control (SPC), none were planning to introduce the technique.

When we turn to how well Japanese companies evaluate their success with these practices, we are limited to our own survey findings; consequently some of the numbers are rather small. Nevertheless, this information (presented in table 5.4) gives some indication of the relative success of these practices.

The first point to note from table 5.4 is how successful on the whole companies have been with these practices, although some variation between practices is apparent. Flexible working, total quality control and the use of work teams all stand out as particularly successful. This pattern broadly follows that of the evaluation made by the emulating companies, although the mean scores − and by implication degree of success − recorded by the Japanese companies is greater for every practice apart from JIT. However, when simple statistical analyses were performed, the Japanese companies came out *significantly* more successful on only one of the above items, namely flexible working. In common with the experiences of the emulating companies, quality circles again come well down the league table in terms of their success. What explanations are there for this pattern, particularly the greater success of the Japanese companies with flexible working?

Anecdotal evidence points to a shopfloor existence markedly different from that in typical British firms. Takamiya (1981) noted much greater attention paid to minor details in the production process. Contrasting British and Japanese practice in printed circuit board assembly, the British strategy to safeguard quality

Table 5.4 Japanese firms' evaluation of manufacturing practices

Practices	Not successful	Quite−very successful	Highly successful	Mean[a]
Flexible working	0	4	8	3.50
Total quality control	0	5	7	3.42
Group working/work teams	1	4	7	3.33
Statistical process control	0	6	3	2.89
Quality circles	1	8	1	2.50
Just-in-time production	1	6	1	2.25

[a] 1 = Not successful, 4 = Highly successful

was to buy an extremely sophisticated and expensive testing machine. The Japanese approach was to organize assembly into three-worker teams, with two workers inserting components and one visually checking and correcting. He recounts:

> Every movement of the operators is closely watched and constantly improved upon. Every mistake they make is constantly and individually fed back to them verbally by supervisors, formally by tables and graphs displayed in front of them and visually by supervisors taking them to the other production section where their mistake is causing trouble. (Takamiya 1981, p. 8)

Many accounts suggest that discipline on the shopfloor is much tighter, which manifests itself in a variety of ways. Reitsperger (1986a) found that Japanese TV companies in Britain exacted much stricter work discipline, discouraged social interaction of semiskilled workers on the assembly line, and meticulously enforced work standards and procedures in comparison to equivalent British and American companies. Takamiya (1981, p. 9), also comparing Japanese firms with British and American ones noted:

> While both British and American companies allow eating, drinking and smoking on the shopfloor, the Japanese strictly prohibit such activities even during breaks. Sometimes chatting can be cause for a warning.

Another characteristic of Japanese companies which is frequently commented upon is an insistence on bell-to-bell working. As a senior official from the EETPU, who had negotiated a number of agreements with Japanese firms, remarked to the authors:

> The Japanese believe in bell-to-bell working. They cannot understand the mentality of the British people where they have to go to the toilet at times other than their natural break because they have conditioned themselves to do that. They can't understand why they are not prepared to co-operate with the company and give back to the company the two and a half minute washing time before the end of the bell because the Japanese say 'Well it's our company and that two and a half minutes, if added up throughout the week is 70 television sets'. Whichever way you look at it they are absolutely right.

In some cases, bell-to-bell working is written into union agreements. The Nissan-AEU agreement, for example, states 'Employees will be prepared for work at the start and end of their normal working day/shift' (Wickens 1985). A supervisor from Komatsu, quoted in chapter 3, also felt that such discipline was important in Japanese companies' success, going so far as to say that:

> All that the British worker has got to do to work to the Japanese system is to work during the time he is paid ... once the British worker has done that he has fulfilled the Japanese system. (BBC 1987)

Quality circles in Japanese companies provide instances of both relative successes and failures. For example, the industrial relations executive of a Japanese colour TV manufacturer described the company's success with quality circles as 'patchy'. Most of their 'quality activity groups' were supervisor led in order to provide a focus; people were generally reluctant to take the initiative themselves. On the other hand, there have been reports from Komatsu of workers forming quality circles and meeting after work (without pay) to discuss quality problems, indicating success — from the company's point of view at least (BBC 1987). Mitsubishi, located in Livingston new town, also report success with what their personnel officer describes as a 'bastardized' system of quality circles. This involves splitting its operators into teams which seek to achieve performance targets for attendance, housekeeping and 'zero defects'. A tactic used to maintain dedication at Mitsubishi, also reported in Nissan (see chapter 3) is to publicly display performance. At Mitsubishi the weekly performance ratings of operators are displayed on charts above their heads, and charts at the end of assembly lines show the performance of the quality circle (*Financial Times* 18 January 1988).

Flexible working stands out as the area in which the Japanese companies have been particularly successful in comparison to their British counterparts, both in our survey, and according to other published accounts. For example, Takamiya (1981) reports the case of a Japanese colour TV manufacturer in Britain in which secretaries and clerical workers helped out on the shopfloor with insertion and packing when adverse weather conditions led to a shortage of operators. At the same company there were also instances of supervisors, operators and technicians installing a conveyor because of delays with a subcontractor. We also came across some problems with flexible working at a TV manufacturer, but these centred around limitations of ability rather than motivation.

A number of conditions present in the Japanese companies appear to facilitate flexibility, tight discipline and bell-to-bell working, and hence relative success in the sphere of production. These are related to their personnel practices, to which we now turn attention.

Personnel and Industrial Relations Practices

The usage of six practices is explored in this section: single status facilities, systems of communication and involvement, the provision of staff benefits to all, job security and temporary workers. The results are shown in table 5.5.

Single status is practised in all but two companies. Of the two that did not have single status conditions one was very small, employing only three people, and the other a long established British company taken into Japanese ownership only in 1986. In all the other companies, single status is currently in use. Almost as high a proportion of companies use some form of direct communication with workers, although this takes a variety of forms. It often involves regular team briefings, which can also function as a forum for discussion.

A majority of the companies reported that they offered high job security for their core workers, although as in Japan this was never offered contractually, but rather as a matter of general policy. In his study of five Japanese companies

Table 5.5   Status of personnel practices in Japanese firms

Practices	Never used (%)	In use, planned or implementing (%)	Number in sample
Single status facilities	12	88	24
In-company communications/ employee involvement	17	83	18
'Staff' benefits at all levels	25	75	16
High job security for core workers	27	73	22
Company representative bodies	45	55	20
Use of temporary workers	67	33	21

Sources: authors' survey; Gleave (1987); Pang (1987)

Gleave (1987) suggests that this policy is largely attributable to influence by the parent companies.

Company representative bodies exist in just over half the companies in the combined sample. As these carry important implications for industrial relations they will be discussed in some detail below.

As we saw in chapter 1, in Japan the major corporations segment their labour markets, and make extensive use of temporary and other peripheral workers. In the UK a significant minority of companies (33 per cent) on which we have data routinely use temporary workers, which is in fact smaller than the proportion reported by our emulating companies. However, some Japanese companies have deployed temporary workers in positions traditionally the prerogative of permanent employees. Nissan, for example, employed temporary workers on its production line, the first time temporary workers had been used on a car assembly line in Britain since the Second World War (*Financial Times* 16 February 1987).

Table 5.6   Japanese companies' evaluation of personnel practices

Practices	Not successful	Quite–very successful	Highly successful	Mean[a]
10% + temporary workers	0	1	2	3.67
In-company communications	0	3	8	3.64
Single status facilities	0	4	6	3.60
'Staff' benefits at all levels	0	3	5	3.50
High job security for blue collar workers	0	3	5	3.50
Employee involvement	1	4	6	3.27

[a] 1 = Not successful, 4 = Highly successful

Turning to how the Japanese companies evaluate their success with personnel practices, a generally favourable picture emerges with a majority of companies considering these practices 'highly successful'. Two qualifications should, however, be made. First, and self-evidently, the number of companies reporting is small — only three in the case of temporary workers, for example. Secondly, success is defined by the companies themselves, and therefore may mean different things to different organizations, according to what their objectives were in using such practices in the first place.

In addition to discussing Japanese companies' experiences with some of the practices listed in the above table, we shall also consider aspects of personnel practices such as selection, recruitment and training.

Direct Communication and Single Status

In-company communications, single status facilities and the provision of staff benefits for blue collar workers may of course take a variety of forms. From the companies' perspectives these practices are regarded favourably, although other evidence suggests the picture is a little more mixed lower down the organization. Single status appears to have been generally welcomed by direct employees and by trade unions, although some of its trappings — for example the wearing of uniforms — have not always been whole-heartedly appreciated. At Matsushita in Cardiff, for example, some of the female administrative workers were reluctant to wear uniforms as they considered them unflattering; at Hoya, the managing director had a problem convincing a delivery driver that he was in fact the managing director, because of the uniform he was wearing (Gleave 1987).

Single status is generally welcomed by those who would otherwise be well down the status hierarchy, but what about those who would traditionally be at an advantage status-wise? In general this does not appear to have caused many problems, although there are signs from some of the longer established companies that the homogeneity generated by single status tends to degenerate over time, partly due to the existence of status differentials in the wider industrial environment. Commenting on the situation at a TV manufacturer, a trade union official remarked to us:

> When senior management are taken on they ask 'What's the pension scheme? Is there a special incentive scheme?' They are told that it's the same as the guy on the shopfloor. So there is a little bit of change and resentment about the old British type of understanding about perks creeping back into the company.

The case of the newly-appointed supervisor at Komatsu, ruefully reflecting on how he used to dream about the day he would come to work in a suit and tie (reported in chapter 3) provides another example of this sentiment, and at Mitsubishi managers have 'quietly' ceased wearing uniforms (*Financial Times* 18 January 1988). We have no information on managerial turnover in the Japanese companies, but one might expect it to be relatively high unless the lack of status-related rewards is compensated for by more pronounced salary differentials. Pang and Oliver (1988) found that seven Japanese companies out of a sample of 11 offered salaries and wages greater than those offered by comparable local firms; the other four all claimed to offer rates which were the same.

Selection and Recruitment

Another notable aspect of Japanese companies' personnel practices lies in their selection and recruitment criteria, and some explanation for their success with flexible working and the apparent willingness to accept bell-to-bell discipline may plausibly be ascribed to this. Morris (1988b) noted that 15 out of 20 companies approached recruited young, unskilled labour – generally school leavers – to perform production jobs. The commercial director of Livingston Development Corporation refers to a preference on the part of newly-investing companies for 'uncontaminated' labour (*Financial Times* 18 January 1988). Pang (1987) found a similar emphasis in seven out of eleven companies, although there was a marked tendency for managerial talent to be 'bought in'. This pattern may be partly explained by the generally low skill levels required in many of these companies, but also, we suspect, due to a desire to have a reasonably compliant and flexible workforce. For instance NEC's personnel manager, responsible for the employment of 280 operators whose average age is 18.5, argued that the company needed a young workforce willing to undergo frequent training. As he put it: 'We cannot offer them a long-term job. But we are guaranteeing them long-term employment'.

It is possible that the emphasis on raw recruits at all levels may increase as Japanese companies establish themselves and have to rely less on externally-acquired professionals and skilled workers. Certainly a strong internal training capability is being developed within these companies (Gleave 1987; Pang 1987). One exception to the 'raw recruit' policy is Takiron, a Japanese company established in Wales with a single union agreement with the TGWU. Their policy is to recruit young married men because of their ability to work shifts (Gleave 1987).

Whether or not Japanese companies have this in mind, the effect is to take on a workforce untainted by working habits which might not fit the company culture. Neither is it likely for such a workforce to have any previous experience of, or involvement in, trade union activity of any kind. Hence recruits are more easily socialized into the ways of the company, and if the company does have a trade union, more easily socialized into co-operative union–management relations. Some companies, of which Komatsu is an example, make use of a variety of attitude tests in their selection procedures.

Following recruitment, a company-organized induction programme typically awaits the candidates in Japanese companies in Britain (Gleave 1987), the length of which varies from company to company. At Matsushita's Panasonic plant in Cardiff the formal induction lasts only one day, for instance, whereas at Komatsu in Sunderland there are ten full day sessions spread over the first ten weeks at work, including Japan familiarization courses. Further initial socialization is typically given with immediate on-the-job training in a variety of tasks or jobs. At Mazak, the Japanese machine tool plant in Worcester, this involves the trainee submitting weekly reports on progress, serving to impress the importance of flexible working on the recruit.

One final set of personnel practices which merits some attention is systems of reward. Toshiba has developed a reward system specifically designed to encourage flexibility. In a similar manner to the system at Pirelli described in the previous chapter, the system pays workers to be flexible; there are 18 recognized production skills, and increments are paid for each one mastered. A formal assessment of each employee is carried out annually. Some other companies are also going for systems of performance appraisal, in which employees are evaluated against a range of criteria. At Komatsu, this procedure is particularly sophisticated, and goes well beyond on-the-job performance. Employees are assessed on their flexibility, teamwork and communications skills and activities 'Beyond the contract' (Komatsu Employee Handbook 1987).

Management−Union Relations

Given the extensive use of company based representative bodies, what role do such bodies play, and how does their role relate to that of the trade unions in these Japanese companies?

At Toshiba the company advisory board, or CoAB, consists of 14 elected representatives from all areas of the company, plus the senior union representative with the managing director in the chair. Representatives need not be union members. The CoAB can discuss 'any subject from the size of the managing director's car to the annual salary review' (Trevor 1988). Management−union bargaining is there as the 'backstop' if agreement cannot be reached in the CoAB. Gleave reports a similar backstop role for the AEU at Komatsu, and suggests that there is a feeling within the company that management and workers sitting on the Advisory Council have 'failed' if they have to resort to official company/union bargaining.

Some elements of bargaining are inevitable between the agents who sit on these bodies (implicitly if not explicitly), but in general they are rarely construed, by management at least, as bargaining or decision-making agencies. The emphasis is on consultation, an ambiguity which can lead to cynicism about the role of such bodies, as the case of the Komatsu Advisory Council reported in chapter 3 illustrates. At Toshiba, the model on which many other company representative bodies are based, there was some initial confusion about the role of shop stewards on the company advisory board. The traditional view that shop stewards should not sit on such bodies meant that it was primarily non-union members who were sitting on the board − something which alarmed the EETPU, as it implied a short-circuiting of the trade union structure. Subsequently, EETPU policy has been that stewards should seek election to the CoAB, and EETPU official Wyn Bevan (in an interview with the authors) pointed out that this was one of the reasons why the EETPU had retained a credible role in the eyes of its membership and hence kept relatively high membership levels.

Of the 31 Japanese companies in our combined sample, 21 (68 per cent) recognize trade unions. Of these 21 all but one have single union agreements. One of the major motivations behind this is clearly a concern for labour force flexibility. The sole multi-union company had seven trade unions, though this was originally a British company which had been taken into Japanese ownership in 1984. The single union deals are concentrated in the hands of a relatively small set of unions, as is shown in table 5.7.

Unsurprisingly, those unions with 'progressive' reputations such as the EETPU and the AEU have been accepted as single unions in rather more Japanese companies than those with a more traditional image, such as the TGWU. Because of the membership crisis in the trade union movement, competition between unions for single union deals with inwardly investing companies has led to conflict. For example, in a 1987 TV interview one trade unionist described some of his colleagues in other trade unions as 'pigs at the trough of Thatcherism' because of their behaviour towards inwardly investing companies in South Wales. The TGWU has been one of the bitterest critics of single union deals, particularly those which contain so-called no-strike clauses. Indeed, in January 1988 the regional secretary of the TGWU in Wales appealed to the Japanese government to urge companies setting up in the UK to do so without reaching strike-free agreements with British unions. This move was intended to block companies signing agreements with the EETPU in preference to other unions, on the grounds that the former would offer a 'strike-free' package (*Financial Times* 20 January 1988).

Contrary to the impression which might be gained from some reports in the press about very low levels of union membership, our results indicate a wide range of variation in membership levels, from a low of 25 per cent up to a claimed 100 per cent. Average union membership reported by the 16 Japanese companies on which we have data was 59 per cent.

Given the extensive use of company-based representative bodies, there is potential for confusion between the role of these bodies and the role of trade unions. It could be argued that company-based bodies serve to ease out trade unions, or prevent their penetration in the first place. At Mitsubishi, for instance, approaches for recognition by the EETPU were rebutted by the company on the grounds that its elected staff consultative committee eliminates the need for union recognition (*Financial Times* 18 January 1988). However, if company-based bodies are generally being successfully used to keep trade unions out, we would expect

Table 5.7   Trade unions in Japanese companies

Union	Number of companies	Average membership density
EETPU	8	64%
AEU	5	58%
GMB	3	65%
TGWU	2	60%
Number in sample	18	12

Sources: authors' survey; Pang and Oliver (1988)

unionized companies to have a lower proportion of company representative bodies, and vice versa for non-union companies. As table 5.8 shows, such a pattern does not exist among our sample of companies.

Of the four configurations of company representative bodies and unions, the one most frequently found is the combination of a union presence plus a company representative body. This effectively refutes the idea that there is an either/or situation between company representative bodies and trade unions. If that were the case we would expect companies to be clustered in categories 2 and 3 in table 5.8; that is, unionized companies would be less likely to possess a company representative body and vice versa.

It could be argued that the recognition of a trade union in itself is a poor index of the effect of company-based representation, and that trade union membership levels are a more meaningful indicator of union status. Comparing these, the average membership in firms with company-based representation is 62 per cent (eight firms), compared with 87 per cent in firms without such representative apparatus (three firms). With such small numbers, there are obviously limits to how far one can extrapolate from these results, but they do suggest a link between trade union membership and the presence of company-based representative bodies.

These Japanese companies are clearly not conforming to the standard British multi-union model of industrial relations. With the exception of a recent multi-union acquisition, all 31 companies pursued either single or non-union policies. Reitsperger (1986a, p. 75) has suggested that:

> Multi-union representation, and a resultant difficulty in flexibility and labour utilization, problems of demarcation and the complexity of multi-union bargaining are deeply worrying and seen by Japanese management as impediments to productive performance improvement.

He goes on to argue that Japanese companies operating in the UK face essentially three industrial relations options; to accept unionization in its usual (multi-union) form; to avoid it altogether; or to accept unionization but to utilize strategies to neutralize its negative (from a managerial perspective) consequences. On the basis of our evidence, it appears that most Japanese companies are going for the second, and particularly the third of these options, and it seems likely that the use of company representative bodies may indeed be one means of 'neutralizing' the

Table 5.8   Trade unions and company representative bodies

Unionized, with company representative body	8	(40%)
Unionized, no company representative body	4	(20%)
Not unionized, with company representative body	3	(15%)
Not unionized, no company representative body	5	(25%)
	(20)	(100%)

Sources: authors' survey; Gleave (1987); Pang and Oliver (1988)

negative consequences of trade union presence. In chapter 6 we explore the idea that Company Advisory Boards are used to incorporate trade unions, and investigate the evidence for and against this argument.

Buyer—Supplier Relations

This section provides an overview of Japanese companies' relations with their suppliers, and examines how successful they consider these practices to be. The status of four aspects of supplier relations is shown in table 5.9. All the companies in our sample considered themselves to be collaborating very closely with their suppliers; the other three aspects of supplier relations — quality assured supplies, the subcontracting of non-core activities and JIT, were used with decreasing degrees of frequency. Moreover, the proportion of companies planning or implementing these practices (as distinct from already using them) increases as one moves down the table; the 62 per cent of companies using, planning or implementing the subcontracting of non-core activities were virtually evenly divided between those already doing so and those planning to do so. We now turn to the evaluation of these practices.

In terms of favourableness or otherwise of evaluation, supplier relations all receive less favourable ratings than do the personnel practices, with the 'mechanics' of buyer—supplier relations such as quality and JIT delivery of purchased supplies coming in the lower half of the list. Other published accounts and our own anecdotal evidence suggest some explanations for this. Accounts of Japanese companies' concern about the quality of locally sourced parts are frequent. In the words of a Japanese colour TV manufacturer:

> In deciding where to buy our components from, quality availability is the key factor, together with continuity of supply. The fact that we do not buy more components from the EEC reflects our inability to persuade suppliers to provide us with components at the right quality and competitive price. (Quoted in Dunning 1986, p. 107)

Table 5.9   Status of buyer—supplier relations in Japanese companies

Practices	Never used (%)	In use, planned or implementing (%)	Number in sample
Close supplier collaboration	0	100	17
Quality assured supplies	21	79	14
Subcontracting non-core activities	38	62	14
Just-in-time supplies	50	50	26

Sources: authors' survey; Morris (1988b)

Table 5.10   Evaluation of buyer—supplier relations by Japanese companies in Britain

Practices	Not successful	Quite—very successful	Highly successful	Mean
Close supplier collaboration	0	7	5	3.00
Subcontracting non-core activities	1	5	2	2.75
Just-in-time supplies	1	6	2	2.56
Quality assured supplies	1	4	4	2.00

Sony, the colour television manufacturers, manage about 80 to 85 per cent local content in their sets, but this is because they make many of their own parts on site — primarily to safeguard quality and permit the use of JIT production. Their TV plant at Bridgend was described to us as 'probably the most vertically integrated TV plant in Europe, if not the world', with a very high proportion of components made on-site. Sony aspire to long-term relationships with their suppliers, with an emphasis on mutual trust and understanding, but that has not always worked out. A Sony executive recounted to us, 'In some cases Sony have ended up managing the supplier's business as well as our own. They have absolutely no idea of how to produce a consistently good quality product.' Dunning (1986, p. 113) recounts similar sentiments, also from a Japanese colour TV manufacturer, 'It's not so much that suppliers do not know what they have to do to satisfy our standards; but they do not pay enough attention to ensuring that these standards are met.'

Instructive examples of the possible shape of things to come are provided by the attempts of Japanese companies to source materials locally. The purchasing activities of Komatsu, which were examined in chapter 3, illustrate a pattern of buyer—supplier relations which appear to be emerging generally within the British vehicle and automotive industry. Hitherto Ford has taken the lead, as was recounted in the previous chapter. The Komatsu engineers looked hard at the manufacturing operations of their potential suppliers, and suggested improvements the suppliers could make in order for the efficiency levels considered appropriate by Komatsu to be met — hence enabling price reductions. The UK suppliers obviously found this 'hands-on' approach unfamiliar and unsettling. Even once the orders had been landed, the closeness of the buyer—supplier relationship expected by the Japanese was startling to the British suppliers:

> The Japanese tend to camp out on your doorstep. We've got English firms that we seen once or twice a year ... it's nothing for the Japanese to turn up two, three or four times a day. (BBC 1987)

This degree of contact is likely to be more intense in the early days of production, so in the case of Komatsu the 'Japanese' effect is being confounded with the 'start-up' effect; nonetheless a clear divide is apparent in the way in which buyer—supplier relations are conducted.

A further area of contrast between Japanese and UK practices lies in the standards of quality expected. Indeed, the poor availability of components of the necessary quality is frequently cited by the Japanese companies as a reason for low content of locally sourced components. Pressure in this area is already high and could increase: presently to escape tariff barriers at least 60 per cent of the input to a product has to be of local (that is EEC) origin. As more Japanese companies set up manufacturing operations overseas, more of their subcontractors are likely to follow them; some already have, such as Ikeda-Hoover who make seats for Nissan. The number of Japanese subcontractors entering Britain could rise to a higher level than would otherwise be the case, we would suggest, because of the lack of confidence by the Japanese in the quality of locally sourced materials.

Conclusions

The most important point arising from the evidence presented in this chapter is that Japanese direct investors *are* bringing with them to the UK many of the manufacturing and personnel practices which they use in Japan. That is, 'adaptation' to the local environment does not necessarily entail the abandoning of the essential elements of the Japanese approach to manufacturing. Certainly, problems have been encountered, particularly with regard to just-in-time supplies; and quality circles and just-in-time production have not always been overwhelmingly successful. Further, there are one or two anomalies — the low level of usage of temporary workers being the most obvious. However, some of these will obviously be related to the fact that most of the companies are in the 'infant' stage — for instance establishing just-in-time supply bases will necessarily be a slow and difficult process, and the use of temporary workers as a 'buffer' may not be a pressing concern in the present stage of rapid growth.

A second point is that the personnel practices for which the Japanese are renowned — consultation, direct communication, highly selective recruitment, long-term employment for core workers and so on — are being introduced, more than in the emulating companies, in tandem with the new manufacturing methods and working practices. Indeed, if anything, our survey evidence suggests the personnel practices are being 'put in place' more rapidly than the manufacturing practices. In terms of our theory of Japanization, this makes sense — Japanese companies may be 'laying the groundwork' for their manufacturing practices. The emulating companies, as we saw in the previous chapter, can face problems if their existing personnel practices, which evolved in a different era, are 'out of synch' with their manufacturing ones. This may explain why, as table 5.11 demonstrates, the Japanese report greater success with *all* practices (excepting JIT) than do the emulators.

Statistical significance tests revealed *significant* differences with regard to four practices — flexible working, in-company communications, single status, and high job security for core workers. Nonetheless the consistency of perceived

Table 5.11   Relative success of Japanese practices: Japanese companies vs emulating companies

Practices	Emulators	Japanese companies
Flexible working	2.91	3.50
Total quality control	2.98	3.42
Group working/work teams	2.78	3.33
Statistical process control	2.60	2.89
Quality circles	2.12	2.50
Just-in-time production	2.45	2.25
10%+ temporary workers	2.69	3.67
In-company communications	2.67	3.54
Single status facilities	3.15	3.60
'Staff' benefits at all levels	3.08	3.50
High job security for blue collar workers	2.97	3.73
Employee involvement	2.76	3.27

1 = Not successful, 4 = Highly successful

relative success by the Japanese compared with the emulators very strongly points to a better overall performance by the Japanese.

This relative success − a success most marked with regard to personnel and working practices − may be explained by the advantages the Japanese companies have in terms of greenfield sites and by implication (selected) green labour. Under such conditions, with no history of adversarial industrial relations and the restrictive practices which typically accompany them, a greater success with Japanese-style practices is to be expected.

A remark made to us by an executive of a Japanese TV manufacturer operating in the UK seemed particularly pertinent to the question of the relationship between manufacturing and personnel strategies in Japanese companies:

> I don't think it is very profitable for companies to come along to Japanese companies and pinch their techniques. They have got to get to the fundamental point and say 'What are we trying to do here?'. In our case it is to create a very high quality product and sell it at a relatively high price ... It is all a question of deciding what the end object of the organization is. Once you've done that it is very easy to begin to see what techniques you should use. If you are producing cheap, nasty products that are disposable where it does not really matter what the appearance is, then why devote an enormous amount of time to the welfare of your employees because it is not going to produce any benefits to you.

What is so significant about this comment is the way in which personnel strategy is unquestionably an integrated part, indeed a necessary element, of a total business strategy, based in the case of the major Japanese corporations around high dependency, low-waste practices. Considered thus, the real issue is not simply one of whether or not particular elements of Japanese business strategy (such as production methods, personnel practices and so on) can be transferred to a different socio-cultural environment. Equally significant is the extent to which these personnel practices fit with other elements of a company's total strategy, such as its manufacturing strategy, which in turn must fit with the organization's marketing strategy. What is noteworthy about the successful Japanese companies (in general) is the goodness of fit between the strategies employed by their various constituent parts, particularly the fit between their manufacturing strategy and their human resource strategy.

It appears, then, that Japanese manufacturers in the UK are more aware of the importance of carefully managing the dependency relationships characteristic of Japanese-style manufacturing systems. Selection and induction procedures ensure a degree of homogeneity amongst recruits, and practices such as long-term employment, relatively good pay for core workers, single status provisions, and frequent and direct consultation and communication decrease the likelihood of production disruption. At the same time they represent a 'return' to workers for their commitment, bell-to-bell discipline, flexibility, and so on. Of course, because they are newly-investing, they are in a better position to introduce the personnel practices of their choice. Where the emulators *are* aware of the need to transform employee relations, they face problems because of entrenched attitudes, interests and power bases. Interestingly, whilst indicating 'never used' and 'not planned', some respondents to our *Times 1,000* survey wrote comments in the questionnaire margin to the effect that they would like to see arrangements such as single union deals and no-strike agreements − if only they were feasible.

In conclusion, we would not wish to over-emphasize the direct impact of the presence of Japanese manufacturers in the UK − the extent of this impact remains to be seen. However, because of their presence, their practices have become more highly visible, and existing companies in the UK are frequently pointing to these companies as models to be emulated.

6

Industrial Relations and Trade Unions

Previous chapters have described how the adoption and introduction of new production systems, employment practices and human resource management strategies by Japanese and Japanizing companies have crucial implications for the structure and distribution of power and control in the workplace, and therefore industrial relations. The new manufacturing systems, and in particular just-in-time, could serve to enhance the power capacity of workers, but the *visibility* characteristic of just-in-time systems and module-based production, together with employment and human resource management practices which facilitate tighter control of workers, are likely to counterbalance this in favour of top managements. Of course, in practice, the relative success or failure of these initiatives is dependent on wider changes in the British political and economic system — on a set of supportive or 'facilitative' conditions — and these will be discussed in the next chapter. Success is also dependent, at least in most large companies, on the trade union response, for trade unions are theoretically in a position to thwart attempts at Japanization with simple tactics entailing little cost to members. For example, the circulation of bad publicity about quality circles could easily breed cynicism among members, and a mere work-to-rule or overtime ban could be as disastrous for a company operating a just-in-time system as could a strike for a company not so doing. Success is dependent, then, on a form of trade unionism which is sympathetic towards, or at least accepting of, the need for the sorts of radical changes we have discussed.

We suggested in chapter 1 that Japanese unions tend to have relationships with employers making for relatively stable industrial relations. At least since the 1950s unions have been enterprise-based and company-oriented to the extent that supervisors and middle managers are frequently found in official union positions, and the union is sometimes a career route into senior management. This situation, which in large part accounts for the low level of industrial action in Japan, emerged in the context of state initiatives (with the blessing of the US in the 1950s) which curbed the rise of a budding independent trade union movement.

While Japan enjoys (for the moment) a relatively stable industrial relations environment, British trade unionism is perhaps less likely to be so facilitative of manufacturing systems which are inherently vulnerable. Britain experiences more industrial disputes and British unions are more independent and exert greater influence at both local and national levels. In addition, occupation- and industry-wide unions are the norm. However, in the mid-1980s British trade unions are undergoing changes which, if not making them more akin to their Japanese counterparts, are at least making them more receptive to the new initiatives.

This chapter summarizes the position of trade unions in Britain in the 1980s and argues that the industrial relations climate is facilitative of radical changes in management strategies and working practices. It then examines the manifest implications of Japanization — that is the form of trade unionism implied by, indeed often demanded by, Japanese and Japanizing companies — and ends with a discussion of the latent implications which, we would argue, could have equally profound consequences.

Contemporary Trade Unionism in Context

The ascendancy of a new movement in British trade unionism is captured by the term 'new realism'. 'New realism' is described in Bassett's popular book as an:

> explicit rejection of class-based industrial enmity in favour of mutually beneficial co-operation, pragmatically embracing social and technological change, resting (its) market based vanguardism on the aggregated assent of the individual. (Bassett 1986, pp. 1–2)

The adoption of *new realism* is not, of course, complete: many of the leaders of some of Britain's largest unions — the TGWU and NUM for instance — have provided vociferous resistance. But new realism does enjoy massive popular support, having been presented as a pragmatic and logical response to radical political, social and economic change. The context of the emergence of new realism is one of a decline in trade union membership and power. Probably the best account and analysis of this decline is provided by Beaumont (1987), who identifies a drop in union membership in Britain of over 10 per cent between 1979 and 1984, and a decline of around 5 per cent in union density, *excluding* the unemployed, over the same period. The decline has continued since then — between 1985 and 1986 alone membership levels of TUC-affiliated unions fell by 3.6 per cent (*Financial Times* 25 June 1987).

Beaumont identifies the problems underlying the decline in membership and power as many and varied, but worryingly for unions most are related to deep-seated changes in industrial and economic structure. Perhaps most important has been the trend in employment in the private sector away from manufacturing towards the services, which are more difficult (and costly) to organize for reasons such as the relatively small size of establishments and high labour turnover. The level of trade union membership in the private services sector is currently around

15 per cent, compared with 60 per cent in manufacturing (*Financial Times* 2 October 1987). It has been estimated that two-thirds of net new jobs created between 1985 and 1990 will be in this sector. Other changes which are contributing to the declining membership and power of trade unions include: increased corporate divisionalization and further subdivisions into wholly-owned limited liability companies — union recognition in one legal entity does not necessarily mean unionization of a division, let alone the whole corporation, as the GMB recently discovered in its dealings with Matsushita (discussed shortly); a trend towards manufacturing employment growth in small towns, new towns and rural areas rather than the old conurbations — workers in these areas are less likely to have traditions of trade union organization; privatization — the private sector is much less densely organized than the public (membership density in the latter is currently around 80 per cent); and a trend towards more subcontracting of non-core operations, more fixed-term contracts and increasing use of part-time, mostly female, workers — all of these 'peripheral' categories of employee are more difficult for trade unions to organize.

In addition to these structural changes, the 1980s have seen government attempts to limit trade union power through legislation, a break from the tradition of active encouragement by governments of union membership in the public sector (perhaps also thereby providing a lead for the private sector) and generally a political climate hostile to militant trade unionism (Beaumont 1987). Though the precise impact of these political changes on union membership and power is unclear, one might safely assume some detrimental effect.

Finally there are the new human resource management and industrial relations strategies of companies, which are the focus of this chapter. These can be seen both as a contributor (probably small so far according to Beaumont) towards a declining union membership, and as an attempt to take advantage of the weakened unions in the face of their declining membership: besides anything else, management might identify a cost incentive in moving away from a philosophy of 'union acceptance' — one study suggests that the union 'mark-up' (the extra amount the average worker receives when represented in pay bargaining by a trade union) has increased from 4.7 per cent in the 1960s, to 7.5 per cent in the 1970s, to 11.1 per cent in the early 1980s (Beaumont 1987). (This is notwithstanding the fact that *some* companies pay premium wages as part of a non-union strategy.)

Trade union responses to these changes in economic structure, political climate and management strategies have so far not significantly slowed or diverted the trends. Perhaps most importantly, the industrial restructuring of Britain's traditional heavy industries — steel, shipbuilding and coal in particular — has been largely achieved despite bitter disputes. Workers from these sectors, traditionally well organized in strong unions (where they have not joined the ranks of the unemployed) have been scattered across new occupations where union density is often lower and union power normally weaker. The political climate has of course made things more difficult for trade unions, and three successive general election victories for the Conservatives have forced the Labour movement in general and trade unions in particular to rethink their position. This situation was summed up in a typical comment from one trade union official interviewed by the authors as follows:

> I use Merthyr Tydfil as the barometer. From coming here until four years ago, about four times a year I had to go there and persuade the refuse men to go back to work. The last time I went I was trying to persuade them to come out. They wouldn't.

Given that part-time and temporary workers are today an important segment of the workforce, that the private services sector is rapidly rising in importance, that any manufacturing employment growth is more likely to be on greenfield rather than established sites, and that militant union activity is less likely to receive popular or practical support in the current political climate, unions have looked closely at their recruitment and organizing strategies, at the services they provide to their members, and even at the image they present to potential recruits and the public generally.

The increasing use of part-time and temporary workers is generally blamed by the unions on employer attempts to cut costs — the TUC General Council for instance recently calculated that an hourly paid part-time manual female worker earns 63 per cent of the wage of a male manual worker. The TUC further argues that the position of part-timers — today accounting for almost one in five of the labour force — is being further undermined by a government cutting back on their legal protections (*Guardian* 8 September 1987). However, there is little the unions can do to halt or change legislation, and many unions have publicly acknowledged that increasing numbers of people work part-time out of choice — women with child-rearing responsibilities or people pursuing higher education, for instance.

Several unions have hence turned their recruiters' attention to part-timers, the TGWU having launched a *Link Up* campaign and the GMB a *Flair* campaign. Unions have similarly turned attention to temporary or fixed-term contract workers, offering to attempt to gain for them better terms and conditions. So far these initiatives have had little success, though the GMB recently won acceptance of its model agreement on temporary labour at British Cable Services. This agreement lays down the circumstances under which temporary labour may be employed and the terms and conditions under which such employees will operate (*Incomes Data Services Report*, no. 502, August 1987). Temporary workers will be eligible for union membership on the first day of their employment.

The TUC has been taking an increasing interest in recruitment, traditionally a responsibility and prerogative of individual unions — and among other things has announced campaigns in non-union areas such as Milton Keynes, the new town which Bassett describes as a 'foreshadow of the future ... almost a paradigm of how government ministers would like the UK economy, labour market and industrial relations to be', with two-thirds of all jobs in services, 27 per cent in production, many small employers with only three employing over 1,000 workers, a large number of foreign-owned companies, and increasing numbers of women in the labour force (*Financial Times* 9 May 1987).

Compared with these sorts of problem explicit de-unionization moves have not so far been of enormous import. They are in any case rare, most employers (British Coal is a significant exception) appearing satisfied that their flexibility initiatives are being embraced more or less willingly by trade unions. Two notable exceptions are a trend away from union recognition at senior management levels in industry (*Financial Times* 3 July 1987) and de-recognition moves in hotel chains following the elimination of national bargaining over hotel staff conditions under the 1986 Wages Act (*Financial Times* 13 August 1987).

Estimating that union membership could decline from its present 9.2 million to 7 million by the end of the century, GMB general secretary John Edmunds, among others, has called for a radical change in union strategy to halt a potential 'terminal decline' (*Financial Times* 8 May 1987). Recruitment, rather than bargaining, is to be the crucial issue. As well as aiming at temporary and part-time workers, and at the 'non-union' new town areas, some unions, notably the EETPU, are increasingly offering extended services to their members such as discount cards and special deals on life assurance. Recently, for instance, the EETPU bought for its members a £6 million Georgian mansion in Sussex to become a holiday centre, and began offering a free legal advice service — extensions of what Bassett refers to as 'market unionism' (*Financial Times* 30 July 1987). Others are cynical of these initiatives, Ron Todd, TGWU general secretary, stating that 'we are not going down the road of gimmicks and treating our members as customers' (*Financial Times* 23 February 1987). Unions are also going to great lengths to change their image, the GMB for instance dropping its 'unity is strength' slogan in favour of a 'welcoming, lively and friendly' image (*Financial Times* 23 June 1987).

Perhaps predictably, as membership levels have declined, so the number of inter-union disputes over recognition rights has risen, the problem being worsened as traditional demarcations are broken down and previously craft- or occupation-based unions become 'general' unions (the latter is, of course, a long-term trend). A sign of the times is that when British Coal stated it would consider negotiating with unions other than the NUM at the proposed Margam 'superpit' in South Wales, the leaderships of the TGWU and the EETPU as well as the UDM were reported as offering to organize the Margam miners and accept flexible shift working (*Financial Times* 24 June 1987).

A related factor in the rise in inter-union competition in the 1980s, described at length below, is the increasing number of single-union deals sought by inward-investing companies. Inter-union rivalry over these deals accounted for the majority of the 23 inter-union disputes being examined by the TUC's inter-union disputes committee in June 1987 (*Financial Times* 25 June 1987). It is in this context that the TUC has attempted to become involved in recruitment, with suggestions for the establishment of specially designated organizing areas to give individual unions a 'clear run' at non-union companies, and for an agreement that if the membership level is found wanting after a period of time, other unions have the right to attempt recruitment and organization. At the end of 1987, however, inter-union disputes continued.

Finally, and again a subject to be expanded below, there is the offer by some unions — notably the EETPU — of agreements which make strikes or other industrial action extremely unlikely. Referred to as 'no-strike agreements' proudly by some EETPU leaders (Bevan 1987) and cynically by leaders of many other unions, they have become a condition for recognition in many newly-establishing companies. The no-strike deal is possibly the most radical response by trade unions to the situation of declining membership, and though it is difficult to say to what extent they are a pointer for the future, the EETPU at least is determined to continue signing such agreements.

It is in the face of declining membership and power, inter-union rivalry, and uncertainty and disagreement as to the strategies unions should adopt, that Japanese and Japanizing companies are introducing radically different production, management, and industrial relations practices. As we shall see, change is not unproblematic, but certainly the current defensive position of *all* unions, and the *new realism* of some, makes it easier.

The implications of Japanization for patterns of industrial relations and trade unions will be considered in two parts. First, in terms of the types of agreements which unions are currently making with companies, particularly with inwardly investing companies. Such agreements have been the subject of popular debate and have caught the attention of national and local newspapers — the signing of single union deals and flexibility agreements in particular. Secondly we consider the probably less well understood *latent* implications of the new management practices which, we argue, may have equally serious consequences for traditional union organization if managements can achieve their objectives of reorienting the attitudes and allegiances of workers on a significant scale.

New Style Company—Union Agreements

No-strike Deals and Binding Arbitration
Partly because of a search by employers for flexibility and industrial relations stability, the 1980s has seen the establishment of many single-union deals by newly-investing companies — the Japanese providing the lead. In themselves single-union deals are not new, but their increased rate of adoption in the 1980s is of note; more significantly the typical contents of recent deals, which provide for virtually complete flexibility of the labour force and often for binding arbitration in the case of failure to reach agreement during bargaining, represent a radical break from traditional British employer—union relations. Bassett (1986) describes EETPU national engineering officer Roy Sanderson as the 'principal architect' of the 1980s 'strike-free package', and the 1981 agreement between Plymouth-based Toshiba and the EETPU as its 'testbed'. Sanderson has been reported as an admirer of Japanese employee relations practices, though insisting that strike-free deals are a British solution to British industrial relations problems even though the coincidence between these deals and practices in Japan are significant.

Since the signing of the first 'no-strike deal' other companies have followed the Japanese lead. By the end of 1987, 28 companies in Britain were known to have strike-free agreements. These included nine Japanese, three American and twelve British companies. The EETPU was involved in twenty-one of these deals, and the GMB in three. AEU shop stewards were involved in another deal, though in this case without the sanction of the local district committee (Gregory 1986). Bassett (1986) estimated that a total of 9,000 workers were covered by strike-free deals, and Gregory (1986) that around 5,000 trade union members were subject to the deals. Another 2,000 or so workers were encompassed by the deals in 1987. Hence in 1987 these were small numbers. However, with some trade unions advertising their model agreements encompassing binding arbitration to prospective employers the numbers could well increase rapidly. Further, these figures relate only to those deals with *binding arbitration* — many other deals are similar in content in all but this respect.

Before describing the typical contents of the deals, it is worth commenting on exactly what is meant by binding arbitration and making a clear distinction between this and another recently emerging practice — pendulum arbitration. When employer and union agree on binding arbitration then they agree that if a dispute is not resolved after exhausting other procedures (the last but one normally being conciliation) the dispute will be referred to an independent arbitrator (to be appointed by ACAS) whose findings are binding on both parties. Pendulum arbitration simply means that the arbitrator is obliged to find wholly in favour of one side or the other when asked to adjudicate in a dispute. Pendulum arbitration may or may not be binding. Hence an agreement which incorporates pendulum arbitration does not necessarily imply binding arbitration, or *vice versa*.

Pendulum arbitration has been adopted recently in a number of agreements in Britain, copying a practice widely used in the public sector (interestingly, rarely in the private) in the United States (Bassett 1986). The EETPU tends to favour pendulum arbitration in its strike-free agreements — the advantage claimed is that it makes industrial action improbable because each side is more likely to make 'realistic' opening bids lest they lose the dispute altogether. For example, the EETPU's pioneering agreement with Toshiba reads:

> Both the company and the trade union shall represent their case to an agreed independent arbitrator. The terms of reference to the arbitrator will be to find in favour of either the company or the trade union. A compromise solution shall not be recommended. Both parties agree to abide by the decision of the arbitrator.

MATSA, the GMB's white-collar section, on the other hand, prefers binding but not pendulum arbitration. In its glossy draft agreement offered to employers, it suggests simply:

> If conciliation fails then the difference may be referred by either side to arbitration. If arbitration is used then both parties are considered bound by the findings of the arbitrator.

In both cases, and as far as we know in all cases to date, binding arbitration is invoked only after other lengthy procedures are exhausted, the last but one being ACAS conciliation.

Binding arbitration may not be enforceable under present legislation but it is difficult to imagine a party to such a deal taking industrial action in other than exceptional circumstances. Hence the term 'strike-free' deal is for most intents and purposes appropriate. It may be going too far, on the other hand, to extend the term to include the large number of other deals which make strike action unlikely. These deals, like the one signed by Nissan and the AEU, rule out industrial action while disputes are in procedure, and spell out union respect for managerial prerogatives and the commitment of the union towards company goals, but although action is unlikely it is still in principle possible. The deal between Komatsu and the AEU, for instance, states after describing elaborate procedures involving the Advisory Council:

> The company and the union are totally committed to resolving negotiations as above within the domestic procedure. However, exceptionally, in the case of non-resolution by domestic procedure, both parties agree to refer the matter for conciliation to the Advisory Conciliation and Arbitration Service.

> If the matter is still unresolved, both parties may agree to refer to an independent arbitrator who will determine positively in favour of one side or the other. They will take into account the common ground achieved between the parties. Both parties agree to accept the decision of the arbitrator.

> There will be no industrial action of any kind while an issue is in procedure or the subject of conciliation and arbitration. In the unlikely event of total exhaustion of the above procedure without resolution, no industrial action will be taken without a full, secret, audited ballot of all affected employees.

Given that deals such as Nissan-AEU and Komatsu-AEU are similar in most respects to the strike-free deals described by Gregory (1986), we shall consider them together. These 'new realist' deals, we will argue, are facilitative of Japanization, and indeed are frequently sought by Japanese and Japanizing firms. This is no coincidence for, we suggest, the *new realist deal* makes up a crucial part of the package of changes currently being sought.

Such deals are characterized by the inclusion of *most or all* of the following: a unitarist ideological preface (that is, an emphasis on co-operation and common purpose), denying a conflict of interest between employer and employee; binding arbitration; an agreement for extensive labour flexibility; the harmonization of terms and conditions; the establishment of company advisory boards independent of the trade union; and sole recognition of the signing union. Each element in itself is not new, but taken together these features make for deals characteristic only of the 1980s, and, binding arbitration apart, their adoption is very wide. We will now examine each element of the *new realist deal* in detail.

Trade Union Roles

The ideological prefaces which typify the deals are quite remarkable in that they appear to redefine the role of the trade union as *partner in commercial success* rather than *company adversary*. Toshiba's agreement with the EETPU, for instance, reads:

> The company ... and the trade union ... in reaching this agreement wish to establish and operate policies and procedures which will ensure that the company and its employees enjoy a harmonious relationship to their mutual benefit. Both parties recognize, in this joint approach, that the security of employment and advancement of all employees can only be through the company's commercial success and through the common purpose and involvement of all employees in the company's activities.

'Harmony', 'mutual benificence' and a 'commitment to company success' feature prominently in other new realist deals. At Nissan in Sunderland the AEU signed an agreement with the company which states that the objectives of the agreement are:

> to develop and maintain the prosperity of the company and its employees ... to promote and maintain mutual trust and co-operation between the company, its employees and the union (and) to establish an enterprise committed to the highest levels of quality, productivity and competitiveness using modern technology and working practices and to make such changes to this technology and working practices as will maintain this position. (Quoted in Crowther and Garrahan 1988)

Another illustration of a union accepting a role as *partner* rather than *adversary* comes from a deal between a British company, INMOS, and the EETPU. This agreement states that to meet their objectives the union and the company agree on the need to:

> Keep open and direct communication with all employees on matters of mutual interest and concern. Avoid any action which interrupts the continuity of production. Respond flexibly and quickly to changes in the pattern of demand for the company's products and to technological innovation.

This assertion of a unitarist ideology is all the more remarkable for the fact that the initiative is frequently taken by the trade unions themselves, whose rationale for existence is based on relations which are at root adversarial. The GMB's MATSA, for instance, who recently signed a single-union no-strike deal with a Pirelli subsidiary in South Wales, offers employers a draft agreement intended to:

> form the basis of a progressive, responsible and stable relationship between the company and its employees ... an agreement based on *realism* and *mutuality*. [MATSA's emphasis]

The Wales TUC's general secretary David Jenkins, responsible for overseeing many no-strike agreements, in a public statement targeted at potential inward investors to Wales, starts:

> from the basis that industrial disruption is contrary to the interests of management, the workforce, the company as a whole ... I would ask you to

consider myself and my trade union colleagues as potential allies should
you be considering investment in Wales, a country within the UK where
industrial relations are making a positive contribution towards securing
economic success. (ACAS/WINvest 1986)

Some of Britain's largest unions, with the blessing of at least the Wales TUC,
have defined for themselves roles as allies of management in a search for
competitiveness. On the evidence presented it would be going too far to refer
to them as *socializers* rather than *representatives* of their workforces — a role
taken by unions in Japan — and indeed we shall see later that the ambiguities
apparent in the new realist position make talk of any 'Japanization' of British
trade unions problematic. Nonetheless, non-adversarial trade unions identifying
mutual benefit in collaboration with the company are clearly in line with the shift
to the new manufacturing and management methods we have described.

Strike-free deals have virtually all been signed with single unions on greenfield sites or in the context of an enterprise being re-established out of the collapse
of a previous business (Gregory 1986). The latter includes the pioneering Toshiba-
EETPU deal at Plymouth and the deal between Hitachi and the EETPU at Hirwaun
(Pegge 1986). Hence the argument that the alternative was probably no union
at all could hold some weight. GMB general secretary John Edmunds, for instance,
summarized the position of his union's willingness to sign single union deals on
new sites as 'not a very noble policy, but a pragmatic one' (*Financial Times*
29 December 1986). However, new realist unions have increasingly provided
legitimations of strike-free deals as politically and morally desirable. For instance
Roy Sanderson of the EETPU describes his union's strike-free package as
'designed to enhance the collective and individual rights of workers' (quoted in
Bassett 1986, p. 111). We shall return to the arguments for and against the deals
later in the chapter.

While agreements encompassing binding arbitration have (so far) been limited
to new sites or takeovers (an exception is the AEU stewards agreement with Eaton,
a US vehicle components manufacturer with a history of union militancy (Gregory
1986)), other aspects of the new realist deal have not.

Flexibility Agreements

Flexibility in particular has been pushed by many companies and accepted by
trade unions, often in return for the harmonization of terms and conditions. These
include recent Japanese investors such as Nissan and Komatsu, and most significantly many British companies and companies long established in Britain. Typically
the new realist deal declares complete labour flexibility, traditional demarcations
being broken down and managerial prerogatives over labour deployment being
unambiguously established. The Komatsu-AEU agreement, for instance, states
that the following work practices are agreed:

Complete flexibility and mobility of employees; Changes in processes and
practices will be introduced to increase competitiveness and that these will
improve productivity and affect manning levels; To achieve such change

employees will work as required by the company and participate in training of themselves or other employees as required; Manning levels will be determined by the company using appropriate industrial engineering and manpower planning techniques.

Ironically, British trade unionists have pushed for many years for the single status arrangements which often accompany flexibility agreements, with common provisions for staff and manual workers on items such as the working week, sick pay, holidays, pensions and toilet and canteen facilities. Hence the EETPU has been able to celebrate their contribution to the breakdown of the British system of 'industrial apartheid' (Gregory 1986), and that single status provisions in the no-strike package are one of the real benefits to workers which justify the signing of such deals (Bevan 1987). This is not only because discrimination against blue collar workers is removed, but also because single status and flexible working arrangements facilitate a commitment by the company to the provision of training in a variety of skills which could enhance the worker's development. The EETPU's agreement with Hitachi, for instance, states that:

All company members will agree the complete flexibility of jobs and duties within and between the various company functions and departments. The main flexibility principle will be that when necessary to fit the needs of the business, all company members may be required to perform whatever jobs and duties are within their capability.

The company accepts its responsibility to train, retrain and develop company members to broaden their skills, grow their potential and meet the needs of rapid technological change. The company also accepts that in the instances where more competitive manning levels can be achieved by agreed flexibility, any directly related manning reductions will be achieved without compulsory redundancy.

Established companies with established unions and established agreements obviously have more difficulty in introducing such industrial relations agreements and practices, and indeed while the UK motor industry has, as we have shown in previous chapters, gone well down the road in terms of Japanese manufacturing techniques, it has been slower in changing its industrial relations.

This was demonstrated in 1987 most clearly at General Motors' Vauxhall and Bedford plants. In 1986, John Bagshaw, chairman of Vauxhall, was claiming that poor industrial relations and restrictive practices were preventing the company winning more investment from the US parent, and declared a need for no-strike agreements and new work practices (*Guardian* 16 December 1986). His justification involved a comparison with Nissan's new plant in the UK which, he declared, had cost advantages of between £250 to £500 per car. The first major move by GM in the UK has been to push through a 'Nissan Washington-style' flexibility agreement at its Bedford van plant in Luton. The unions eventually signed, however, only under GM's threat that Japanese company Isuzu, which was to take a 40 per cent stake in a new company to run the Bedford van plant, might withdraw and the plant be closed altogether (*Financial Times* 26 June 1987).

Eventually GM gave way on its initial demand for binding arbitration, but gained agreement from the several major unions representing the workforce for total shopfloor flexibility, together with most other aspects of the 'Nissan package' such as a simplified pay structure, the establishment of a works council, and the right to use temporary workers and subcontractors where considered appropriate by management (*Financial Times* 25 July 1987). By way of concessions, GM agreed to a one-off cash payment of £500 per employee, and to enlarge the works council to include five full-time union officials.

Having gained acceptance at the van plant, GM immediately indicated its intention to seek similar changes at its Vauxhall car plants. Here their declared intention with regard to flexibility relates to production worker responsibility for quality control, the breakdown of demarcations between trades, and production workers taking responsibility for cleaning and routine maintenance (*Financial Times* 21 August 1987). The search for flexibility is not, of course, a new phenomenon, but does appear to have heightened in the 1980s (Atkinson 1987) and is a key feature of the new realist deal.

It is worth repeating here that flexible working arrangements are crucially important to total quality organizations and just-in-time systems of production – without such arrangements any sudden change in customer demand or any technical 'hiccup' in the production process could prove seriously damaging.

Company Advisory Boards

The next element of the new realist deal to be discussed is the Company Advisory Board (CoAB). These are frequently sought by both Japanese and Japanizing companies as an additional means to gain the stability and predictability in industrial relations so crucial to their manufacturing systems. The CoAB appears under a variety of names such as company council (Nissan), company members' board (Hitachi), advisory committee (Orion), staff council (Kyushu Matsushita), advisory council (Komatsu and Norsk-Hydro) or works council (GM). What they share in common, however, is that first, unlike the Joint Consultative Committee (JCC) its elected employee representatives (elections are normally by secret ballot) are not necessarily shop stewards, nor necessarily trade union members, and are chosen by non-union employees as well as union members. Occasionally a few places on the board might be reserved for shop stewards, as at GM, and the local district official of the recognized union sometimes has the right to attend board meetings, but the principle and the practice that the board is independent of the union remains. Secondly, also unlike Britain's traditional JCCs which normally limit themselves to non-collective bargaining issues (Marchington and Armstrong 1986), CoABs typically go beyond 'tea and toilets', providing a forum for negotiations on pay and conditions. Hence they break down the traditional distinction between consultation and bargaining. For instance the EETPU's agreements with Control Data (now Xidex), Hitachi, Inmos, Yuasa Battery, Orion and Kyushu Matsushita, all place responsibility for the first stage in collective bargaining on the CoAB. If agreement is achieved then the union and the company consider the CoAB's recommendations and union involvement in negotiation begins only if either party do not accept the recommendation. Provisions for secret ballots are typically made towards the latter stages of procedure, and as described, procedure often ends with binding arbitration.

In these circumstances the role of the trade union representative is called into question. The Toshiba agreement with the EETPU makes this clear in stating that:

> The function of the (union) representative will be *to represent trade union members on those issues which cannot be resolved through the Company Advisory Board* and to represent individual members of the trade union in cases of individual grievances, discipline or other related matters. [Emphasis added]

Toshiba also request new union representatives to sign a form, together with the trade union official and personnel manager, stating:

> It is recognized that the Company Advisory Board is the best and first means of resolving all collective issues between the company and its employees, and *the representative fully supports and encourages the role of the Company Advisory Board* in the conduct of relationships between the company and its employees. [Emphasis added]

The shift of important responsibilities from shop stewards to CoABs which is typical of the new realist deal has been the subject of criticism. Crowther and Garrahan (1988), in describing Nissan's deal with the AEU, claim that:

> it allows virtually no independent role for shop stewards, and whilst it appears that the company does not intend to actively obstruct union activities, the mechanisms for representation are highly supportive of non-union participation.

This is one explanation, they suggest, for the low membership density at Nissan, claimed by some to be no more than 10 per cent, and at most to be 30 per cent. On the other hand, membership densities are normally much higher, and it should be pointed out that in signing single union deals with various companies, the EETPU has often persuaded managements to encourage union membership. This is achieved largely through managements offering union membership forms and displaying positive attitudes to the union to new recruits, and through the provision of 'check-off' arrangements. (A check-off facility means that union subscriptions are automatically deducted from union members' pay until the member gives written notice that it should cease – this makes withdrawal from union membership due to allowing subscriptions to lapse impossible, and eases the burden of the shop steward as money collector.) A commitment to company encouragement of union membership is actually written into the deals with Yuasa, Hitachi and Orion, and Kyushu Matsushita state that they will provide check-off facilities.

Linn (1986, p. 28), in a detailed study of the new realist deal between the TGWU and Norsk-Hydro in Humberside, concisely summarizes the problems for trade union organization:

> Should the TGWU change its stewards' constituencies to correspond with

those of the advisory council? Should it persist in putting up candidates for the advisory council or should it play a very low profile in that arena, to effectively allow the 'supervisory types' that the ex-TGWU convenors believe will dominate the employee constituencies to do so, and thereby discredit it in the eyes of the workforce? Is the union organization equipped to counter the arguments of those who will start to question why they should join the union when they can have a say in collective issues through their representative on the advisory council?

A defence of the CoAB often posited is that it is a consultative mechanism which makes available company information on important matters which companies in the UK have tended to keep secret. Kyushu Matsushita state in their agreement that the staff council is to be used for the provision of information and consultation on 'company investment and business plans' and 'company operating efficiency and manpower plans' as well as terms and conditions, pay and benefits, and health and safety. A high level of access to information normally the sole preserve of management is, like single status arrangements, considered quite a coup by EETPU leaders, and further justification for the new realist deal. (Critics, of course, would point out that the seriousness and extent of information provision remain dependent on the goodwill of management.)

Single Union Status

The final element of the new realist deal favoured by Japanese and Japanizing companies to be dealt with is single union status. Of course, established companies with established multi-union deals generally have to manage without this part of the package, though it is worth noting that the UDM has made overtures to British Coal regarding the possibility of a single union deal at the new Ashfordby superpit in Leicestershire (*Financial Times* 9 November 1987). The advantages are that bargaining and consultation are made far simpler, that 'spillover' disputes are made less likely, and perhaps most importantly that introducing flexible working arrangements is made easier. As Bevan (1987, p. 9) put it:

> Obviously, the fact the agreements are single union, at a stroke, removes many of the potential obstacles to flexibility. Inter-union demarcation lines are a thing of the past and flexibility depends on nothing more than receiving the necessary training to carry out the task required.

Industrial relations stability and workforce flexibility, to reiterate, are crucial to the effective operation of a Japanese-style production system. As with other aspects of the new realist deal, single union recognition is hardly new — indeed Eric Hammond had pointed out that the TGWU holds 76 such deals, the AEU 65, and the GMB 25. On this basis he claims other unions are 'hypocritical' and 'envious' of the EETPU's recent activities (*Financial Times* 3 June 1987). The single union deal simply entails that the signing company recognizes only the one union which has sole bargaining rights. Employees are free to join any other union they wish, or not to join any union at all, but collective representation is only allowed via the signing union.

The case of Matsushita is particularly interesting in that the GMB already had a single-union deal at their first UK plant in Cardiff. A new deal with the EETPU for a second plant in nearby Newport took many by surprise, including the GMB itself, though a separate deal would fit the logic of a manufacturing system vulnerable to disruption – a separate deal with a separate union ensures that bargaining does not become centralized for all Matsushita subsidiaries in the UK and makes less likely the possibility of plant-to-plant comparisons and the 'spillover' of any dispute from one plant to the other.

Previous chapters have described the new business strategies and manufacturing practices, and it has been made clear that these are dependent on high degrees of industrial relations stability and workforce flexibility. These are exactly what the new realist deals provide. The declared ideology of the deals attempts to impart moral obligations on the parties to the deal to work together in a 'spirit of co-operation'. Binding arbitration and other procedures making industrial action less likely – at least in the short-term – make for greater industrial relations stability and predictability. Harmonization, flexibility and single union agreements facilitate the degree of workforce flexibility necessary for a system of production based on low stocks and inventories, total quality control, and production modules. And CoABs provide management with the opportunity for direct consultation and communication with the workforce, circumventing the shop steward organization and thereby ensuring every opportunity to identify problems and grievances directly and immediately.

Given these developments in the area of company–union agreements, how have unions responded thus far? It is this question which is the focus of the section which follows.

Trade Union Responses

With the declining membership and influence of trade unions in the 1980s and the resultant scramble for membership, newly investing companies have found themselves in the enviable position of being able to play off one union against the other in their search for stability and control. As Crowther and Garrahan (1988, p. 56), describing Nissan, put it, 'Nissan was in a position to offer a non-negotiable agreement, and watch regional union officials struggle with their consciences as to whether they should accept.'

In an interview with the authors a GMB officer further confirmed the strength of the employer's position. Explaining the difference between Matsushita management's approach to trade unions in the 1970s, when they set up a plant in Cardiff, and the 1980s when another, as a separate company, was set up in Newport, he said of the first plant:

> They plumped for us before we started negotiating an agreement. The talks and discussions were long and drawn out, but there was never any question that they might go elsewhere. Today companies won't indicate which union they will recognize until they've got the agreement tied up. . . . Panasonic (the Matsushita Cardiff company) were looking for single union status. But we talked initially about a section of the plant which involved skilled

electronics workers which might need to be organized by the EETPU or AEU. Now it's not just a preference for a single union — it's there at the top. ... At Panasonic we said we'd do everything we could to avoid industrial action. In agreements of late that's become written in bright colours.

Regarding the second plant at Newport:

At Newport they deliberately chose another union (the EETPU) to prevent cross-pollenization. What the Japanese were saying was that policy would not let the management of the Newport project go to the GMB — they were worried about sympathetic disputes, cross-fertilization, comparisons of pay and conditions and therefore parity demands ... they wanted to compartmentalize it.

The Newport deal, unlike the Cardiff deal, contains a no-strike provision. The same officer's comments on a very recent (1987) no-strike deal between Pirelli and the GMB's white collar section MATSA is perhaps even more telling:

The negotiations were of the new type. They'd got to the third draft of an agreement before the company said 'Well we've been talking to the three of you, we're not certain, but we're approaching a decision'. I thought fucking hell, is it worth it — a couple of hundred members?

He went on:

This [membership problem] is what leads trade unions to sign these sorts of agreements — the chase, the desperate need for membership — but then the Nissan's and Hitachi's make them a waste of time altogether.

Waste of time or not, inter-union competition has been the most dramatic response of the trade union movement to the new industrial relations strategies of newly-investing companies. In June 1987 the EETPU was involved in 11 of the 23 disputes then under examination by the TUC's inter-union-disputes committee (*Financial Times* 25 June 1987), and indeed the EETPU has been in the firing line more than any union in attacks against new realism by the union movement's left.

Critics of new realist deals have been damning in their comments. Ken Gill, general secretary of TASS, has stated that:

The difference between a slave and a worker is the right to withdraw his labour. So while the pendulum arbitration agreement does not specifically forbid strikes, it obliges both sides to accept the arbitrator's verdict, thereby denying the workers the ultimate expression of rejection. (Quoted in Bassett 1986, p. 2)

And Rodney Bickerstaffe, NUPE's general secretary, claimed:

What such organizations are saying is 'we will be less militant, we will be more accommodating, we will crawl lower and further, if you will give us the membership'. (Quoted in Bassett 1986, p. 2)

The competition — 'beauty parades' between rival unions seeking sole recognition rights — has been characterized by the TGWU North Eastern Region secretary Joe Mills as follows:

> Because of high unemployment and in desperation to co-operate with inward investment some unions are ignoring their traditional role ... they are standing back and allowing companies to choose which union they want, similar to choosing washing powder from a supermarket. (*Financial Times* 30 December 1986)

Perhaps the most dramatic outburst from a trade union leader came at the height of recognition disputes at two Japanese companies in South Wales. George Wright of the TGWU attacked the companies as well as the EETPU at a Wales TUC conference where he accused some Japanese firms of using 'samurai management' and expecting to operate in a 'coolie economy' (*South Wales Echo* 1 May 1987). The EETPU, he implied, were encouraging them with 'sweetheart deals'. Complaining of a change in industrial relations strategy by inwardly-investing Japanese companies since 1980, he declared:

> Enough is enough. They had better change their ways. If you operate in this country you live by our standards and observe the rights of democratic people.

After protracted disputes and TUC investigation the deals between the EETPU and Orion and Yuasa went through, though other disputes have continued to surface, including one recent case over the proposed new Ford plant in Dundee for the production of electronic components. In this case the AEU signed a single union, new realist deal with Ford, and this led to Mick Murphy, the TGWU's automotive officer, accusing the AEU of abusing its links with the Scottish Development Agency which had lured Ford to Dundee. The TGWU, which represents assembly workers at Ford plants throughout the UK, refused to accept the validity of the agreement, and threatened to black the handling of all components produced at the plant. Ford responded with the threat to locate elsewhere in Europe (*Guardian* 31 October 1987) and at the time of writing the dispute continued.

The TUC has regularly been called upon to offer more detailed policy guidelines regarding single union deals: since 1985 there has been a TUC ban on single union deals except on 'greenfield sites' or where the consent of other unions involved is gained (Linn 1986), but this has been insufficient to prevent disputes. What counts as a 'greenfield site', for instance, is highly debatable, as in the Ford Dundee case. Leaders of the GMB and TGWU have called for a 'minimum standards code' which would rule out binding arbitration (*Financial Times* 1 June 1987) and for occasional audits of companies with single union deals such that if membership levels fell below designated levels, other unions would have the right to recruit and attempt recognition instead (*Financial Times* 30 December 1986). The 1987 TUC conference, however, resulted only in general secretary Norman Willis 'winning time' for further investigation, and in October it was announced that a TUC review body should report by March 1988 on the related issues of inter-union disputes, single union deals and no-strike agreements (*Guardian* 24 October 1987). The TUC appear reluctant to make strong rulings, probably for two reasons. First, TUC interference in union recruitment strategy and tactics has traditionally been minimal, and unions have on the whole, until recently, managed to sort out their own disputes without reference to the TUC. Norman Willis has hence suggested that rather than rely on the TUC's inter-union disputes committee after deals have been signed, unions should come to an informal agreement with regard to recruitment and organizing 'territories' for newly-investing companies (*Financial Times* 5 June 1987); at the end of 1987 there were no signs that unions would take this seriously. Second, and of far deeper significance, is the obvious danger of a split in the TUC which could lead to the EETPU and the AEU being expelled, or voluntarily leaving, perhaps to form a second TUC. It is in this context that the 1987 TUC conference, as predicted by officers of the GMB and EETPU in interviews with the authors, 'fudged' the issue again.

Critical trade union leaders, to recap, have referred to the new realist deals as unprincipled 'loathsome alliances' and 'yellow deals' between 'crawling unions' and 'samurai managements' with the blessing of Mrs Thatcher and in the context of the creation of a 'coolie economy' where workers' 'democratic rights' are on the wane. EETPU leaders on the other hand have denied any such conspiracy, and Eric Hammond has referred to other unions as 'envious' and 'hypocritical' (*Financial Times* 3 June 1987). Here it is worth delving into the new realist position in a little more detail.

Perhaps the most obvious and immediate defence of new realist agreements is that the alternative might be no unions at all. As Eric Hammond put it:

> in some cases, it has been clear that the alternative to an employer's package deal with us has been a closure or a non-union plant. Rival unions prefer that to seeing us make an agreement. Some principle. (Quoted in Bevan 1987)

Others have talked of the need for trade unions to 'rise to the challenge' to prevent 'the spread of the IBM approach to industrial relations across the hi-tech sector' (Bevan 1987). It is impossible to test the 'non-union alternative' thesis, but it does appear feasible, as Hammond suggests, in many cases. For instance a first can be claimed at Orion; before the agreement with the EETPU the Osake corporation, of which Orion is a part, had never signed a collective bargaining agreement with any union anywhere in the world (*Financial Times* 3 June 1987). Similarly, the personnel director of Ford's electrical and electronics division told unions, in the light of debate over the proposed Dundee plant, that the company would not reconsider its single union agreement with the AEU, and that Ford would have preferred a non-union factory (*Guardian* 31 October 1987). The threat of an 'investment strike' by Isuzu was also held over the heads of workers at the Bedford van plant when negotiations over the flexibility package were at stalemate (*Financial Times* 6 June 1987). Yet another case supporting Hammond's contention is recently-privatized British Telecom, where moves towards a 'non-union culture' are being made at the same time as flexible staffing and work practices have been introduced. Increasingly, non-unionized subsidiaries such as Mitel are being used to develop new services and products, and the National Communications Union (NCU) has been reported as considering offering a no-strike agreement at Mitel as the price for gaining bargaining rights (*Financial Times* 4 June 1987). A final example relates to luxury coach manufacturer Plaxtons of West London, which insisted on a no-strike deal with its four unions (for all disputes excepting the annual pay review) before giving the go-ahead for a £1.25 million investment programme (*Financial Times* 26 October 1987).

Most new realists, of course, go beyond pure pragmatism in defence of the new realist deal and the no-strike agreement. Positive benefits are claimed for workers in the form of open and extensive consultation, single status terms and conditions, training in a range of skills, and greater union democracy. Bevan (1987) in a speech to the CBI, made it clear that the EETPU did not intend to be a 'crawling union':

> One ... possibility that we are determined will not happen is that the agreements could be used, no doubt by more unscrupulous employers, as a front for what is, in effect, an anti-union policy. In other words, as a paper agreement, to wave in the faces of other unions who attempt to recruit on site.

Referring to Nissan, he went on:

> the reason they decided to sign the agreement ... was the fact that it was the lesser of two evils. That is, the soft option between traditional trade unionism and anti-unionism as was desired by the parent company and as is operated at its American plant. Since the agreement was signed, the union has struggled to maintain membership above 25 per cent. Moreover, the company remains adamant that it will not and cannot recommend union membership to its employees. One wonders why they signed the agreement if they are prepared to operate it with a density of membership that renders the agreement virtually impotent.

Membership densities in companies which have new realist deals with the EETPU have been far higher, and as mentioned some EETPU agreements specifically state that the company will encourage employees to join the trade union.

One may or may not support the new realist position with regard to these deals. However, it is clear, and certainly agreed among trade unionists, that the challenge in the 1980s from the new industrial relations strategies of many companies, and particularly Japanese and Japanizing companies, is a radically new one. What is less well known is the latent implications of Japanization for trade unions and worker organization, implications which, we would suggest, could be equally important in the long term.

Latent Implications of Japanization
As we have argued in previous chapters, a just-in-time system of production, with its low stocks and inventories and high dependence on worker flexibility

and co-operation, renders a company vulnerable to any disruption, including industrial disputes. Industrial disputes are made less likely with new realist deals — indeed this is one of their declared objectives when sold by unions to prospective employers. Kelly (1987) nonetheless believes that flexibility agreements will not necessarily weaken shopfloor union power:

> New systems of labour flexibility often require extensive co-operation from workers in moving from job to job, and if conditions permit, this co-operation can be withheld, as a power resource in bargaining.

He predicts that strike activity in the late 1980s may increase again as the economy recovers. A similar argument is offered in a joint report by the TGWU and Northern College (1987). They argue that in the long-term, flexible work practices and just-in-time production could place workers in a stronger bargaining position to that traditionally enjoyed.

However, other interrelated developments in Japanizing companies, we would argue, are likely to weaken the collective motivation of workers to utilize this power capacity. These include: production modules and group working; flexible work practices and job rotation; individual performance appraisal systems; the transmission of unitarist ideologies; selective recruitment, induction and socialization; and direct communications between company and workers. Such practices, which were discussed in detail in earlier chapters, could potentially change the identifications and orientations of employees away from the occupational group and trade union and towards the work team and employing organization. Here we shall briefly assess the implications of these for union organization at shopfloor level.

Appraisals

The seniority component of wages in Japan may work against individual competitiveness, though as described in an earlier chapter, Japanese companies are attempting to gradually reduce the seniority component and increase the importance of performance considerations in the wage package. Of course in the UK Japanese companies have not been obliged to bring with them seniority based pay systems, and individual merit appraisals are typically used (Pang and Oliver 1988; Gleave 1987). Emulators such as Pirelli and Bedford are also seeking to introduce individual merit appraisals to shopfloor workers. We suggest that such appraisal schemes encourage an individual rather than a collective orientation towards the company, with potentially damaging effects on the solidarity of shopfloor organization.

Individual appraisals do not mean co-operation and loyalty are lost. On the contrary the appraisal is based not just on performance *per se*, but also on a demonstration of co-operative ability and a commitment to the team and company (Robbins 1983). Clegg (1986, p. 36) described the situation in a Canon factory in Japan:

> the worst failing for an employee is to fail to share the overall goals (of the company): this is much worse than failing to achieve certain tasks. Attitude and commitment are highly significant aspects of performance.

Clearly, all this goes against the logic of collective representation by an independent trade union — both individual competition and a requirement to display company loyalty are anathema to union solidarity. As Turnbull (1988) points out, the appraisals, being 'based on company procedures that deliberately exclude existing forms of union regulation and channels of union representation', mean that the whole *rationale* of unionism is brought into question.

Team Spirit

Often written into the new realist deal, a unitarist ideology emphasizing mutual interest in competitiveness and high productivity is typically disseminated at every opportunity in Japanese and Japanizing companies. Efficiency and increasing the workload are particularly emphasized at the level of the team, the result being what Domingo (1985) calls 'crisis management Japanese style'. Slaughter (1987) similarly refers to 'management-by-stress' in relation to the application of the team concept at the GM-Toyota joint venture in California, and one trade union official in an interview with the authors was struck more than anything else in the Japanese companies he had visited in Britain by 'bell-to-bell working'. With little manpower slack, peer pressure to maintain output and meet targets is increased, and absenteeism and lateness may be frowned upon. The working atmosphere is, then, rather different to that in traditional organizations, and so long as management can 'capture' peer pressure and competitive team spirit (and they clearly go out of their way to do this) and put it to its own use, unions may find difficulty in resisting an intensification of work. Indeed, any limits to work intensification could arguably come from labour turnover and low morale, rather than from organized resistance — formal or informal.

The problems of turnover and morale reported at Nissan would make sense in this context — most complaints reported related to work overload (*Daily Telegraph* 6 May 1987; *Guardian* 8 May 1987). Nissan claimed that by June it had reduced its absentee rate to 3 per cent (lower than the British average for the car industry) and publicly defended its working methods (*Guardian* 8 September 1987). Interestingly, the names of absentees and their dates of absence are now publicly displayed for all to see at the Nissan factory, an idea, according to personnel director Peter Wickens, which came from the workforce (*Financial Times* 19 August 1987). The line taken by the AEU on the public shaming of absentees is not recorded.

Selection and Induction

Both Japanese companies and British companies attempting the adoption of methods from Japan have introduced formal induction and new selection criteria — Rover for instance recently adopted a one week induction foundation programme which is preceded by successful applicants and their families being taken around the Longbridge plant. A senior Rover manager was quoted as follows: 'We are not just looking for manual skills and dexterity. We want to know whether their aspirations are the same as the company's' (Smith 1988, p. 47). Similarly, in chapter 4 we recounted the comment of a team leader regarding his selection criteria for his work team — 'You could almost forget the job spec and write attitude'. Within the context of a slack labour market, such philosophies are most unlikely to assist union recruitment unless they change their image and rationales. As we saw, some unions have already taken steps in this regard.

Harmonization
Company identification is further encouraged by single status terms and facilities, which in Japanese companies in Britain as well as in Japan are normally symbolized by company uniforms, common car parks and canteen facilities, and clocking on for *all* followed by exercises at the start of each shift. Pang and Oliver (1988) found extensive provision of single status facilities in Japanese companies in Britain and as we have seen, most Japanese and Japanizing companies seek harmonization, usually with the support of the union. Add to this the typical long-term employment policies for the core workforce, and one can begin to understand some of the difficulties trade unions may face − the reality may still be 'them and us', but the 'them and us' symbols are less readily apparent and core workers may feel privileged and perhaps even 'cared for'.

Ironically, the single status conditions and staff benefits so much sought by trade unions, and suddenly being granted in exchange for flexible working practices and the like, perhaps pose one of the greatest threats to union organization as it currently exists. By removing many of the trappings of the divisions which lead people to join trade unions in the first place, harmonization may be undermining one of the premises on which membership is based. Wickens (1985) points out that in Japan subtle differences are still evident. For instance the uniform wearer's rank may be distinguished by the number and width of bands around his cap, and only managers wear a collar and tie underneath the jacket of their uniform. Similarly we recorded instances in the UK of subtle status distinctions creeping back in to 'single status' companies. Nonetheless, single status provisions are more prevalent than in the traditional British company, and may serve to reinforce the new orientations of workers under a harmonized system of conditions and benefits.

Direct Communication
Japanese and Japanizing companies use a host of means for communicating directly with their workforces. The clear problem for trade unions is that shop stewards, traditionally the go-between of employer and employee, are bypassed. The most important channel for direct communication which circumvents the union was described earlier in this chapter − the company advisory board (CoAB). As we saw, the CoAB is typically involved in the resolution of issues which are traditionally the preserve of collective bargaining between union and company.

British trade unions, in such a situation, have the choice of using the CoAB as their primary avenue for representing workers in the company by seeking election of union representatives to the board. If they do not, the danger is that they could be 'frozen out' − found irrelevant, as seems to have happened at Nissan. If they do, they may come to have more in common with Japanese enterprise unions than with traditional British unions. David Jenkins, Wales TUC director, suggested to the authors that 'if companies can freeze out unions by establishing good direct communications, then unions should take a look at their own house'. This may be so, but it seems clear that the successful use of systems of direct communication, and especially the CoAB, could pose a challenge to British unions in the 1980s equal to that posed by the new realist deals themselves.

Work Organization

Group working, sometimes in the form of production modules as at Lucas, entails 'semi-autonomy' and heightened responsibility for the foreman or team leader. Each manufacturing cell is responsible and accountable for a definable product, and inputs and outputs come from and go to other cells which are 'clients' and 'customers'. Each cell consists of a team of workers including craftsmen as well as the semiskilled, and flexible work practices mean that the distinctions between occupations is blurred — as described for Lucas and Rover in chapter 3. Identification with the workgroup in the cell rather than with the occupation or craft poses a challenge to the logic of traditional trade union representation. The implications are first, that the representation of members regarding grievances and perhaps even pay is no longer appropriate via a trade-specific union. Second, to the extent that a team spirit does emerge, management have a natural direct communication channel with the workforce via the team leader, and hence the potential to bypass the shop steward. Third, with buffer stocks held to a minimum any lapses in production or quality will be identified immediately — the next cell down the line has problems — meaning that cells are likely to be held accountable not just by management but by other cells as well. In some companies this is reinforced with public displays of cell productivity performance. The potentially divisive effect on workforce solidarity is obvious, particularly if a strong 'customer-driven' ethos pervades the organization.

Temporary Workers

Significantly, Nissan was the first company in Britain to employ auto-assembly workers on temporary contracts since the 1940s (*Financial Times* 16 February 1987), and they will be followed shortly by the GM-Isuzu joint venture where the company demanded complete freedom to contract out work, and to use temporary labour to meet unexpected demand increases (*Financial Times* 26 June 1987). The agreement between Control Data and the EETPU actually stated the policy of creating 'a buffer of approximately 100 jobs to protect the full-time jobs from short-falls in the business'. The buffer here is the use of short-term contracts for new recruits which may be confirmed later. Most agreements do not contain such statements, but it is clear that any increased use of subcontracting and temporary labour pose difficulties for trade unions in that membership densities are typically far lower for those categories of worker. Further, it could be argued that the emergence of core-periphery distinctions among workforces could defeat the object of harmonization in the new realist deal from the point of view of the trade union. Unions at Lucas resisted attempts to increase the use of temporary employees to gain greater flexibility of production (Turnbull 1988), and in January

1988, with the threat of industrial action, so did unions at Ford; but such resistance becomes increasingly difficult in the climate of the 1980s.

Buyer—Supplier Relations and Unions
As pointed out previously, the success of a just-in-time system is dependent on stability not only in the company using the system, but also in its suppliers, raising the question of whether Japanese and Japanizing companies would wish to extend their influence over industrial relations matters, as they do with quality control, pricing, and product development. The high dependency of a company with a just-in-time system on its suppliers would suggest it would, and McFadden and Towler (1987) claim that Nissan, with the largest investment commitment of a Japanese company in the UK to date, lists in its criteria for selection of primary suppliers industrial relations, trade union structure, working practices and strike record. Turnbull (1988) argues that established motor manufacturers, 'will experience far greater difficulty in their attempts to influence the employment practices of their suppliers and to use those suppliers as a device for cutting wages/costs' but indicates that attempts are already being made. Certainly trade union leaders have expressed fears that some large companies have recently attempted to extend their influence to the labour relations practices of suppliers, one instance cited being the controversial no-strike agreement between the EETPU and Christian Salvesen, a supplier to the non-union company Marks and Spencer. Marks and Spencer denied forcing the deal (*Financial Times* 22 June 1987).

Summary

Japanization has important implications for trade unions. Some of these are overt and have manifested themselves in the form of new realist deals, sometimes single union, sometimes strike-free, and more often enshrining clauses on managerial prerogatives over labour deployment, harmonization of terms and conditions, and the establishment of company-based representative bodies. Equally important for the future of trade unionism, we have argued, are the new workplace cultures implied by teamwork, and new selection, payment and other systems. The initiatives of Japanese and Japanizing companies, then, pose serious threats to British trade unionism as we know it. Some further concluding comments on the future for unions will be made in the final chapter.

7

Policy Implications and Conclusions

In our chapter on the theory of Japanization we argued for the importance of the broad social, economic and political environment for the successful functioning of a system of production characterized by — indeed based on — a set of high-dependency relationships. In chapters 3, 4 and 5 we presented evidence in support of our thesis of the Japanization of British industry, and in chapter 6 we explored trade union responses to the new initiatives. In this chapter we seek to consider some of the policy implications which arise out of this evidence. After commenting on the nature of Japanization, these implications will be considered in four areas: organization—employee relations; organization—environment relations; trade unions; and finally public policy. We then spell out what we see as the fundamental dilemmas which underpin the Japanization process.

Japanization as Fundamental Change

As chapters 3 and 4 demonstrate, there is strong evidence of the Japanization process at the level of individual companies, evidence which has led some commentators to claim that 'the Japanization of British industry is now unequivocal' (Turnbull 1987). Our impression is of strong determination among engineers and managers to further advance this process. Some of the writings about Japanese practice do have an almost evangelical flavour about them. For example, an article about recent changes at Lucas carried the title 'Where Lucas Sees the Light', and Lucas' manufacturing director, describing just-in-time production, writes:

> It is not the latest gimmick, *it is fundamental and when completed there can be no other improvement* since it completely tailors a manufacturing strategy to the needs of a market and produces mixed products in exactly the order required. (Parnaby 1987c) [Emphasis added]

Ultimate production system or not, its logic, simplicity, and above all potential results in terms of return on assets are certainly remarkable, and the recent wave of attempts to implement JIT and other Japanese manufacturing practices is indicative of the belief that such a system is crucial to the future of British manufacturing in the face of ever-heightening international competition. If the alternative to Japanization really is to lose out in competition (and given the apparent unavailability of equally promising manufacturing system paradigms in the 1980s this may indeed be the case) then the question becomes not one of whether Japanization will occur, but how much (Japanized) British manufacturing industry will remain in the future. This is not to suggest that manufacturing will cease in Britain altogether. More likely would be a further gradual decline of manufacturing, together with increasing penetration from those corporations capable of facing up to the international competitive climate.

Japanese-style manufacturing systems have captured the imagination of British industry because of the promise of leaps in productivity through efficiency of asset — including human asset — utilization. From a radical perspective, the transformation offers the opportunity to greatly intensify the rate of exploitation of workers and thereby enhance the returns on investments. Hence Graham (1988) suggests the term 'Japanization' may be preferred to alternatives because of its ideological appeal — the implication is that 'we all have to pull together the beat the Japanese at their own game', and divisions due to differences of interest inside (and outside) companies are obscured.

Leaving aside the ideological connotations of the term for the moment, the evidence does suggest that Japanization, from either of the above two perspectives, implies a fundamental change. Japanization is a *high dependence* organizational strategy — and in many respects is the opposite of Taylorism or Fordism. Japanization demands, in return for the organization's dependence on its constituents, a high degree of organizational influence over constituent behaviour — over labour and suppliers, obviously, and arguably over customers, investors, local and national governments. This is achieved, as explained theoretically in chapter 2 and demonstrated empirically in the rest of the book, via resource abundance, making goals homogeneous, and by heightening the dependencies of constituents on the organization. Scientific management, in contrast, is a relatively *low dependence* system. This is reflected, for instance, in the quest for substitutability of labour by deskilling jobs and making work sufficiently routine and pre-determined to be carried on by following the simple rules, in lodging authority and responsibility in a rigid hierarchy, and in the extensive use of indirect labour such as specialists in quality inspection, maintenance and work study (Braverman 1974). Multiple-sourcing — making buyers substitutable — of course fits neatly with the philosophy underlying Taylorism.

The desirability of the transformation from an economic point of view is difficult to refute. Indeed in the absence of powerful protectionist measures British industrial success could depend on the depth and extensiveness of the transformation. Whilst we are reluctant to concur that Japanese-style manufacturing systems are the ultimate in manufacturing organization, they do appear to be suited to the contemporary requirements of many companies, and there appear to be no serious contending alternatives in currency at present. On the other hand, the social, as opposed to purely economic, consequences of adopting such an approach do raise issues of moral and political import which are highly contentious. Such issues are reflected in ambiguities towards Japanization amongst those involved in or observing the process. These will now be addressed by looking first at the implications of heightened internal dependencies, then at those of heightened external dependencies.

Organization—Employee Relations

The experience of work in the Japanized organization is likely to be different to that which most British workers, and indeed managers, are used to. On the one hand work is likely to be more varied and involvement in and 'ownership' of the work one is doing higher. On the other hand, accountability and responsibility are increased, performance is more closely monitored, and the visibility of failings (and successes) is heightened. Quality of working life enthusiasts might hence be confused: is Japanese-style work organization 'humanistic' as many advocates claim, or is it 'manipulative' and 'coercive' as the critics suggest? What is clear is that however much contemporary changes such as cellular or group working and employee involvement resemble the practices peddled by the quality of working life movement in the late 1960s and early 1970s, the driving force behind them is quite different.

The European and American quality of working life initiatives of the 1960s and 1970s — the Volvo plant at Kalmar in Sweden being the most frequently cited example — emerged in the context of rapid economic growth, tight labour markets, associated acute problems of absenteeism and labour turnover, growing trade union strength, and in some countries (particularly Norway, Sweden and West Germany) employment legislation which *enforced* a degree of participation (Friedman 1977; Ramsey 1983). 'Humanistic' forms of work organization — semi-autonomous work groups and the like — were invariably employer *responses* to the lack of control over labour they faced (Lupton et al. 1979). The 'humanism', no doubt genuine on the part of some employers, was an attempt to win labour's affiliations and loyalties by providing for raised expectations associated with affluence and improved education following the Second World War. 'If we are humanistic and respect the demands and rights of workers', the logic went, 'then our employees are more likely to turn up for work, stay with the company for more than a few weeks, and pay more attention to quality'.

Japanization on the other hand, at least in Britain, is an initiative taken by employers not so much in response to problems of labour turnover and absenteeism, but to problems of international competitiveness. The concrete practical problem being addressed by employers is no longer how to create a form of work organization which can cope with the demands of an educated, alienated, affluent and franchized workforce, but how to utilize assets more efficiently. The results, we would argue, are in some respects similar to those of quality of working life initiatives, but in other respects very different.

Efficiency of (human) asset utilization is achieved, on the one hand, through flexible work practices and the pushing of responsibilities previously those of specialist indirect staffs onto production workers (hence eliminating human 'slack') and on the other through increasing the intensity of work as close to the limits as possible. In the light of this distinction between quality of working life and Japanization initiatives, developments at Rover (see chapter 3) begin to make sense. As Smith (1988) relates, the 1970s saw the Ryder 'participation scheme', which was abandoned when Sir Michael Edwardes took over and reasserted managerial prerogatives in the context of recession and the decline of trade union power. The programme of establishing teamwork, and relatedly zone circles, zone briefings, and so on, which has followed in the 1980s, is primarily an exercise in efficiency, not a defensive human relations response.

Japanese practices then, seem to hold out the opportunity for improved quality of working life. Holding responsibility for quality, routine maintenance, and so on, in addition to machine operation means broader tasks and the delegation of authority − including authority to stop the line − 'Jidoka'. But it also means accountability and heightened pressure to produce the right quantity of the right quality products exactly on time. As illustrated elsewhere in the book, a JIT production process heightens the visibility of behaviour and performance, and increases the pressure, including peer pressure, to meet performance targets. Some Japanese companies and other total quality organizations reinforce this visibility through various devices, such as public displays of group or individual output and quality levels. In sum, with more job interest and responsibility necessarily comes more job stress.

An additional aspect of Japanization is the employment contract and career management. Because of the lifetime employment and internal promotion policies associated with a high dependency system, recruitment and selection is rigorous (and considerations of candidate's personal characteristics are paramount), company training and socialization is extensive, and job rotation is desired for promotion among the ranks of management. Each of these serves to contribute towards a homogeneity of goals and a willingness to work flexibly. The effects are twofold. First, employees are being asked in a sense to become more intimately related to their organizations − the contract of employment goes beyond 'a fair day's work for a fair day's pay' towards mutual commitment and identification. This point alone bitterly divides the critics and the advocates of Japanization, as we shall see in the concluding section. Secondly, task flexibility and job rotation serve to reduce the salience of occupational specialisms − craft and professional identifications become difficult to sustain, and departmental allegiances are prevented from dominating. The employee's primary point of reference hence becomes the organization as other 'bonds' are dissolved. Enterprise-based unions working closely with the company and representing all occupational groups fit with this type of employer−employee relationship, and the provision of relatively good wages and working conditions and single status facilities also serve to ensure that organization—employee dependence is mutual. There is some evidence of British cynicism towards attempts to create 'strong culture' organizations Japanese-style. Smith (1988, p. 49) for instance recounts:

> that during the induction course (at Rover) a number of references to Japan ... recalled the last war and, implicitly, the British way of life being defended. It was generally acknowledged that the home came before the company; that you worked for money and not out of slavish devotion; and that when holiday time came round you took your full entitlement. One participant remarked to murmurs of assent that his mortgage was with the Halifax, not the Rover group.

The benefits of such arrangements to workers are clear: relative security of well-paid employment; the opportunity to upgrade and broaden skills and abilities; and the opportunity to pursue a career in line with one's capacity. On the other hand, there are potential costs of being 'tied' to the company because of the implied dilution of occupation-specific expertise and the salience of internal promotion. Relatedly, the invasion of personal privacy and the loss of individual independence associated with paternalistic personnel practices may be difficult for many to swallow. It is of interest that there are some clear parallels between twentieth-century Japanese and nineteenth-century British paternalism (Lewis 1987). Critics will argue then, that employer paternalism was a nineteenth-century British phenomenon — a phenomenon which disappeared in the face of advances in democracy and the extension of individual rights, and that a reversion to paternalism would be a morally and politically backward step.

These then, are the pros and cons of work experience in the Japanese or fully Japanized corporation. There is, however, one final point of crucial importance. Japanization as a strategy includes the building of 'rings of defence' for the protection of the core people and activities. Employees who find themselves on the outer rings — the peripheral workers employed on temporary contracts or the employees of the sub-subcontractors — are likely to have a rather different experience of work. Paternalistic provision is less likely, meaning job insecurity, relatively low wages, harsher working conditions and so on. To the extent that the privileges of the core workforces are provided at the expense of the periphery — and clearly they are — the Japanization of industry is likely to further contribute to the already significant divisions in British society.

Organization—Environment Relations

With regard to relations with suppliers, Japanization implies a high dependency whereby the supplier can be trusted to deliver goods of the right quality, in the right quantity, and just-in-time. Long-term relations and corporate influence over supplier operations are hence necessary.

Whilst significant moves are afoot with regard to changing buyer—supplier relations in British industry, and particularly in the automotive industry, important problems have been encountered, especially with regard to JIT supply. Nonetheless, many organizations do seem to be evolving strategies to enable them to cope with their increased dependencies on their suppliers. Examples are the pursuit of preferred supplier status policies and the establishment of longer-term relationships. Such policies carry a price for suppliers of course. A long-term relationship is liable to involve interference in their internal arrangements such as cost structures, quality control methods, purchasing policy, and sometimes even personnel policies, as Marks and Spencer do with their suppliers (Paton 1985). The advantages to the supplier are equally obvious: a long-term relationship, predictability of the market, help and advice, financial security, and so on. On the other hand, with the buyer constantly 'on the doorstep', with a heavy reliance on the corporation as a long-term major customer, and in many Japanese cases with a financial dependence on the corporation, the supplier is under intense pressure to deliver the goods.

In theory, establishing influence and control over supplier operations should be unproblematic compared with workers. This is because suppliers, unlike workers, do not enjoy the same sort of collective representation. Suppliers have on occasion voiced their concerns about their future with organizations making radical changes to their supplies policies, but taking action is for most companies out of the question — they would simply be struck off the preferred supplier status candidates list. However, there are two reasons why the achievement of Japanese-style supplier relations is problematic. The first reason relates to the obvious temptation of large corporations to use JIT production as nothing more than an excuse to pass on the costs of holding inventories to their suppliers. As we saw in chapters 3 and 4, this seems to have occurred in some cases. In these instances corporations are really abandoning, or at least subverting, the philosophy of total quality, and the whole exercise aimed at improving the relationship of trust and dependability between the two parties is brought into question. With regard to this first problem, one might expect corporations to learn from their mistakes as they come to terms with the theory and practice of the new approach.

The second problem might therefore be more serious. This is related to the fact that Japanese-style supplier relations, and JIT supplies in particular, depend not only on exerting control over suppliers, but also on those agencies who can influence supplier performance — for example trade unions in the supplier. We have already pointed out that reducing inventories increases workers' power capacity, which can be used as a bargaining tool if the need to do so is perceived. Just-in-time supply provides a choke point which can be the target of industrial action. In October 1986, for example, a strike at Lucas Electrical's factory at Cannock in Staffordshire swiftly led to 12,000 lay-offs at Austin Rover. According to Austin Rover, part of the reason for the speed and severity of the disruption was the use of just-in-time supply (*Guardian* 9 October 1986). Not surprisingly Lucas management were put under considerable pressure to sort the dispute out quickly. Hence the introduction of JIT supplies proper implies securing against disruption not just from sources within one's own organization, but from within one's suppliers too. We might expect, then, that in the scramble by suppliers to gain preferred supplier status with the Japanizing companies, that those identified as having poor industrial relations will be less likely to have a long-term future.

Management of the Environment?

There is one final issue which we should touch on before we leave the question of the management of dependency relationships. That concerns the attempts of companies operating 'low waste' systems of production to eliminate uncertainty from whatever source in order to minimize the resources invested in 'insurance' policies — buffer stocks and the like. If, as we have suggested, the elimination of uncertainty is important, then it seems logical that such organizations should attempt to operate on their environments so as to make them more predictable, and less uncertain. Japanese strategic marketing, with an emphasis on market share represents one way of doing this. Market dominance, by reducing the number of competitors, also cuts down uncertainty. In addition, market dominance typically allows one higher margins (by increasing the barriers to entry of that market), which gives a company the elbow room to pay premium salaries, provide staff benefits and high job security for core workers and so on. Once in this position a company may be in a self-sustaining cycle.

This leads us to predict that those corporations without such dominance — and many British companies are in such a position — will face most problems in their attempts to Japanize. If they cannot afford to create the stability and predictability necessary for a low waste production system to operate successfully, then getting into the self-sustaining cycle outlined above may not be possible. Comments such as 'the Japanese have "market share" tattooed across their hearts' (made to one of the authors by a director of an inward investment agency) make sense in this context.

In a similar vein, Crowther and Garrahan (1988) suggest that Nissan took advantage of its ability to influence the local authority in North East England and thereby secure, at low cost, the land necessary for the creation of a 'spatially concentrated' production arrangement facilitative of just-in-time supplies. They claim there was:

> . . . a concerted effort by local 'power brokers' (regional government officials, elected local councillors, the Washington New Town Development Corporation, private sector firms, regional trade unionists and the media) to conform with the pattern *determined by* Nissan. (Crowther and Garrahan 1988, p. 52) [Authors' emphasis]

The extension of mutual dependencies to external constituents may be welcomed by many, due to its implications of co-operation and common purpose. However, critics such as Bonis view this situation less favourably:

> A kind of disguised Imperialism results when the organization seeks to

control the external elements: customers, suppliers, subcontractors, members of other organizations, politicians and political organizations, the press, public opinion, pressure groups . . . (Bonis 1980, p. 163)

Trade Unions

As the previous chapter was devoted to trade unions and industrial relations, we shall briefly summarize the key points pertinent to trade unions. Our argument is that because low waste production systems demand a workforce which is dependable, hard working, flexible, and unlikely to disrupt production, an antagonistic or adversarial form of industrial relations is undesirable. Put simply, the production system provides workers with too great a power base for a company to be able to risk them having goals which radically differ from its own. The typical tactics for coping with the uncertainty generated by having parties upon whom one relies but cannot depend − such as slack resources − go against the low waste philosophy on which Japanese-style production systems are based.

As Reitsperger (1986a) has suggested, the options open to Japanese (and by implication Japanizing) organizations in this situation are stark: either avoid unions altogether or accept them but develop strategies to neutralize potential problems, incorporation being one such approach. As we have seen, about a third of the Japanese organizations in our sample opted for a union avoidance strategy, in common with some of the American owned 'excellent' companies such as IBM and Mars. Where Japanese companies have recognized unions, they have gone for single unions, often accompanied by agreements which reduce the likelihood of industrial disruption (sometimes with a binding arbitration clause) and which explicitly give the union a *collaborative* rather than an *adversarial* role. In nearly half our cases unions coexisted with company advisory boards, the members of which are elected independently of the trade union and subject to company-determined rules. These boards function as the first line of communication between company and worker and handle many issues typically handled by unions via collective bargaining.

The existence of company advisory boards is particularly problematic for unions because ignoring them could lead to marginalization, whilst attempting to use company representative bodies to increase union influence (by seeking election of union representatives to the board) implies incorporation. From the point of view of a company avoiding adversarial relations this situation is ideal, for the union in effect becomes *voluntarily* incorporated − even if the option is marginalization.

The incorporation strategy is manifested in its purest form as the enterprise union in Japan. In Britain, incorporation is achieved, or at least attempted, via the single union deal with the company advisory board as the most important mechanism for resolution of collective issues. In effect, any occupation-wide or industry-wide allegiances which trade unions may have (and as we saw in

chapter 6, these had already significantly declined before the advent of Japanization) are effectively dissolved, leaving the corporation as the union's only point
of reference.

This is not to say that Japanese companies have not been willing to adapt
themselves to local cultural and political realities. When one considers the
geography of union recognition among Japanese companies, the tendency has been
for companies setting up in areas without traditions of collective worker organization — such as new towns — to avoid trade unions, and those setting up in the
older industrial centres to accept trade unions. For instance, ten out of eleven
of the Japanese companies which had located in Wales by the end of 1987 had
recognized trade unions whereas none of those companies located in Livingston,
Telford, Worcester and Northampton had done so. According to the evidence
we have available, there appear to be few exceptions to this tendency. The
important point is, however, that where trade unions *are* accepted a non-adversial
role is sought and, at least judging by the contents of the deals signed, gained.
Either option — union avoidance or incorporation — satisfy the requirements
of a production system based on high-dependency relations because both allow
for frequent and direct communication with the workforce and both serve to
increase goal homogeneity via appeals to principles of co-operation and a sense
of common purpose. The obvious problem that this poses for trade unions is that
they draw the rationale for their very existence from the presence of differences
of interest, and hence goal heterogeneity.

The position of unions in traditional long-established companies is obviously
rather different. Many of these companies have sought Japanese-style 'new realist'
agreements with unions, often as part of a whole programme of Japanization.
Obviously the acceptance of such agreements is more difficult to achieve given
established traditions and vested interests, but the threat of plant closures,
redundancies and investment strikes have been used successfully to gain acceptance
of, for instance, flexible work practices and new pay structures. On the whole,
in these cases unions do appear to have retained a degree of independence from
the companies they operate in, and although the present economic and political
climate may militate against industrial action, and despite a trade union membership crisis in the 1980s, British unions are still capable of posing a challenge to
the introduction and operation of just-in-time systems and total quality methods.
This was demonstrated, for instance, with union resistance to zone briefings and
circles at Rover, and to quality circles and the other elements of the 'After Japan'
campaign at Ford.

Many employers in Britain would dearly love the sorts of single-union agreements as have been signed with Japanese companies, and in 1987 Wales CBI
director Ian Kellsor suggested publicly that the extension of single-union deals
to established companies was desirable. However, even putting aside the political
ramifications of such a shift, the same context of a decline of trade union membership and power and inter-union competition which leads to a scramble to sign
single-union deals with newly-investing companies at the same time reduces the

likelihood of any union giving over membership to a rival union on an established site. With membership on the decline even in the 'new realist' unions and in the absence of clearer direction and policy from the TUC the picture of inter-union rivalry looks unlikely to change in the near future. Adding to this the latent implications of Japanese-style management practices, union organization appears most unlikely to survive in a significant way in its existing form.

Public Policy

The Dual Economy

As explained in chapter 1, in Japan large numbers of temporary workers, part-time workers and those employed by smaller organizations enjoy relatively poor pay and conditions in comparison to their counterparts in the large corporations. The army of peripheral workers serve the functions of bearing the brunt of economic misfortune — that is, providing numerical flexibility or 'rings of defence'. Hence these workers could be construed as supporting the lifetime employment policies, generous benefits and so on enjoyed in the large corporations by 'exporting' potential problems outside these organizations. For example if one has temporary workers or subcontractors to ditch in the event of a downturn, potentially divisive redundancies within the core organization can be avoided. Because the potential 'losers' are kept outside the organization's boundaries a divisive win/lose situation *within* the organization is avoided.

In Britain also there is a substantial peripheral labour force, and this has risen in importance in the 1980s. In 1985, 8.1 million workers, or 34 per cent of those in employment, were either part-timers, temporary workers, or self-employed — a 16 per cent increase since 1981. Over the same period, the number of full-time permanent employees fell by 1.02 million to 15.62 million. The majority (60 per cent) of the peripheral categories were female. According to Rajan (1987) the main factor in the rise in the use of peripheral workers is related to employers' attempts — particularly in the services sector — to gain flexibility to adapt to fluctuating demand and to save on non-wage costs such as sick pay, pensions and holidays. Reports by the white-collar union APEX (1987) and the GMB (reported in *Financial Times* 5 May 1987) confirm this finding. APEX adds that there is a real and significant demand by women for part-time work. This situation, we would suggest, can only facilitate the Japanization process.

Regional disparities are also in evidence in the UK, and again these have been increasing in the 1980s (*Regional Trends* 1987). The North of England, the Midlands, Scotland, Wales and Northern Ireland are all less well off than the South East and East Anglia in terms of earnings and employment levels. Profits per employee, on the other hand, with the exception of Northern Ireland, are lowest in the South — £1,715 per year in the South East compared with £2,481 in the North and £2,836 in Wales, for instance (*Labour Research* August 1987).

Segmented labour markets and regional disparities were growing long before the very recent acceleration of Japanization and Japanese direct investment, which have so far probably made only a minor contribution to the broad trends. This is despite the fact that our survey evidence suggests an increased use of subcontracting to smaller companies and the adoption of temporary workers by some Japanese and Japanizing companies. However, what is important here is the fact that, at least outside the affluent areas of the South, the existence of a dual labour market is facilitative of Japanization − its pre-existence relieves organizations of a potential pitfall because precedents have been set. Fairbrother (1987) argues that the increasing use of subcontracting and part-time and temporary workers in public sector services, in particular, pave the way for their use in private sector manufacturing.

Government Strategy and Support to Industry
In chapter 1 we recounted how some commentators have related Japanese success in penetrating (and in some cases dominating) world markets to a history of government intervention in manufacturing industry and selective support to those sectors considered of strategic importance. If this *is* a key aspect of Japanese success, then there is as yet little sign of it being replicated in Britain. The industrial and economic policies of the Conservative government of the 1980s have been driven by a *laissez-faire* philosophy of minimal government intervention. Looser restrictions on capital movements, deregulation, decreased employment protection, and privatization are examples of this philosophy. (Intervention with regard to trade unions and industrial relations is of course the significant exception.) Despite some successes with regard to inward investment, the overall consequence has been a net outflow of capital from the UK (*British Business* 22 May 1987). Further, the increases in profit margins of manufacturing industry, for which the government may or may not be given credit, have not yet been accompanied by the desired rise in levels of investment.

Despite the productivity gains made in the early 1980s, British manufacturing productivity is very low (as are British wages) compared with the international competition. A 1987 report by the National Institute (*Economic Review* no. 20, summarized in *Financial Times* 28 May 1987) states that Britain's recent 'moderately favourable' productivity performance still leaves a 'formidable' gap with its rivals. Measured by output per hour, American productivity is two and a half times greater, and that of Japan, West Germany and France around 80 per cent higher. In contrast Britain came a clear second bottom (to Ireland in a league table of twelve industrial nations) in terms of unit hourly labour costs when taking employers' social charges into account. America's were 61 per cent higher and Japan's 29 per cent. The report's conclusion was that the British competitive advantage of very cheap labour was 'more than offset' by the very low level of productivity.

Whilst attempting to extend the cheap labour advantage may be the government's strategy for improving competitiveness, Japanization, through tackling the *productivity* problem, is increasingly identified as the solution to the competitiveness problem outside government circles, and especially in industry. In the absence of the financial arrangements necessary for Japanization, we would suggest, only the exceptional British corporation may survive in the long run. After all, there are limits to the depression of wage costs (British wages are continuing to rise faster than inflation despite government policy) and in the long term low wages are likely to further reduce productivity due to low morale and a 'brain drain' of skilled and professional workers.

Import barriers, such as local EEC content requirements, may be serving to slow the impact of international competition, but their design is intended not to halt foreign competition *per se*, only to prevent 'unfair' competition. Their effect is to bring the competition onto British soil, and in doing so the relative inadequacies of British manufacturing have been alarmingly exposed. Indeed, the frequent Japanese claims that 'unfair competition' is not to blame for trade imbalances with Europe and the United States have become more plausible with this exposure – their suggestion that the simple fact is that Europe is 'backward' and 'inefficient' with regard to manufacturing and business practice (*Financial Times* 10 February 1987) is less likely to be given a hostile reaction in the UK now than five years ago.

Economic Structures

Closely related to the problem of government support to manufacturing industry (or the lack of it) is the general problem of finance to manufacturing industry. In the 1980s investment expenditure has remained subdued despite the facts that manufacturing productivity rose by 30 per cent between 1979 and 1986 – an average of around 5 per cent per year – and manufacturers' profit margins rose in every single year over the same period. In 1986 margins were at their highest since the early 1970s (*Financial Times* 13 August 1987). Yet, again over the same period, 1979 to 1986, the top 40 British manufacturers increased their overseas investments and foreign-based workforces, the latter going up from 34 per cent of the total in 1979 to 44 per cent in 1986 (*Financial Times* 5 May 1987). Similar figures were cited, of course, by the opposition parties in the run up to the last General Election to justify their contention that the failure of government to intervene was leading to Britain becoming a 'warehouse economy'.

Manufacturers, then, continue to be dependent on 'the City', a situation which Ackroyd et al. (1988) argue has existed throughout this century, but the City continues to be reluctant to commit itself to manufacturing, at least to British manufacturing. As we pointed out in chapter 1, British banks, unlike their Japanese counterparts, are not in the business of providing low interest, long-term loans, and a short-term profit mentality is reinforced by British companies' typically high dependence on the stock market. The problem for manufacturers is, of course, that the dependence is not reciprocal, and in the absence of measures by the government reciprocal dependence seems unlikely to emerge.

The continued scarcity of long-term investment commitments in British manufacturing industry which result from goverment economic policy and City dominance could, we would argue, place the greatest single limitation on the Japanization of British industry. Without this commitment, production reorganization is made difficult, training and development programmes are less likely to be seen as a wise investment, and creating a situation of market dominance is made problematic. Whilst conducting the research for this book we came across a number of examples of (City-driven) short-termism having detrimental effects in companies attempting to turn themselves around. These manifested themselves in a variety of ways. One example was a company with which one of the authors was working, which was trying to develop a set of 'guiding values' befitting a total quality organization, following Peters and Waterman's ideas. Amidst talk of being 'close to the customer', 'flexibility and excellence' and so on, a senior manager piped up 'Of course these values mustn't damage the bottom line . . .'. This contrasts with the long-termism of many Japanese companies, and with a successfully Japanizing British company — Jaguar. In the words of Jaguar's chairman, John Egan, 'Our business objective is to make money out of satisfying customers . . . We stick to the basics, getting those right usually means a good profit.' (Quoted in Heller 1986).

The same issue arose in many guises — the 'debasement' of total quality principles by their use as a smokescreen to push redundancies through, by the questioning and blocking of factory reorganization costs by company accountants, and the ludicrously short pay back times demanded of projects. Engineers at one of Rolls-Royce's aero-engine plants, currently subject to a Japanese-style reorganization, related their scepticism to one of the present authors. Their scepticism, they said, was due to the 'accountant mentality' which they saw as dominating the company at the top level. Japanese-style ideas, they said, are sound, but they had been presented with similar ideas and reorganization proposals in the past: 'we've heard it all before'. Previous attempts to introduce new ideas and proposals had foundered on the lack of long-term financial commitment, and unless someone had determined a way to provide the resources necesssary for the massive commitment required, they figured, there was no reason why present attempts at reorganization should be a complete success. The ideas would be either diluted in the face of the practical realities of resource constraints, or dropped altogether in the face of failure.

A recent report by the Manpower Services Commission (1987) confirms the notion that Japanese companies' business horizons are of a longer-term nature than those in British ones. As well as paying more attention to employee training and education than their British counterparts, Japanese organizations were found to have higher proportions of technologists at board level. Interestingly, the MSC characterized Japanese companies as 'technology-driven' as opposed to 'finance-driven'. The fact that some companies are manifestly worse than others in this suggests that not all the blame can be laid at the door of the City, but its *modus operandi* are obviously not assisting long-term manufacturing development.

Thus there is a danger that the cost-cutting elements of just-in-time and total quality principles are embraced without the development work essential for their long-term success. Given the extent of the shake-out in British manufacturing in the early 1980s, it seems likely that the cost-cutting knife is beginning to shave the bone. Indeed, the figure of 5 per cent annual productivity growth in the 1980s cited above contrasts with a 'real' productivity growth rate — that is, growth in output per person employed — of 1.9 per cent per year between 1979 and 1985 (Matthews and Minford 1987). This is not an insignificant figure, but it does imply that the gains made so far in this decade relate more to cutting away the 'fat' than to genuine advances in technology and efficiency. The use of JIT supplies simply to pass on the costs of inventories is a good illustration of this danger; failure to provide adequate compensation and promises of long-term employment to workers who accept the flexible working practices and greater demands characteristic of a JIT system would be another. For the same reason, training and development, so crucial to effective Japanization because of the delegation of responsibility and authority lower down the organization, may be skimped on. Training and development entails an investment commitment with only long-term pay-backs, and to the extent that one's profit horizons are short-term, training and investment become *merely* a cost.

We explained the importance of establishing a degree of control over the market for the successful use of Japanese-style methods above. A short-term horizon, of course, is anathema to increasing market share. A survey contrasting British companies' marketing strategies with those of Japanese companies in the UK makes this clear. The study found that of the British companies, 80 per cent of the sample had a strategy described as 'prevent decline', 'defensive', or 'maintain position'. In contrast, *all* the Japanese companies described their strategy as either 'steady growth', 'aggressive growth', or 'dominate market' (Wong, Saunders and Doyle 1987). Wong et al. (p. 62) argue that too many British companies:

> are dominated by short-term profit considerations or over-emphasis on internal production capabilities. To improve competitiveness, there is need for re-orientation at the top. The chief executive should take the lead in demonstrating his commitment to marketing and stimulate continuous, informal monitoring and anticipation of developments in the market.

They go on to suggest that better professional education in marketing for British managers is required. This may be so, but unless short-term business horizons can somehow be changed to long-term ones, it seems unlikely that growth strategies could be aggressively pursued regardless of marketing philosophy and skills.

Japanese companies investing in the UK, being financed from Japan, appear to be willing (as ever) to forgo short-term gains in their quest for market share in Europe. This is indicated in the extremely slow (and expensive) planning process they go through before choosing location (see the Nissan case for instance), and was confirmed in comments to the authors from representatives of an inward investment agency and from representatives of various Japanese companies in the UK. The findings of Wong et al.'s (1987) survey on Japanese marketing strategies in Britain would also support this argument — their aggressive market share strategies would simply not be possible if short-term profitability were of primary importance. A growth in the importance of 'direct' Japanization is therefore to be expected — the Japanese companies with 'toeholds' in Britain will expand (many have indeed already announced plans for significant expansion) and they will be followed by their suppliers who are dependent on them, and who are in any case often difficult to replace due to the present unavailability of competent British suppliers.

Successful multinationals from other countries would, of course, be equally willing to extend their presence in Britain — the fact is that the UK is in many respects a desirable country to locate manufacturing plants, so long as one is not dependent on the City. Recent comments by government ministers (for instance in response to concerns raised by the British car industry when Nissan announced its expansion plans in December 1987, to the effect that the nationality of the investing company is less important than the fact of investment) would seem to indicate that any decline of British-owned industry is not considered a central problem. Of course, the government's argument against this assertion is that the concern is there, but the best way for British industry to solve its problems is to learn to look after itself. The fact that Japanese industry appears to have thrived on intervention, however, seems to be overlooked. Also overlooked is the potential danger that 'sharp-end' high technology activities, to the extent that basic R&D is retained in the multinational's parent country, become less commonplace in Britain: Britain may not become a 'warehouse economy', but the alternative might be Britain as an off-shore 'screwdriver' assembly plant.

In sum, it seems likely that the Japanization of British manufacturing industry *will* go ahead on a significant scale, but unless there is a change in the structure of finance to industry, this will be at the expense of British-owned companies, and a further decline in the quality, if not quantity, of Britain's overall manufacturing base.

As we argued in chapter 2, various authors have offered their comments on the key factors in Japan's success, but these have mostly been one-dimensional formulas. For instance Pascale and Athos (1982) suggest the secret is their human asset management. Schonberger (1982) and Parnaby (1987a) argue for their skills in manufacturing organization. And Wong et al. (1987) point to the significance of Japanese companies' aggressive marketing strategies. Our own very clear conclusion on the basis of the extensive evidence presented is that the high interdependencies characteristic of the flagship Japanese corporations mean it is *all* these things, and that *none* of them can be achieved in the absence of the potential for long-term strategic planning provided by long-term financial guarantees.

Conclusions

At a number of points in this book a marked divergence in perspective has been apparent between the various commentators on Japanese practice (both here and in Japan). An example of this is the description of Toyota's production system as 'a respect-for-human' system by one set of commentators and as 'inhuman' by another. It is reflected in the description of a Japanese production system as one over which, when implemented, 'there can be no other improvement', but on the other hand eliciting the comment, 'Faced with the choice of going on the dole or working like the Japanese the men so far would prefer the dole. It's as simple as that' (Turnbull 1987).

The criticisms of Japanese practices centre on claims that they entail work intensification and heightened control by companies over their constituent agencies — their workers, their suppliers and so on. On the other hand the advocates of the Japanization of British industry point to its benefits in terms of business efficiency, and hence the competitiveness of British companies in world markets, arguing that British industry either becomes more competitive internationally or ceases to exist in a significant form. Both critics and advocates would probably agree on the question of work intensification; Nissan's statements on its application forms (quoted in chapter 3) indicate this, along with other evidence we have presented. The advocates would probably argue that the benefits of Japanese-style personnel practices (where they exist) compensate for this intensification; the critics may be unconvinced of this.

Where the two sides appear to have an *unbridgeable* gap is in their perspective on control. In chapter 2 we argued that low waste, high dependency systems require that uncertainty from whatever source is minimized, if not eliminated, if such systems are to operate successfully. This implies tight *control* over the resources involved in the production process, mechanical and human. It is on this issue that opinions most sharply divide. The critics view Japanese-style practices as insidious control devices, the most immoral of which are represented by strategies to elicit loyalty and commitment to the company. The advocates see loyalty and commitment as desirable and morally acceptable on the grounds that everyone benefits in the long run:

> It is the concept of loyalty to the company which so rankles left wing opponents of these new initiatives. Failing to realize that the intention is that all shall benefit, they attack what they believe are companies' attempts to usurp the traditional loyalty of workers to union . . . Companies *do* seek employee loyalty and they *do* want to develop an environment where industrial action is inconceivable! (Wickens 1987, p. 158)

Ironically, it is the very conditions most celebrated by the advocates, such as single status, long-term employment and identification with one's work team, which create the conditions most scorned by the critics: 'The Japanese corporation [operates] as a culturally homogeneous social system that . . . can withstand no internal cultural diversity' (Ouchi 1981).

While one side applauds the Japanese corporations for their unity and apparent ability to create a homogeneous culture and a sense of common purpose, the other castigates them for it. Advocates claim the removal of 'artificial' barriers through the harmonization of employment conditions and the removal of tangible divisions of status within the organization; critics point to a false consensus and the obscuration of 'real' interests.

What is clear is that Japanization entails the nurturing of constituent dependence, and by the same token the erosion of constituent independence. Japanese-style organization is a very different form of organization to that with which most people in the West are familiar. We leave it to readers to make their own judgement.

References

ACAS/WINvest (1986), *Successful Industrial Relations: The Experience of Overseas Companies in Wales*, Cardiff, ACAS Wales.

Ackroyd, S., Burrell, G., Hughes, M. and Whitaker, A. (1988), 'The Japanization of British Industry?', *Industrial Relations Journal*, vol. 19, no. 1, pp. 11–23.

Anglo-Japanese Economic Institute (1987), *News and Views from Japan*, no. 268.

APEX (1987), *Less than Full-time Working*, London, APEX.

Atkinson, J. (1987), 'Flexibility or Fragmentation? The United Kingdom Labour Market in the Eighties', *Labour and Society*, vol. 12, no. 1, pp. 87–105.

Azumi, K. (1969), *Higher Education and Business Recruitment in Japan*, New York, Columbia University Press.

BBC/OU (1986a), 'Strategies for Change: The Task Force', *The Structure and Design of Manufacturing Systems*, Pt 611, Open University/BBC Productions [film].

BBC/OU (1986b), 'Process Capability and Control', *Quality Techniques*, Pt 619, Open University/BBC Productions [film].

BBC (1987), *Chopsticks, Bulldozers and Newcastle Brown*, BBC Productions [film documentary].

BS 5750 (1979), *Quality Systems*, Parts 1–6, British Standards Institution.

Bassett, P. (1986), *Strike-free: New Industrial Relations in Britain*, London, Macmillan.

Beasley, M. (1984), 'Participation in Jaguar Cars', *Industrial Participation*, no. 586, pp. 18–21.

Beaumont, P. (1987), *The Decline of Trade Union Organization*, London, Croom Helm.

Bevan, W. (1987), *Creating a 'No Strike' Environment: The Trade Union View*. Text of a speech given to the CBI Conference on Strike-Free Deals, London, 24 June 1987.

Bicheno, J. (1987), 'A Framework for JIT Implementation', in Voss, C. (ed.), *Just-in-Time Manufacture*, London, IFS, pp. 191–204.

Blauner, R. (1964), *Alienation and Freedom*, Chicago, University of Chicago Press.

Bonis, J. (1980), 'Organization and Environment', in Lockett, M. and Spear, R. (eds.), *Organizations as Systems*, Milton Keynes, Open University Press.

Boyer, E. (1983), 'How Japan Manages Declining Industries', *Fortune*, 10 January, pp. 58–63.

Braverman, H. (1974), *Labor and Monopoly Capital: the Degradation of Work in the Twentieth Century*, New York, Monthly Review Press.

Briggs, P. (1988), 'The Japanese at Work: Illusions of the Ideal', *Industrial Relations Journal*, vol. 19, no. 1, pp. 24–30.

Buchanan, D. and Bessant, J. (1985), 'Failure, Uncertainty and Control: The Role of Operators in a Computer Integrated Production System', *Journal of Management Studies*, vol. 22, no. 3, pp. 292–308.

Burbidge, J. (1979), *Group Technology in the Mechanical Engineering Industry*, London, Mechanical Engineering Publications.

Burbidge, J. (1982), 'Japanese Kanban System', *Production Management and Control*, January/February, pp. 1–5.

Clegg, C. (1986), 'Trip to Japan: A Synergistic Approach to Managing Human Resources', *Personnel Management*, August, pp. 35–9.

Clutterbuck, D. (ed.) (1985), *New Patterns of Work*, Aldershot, Gower.

Cooper, C. (1988), 'Executive Stress Around the World', *University of Wales Business Review*, forthcoming.

Crowther, S. and Garrahan, P. (1988), 'Invitation to Sunderland: Corporate Power and the Local Economy', *Industrial Relations Journal*, vol. 19, no. 1, pp. 51–9.

Cusumano, M. (1986), *The Japanese Automobile Industry: Technology and Management at Nissan and Toyota*, Cambridge, Mass., Harvard University Press.

Dace, R. (1987), *Japanese Strategic Marketing: An Insight into Product and Market Plans of Japanese Companies*. Paper presented to the Conference on the Japanization of British Industry, Cardiff Business School, 17–18 September.

Dale, B. and Barlow, E. (1984), 'Facilitator Viewpoints on Specific Aspects of Quality Circle Programmes', *Personnel Review*, vol. 13, no. 4, pp. 22–9.

Dale, B. and Hayward, S. (1984), *A Study of Quality Circle Failures*, UMIST Occasional Paper, Manchester.

Dickens, P. and Savage, M. (1988), 'The Japanization of British Industry? Instances from a High Growth Area', *Industrial Relations Journal*, vol. 19, no. 1, pp. 60–8.

Domingo, R. (1985), '"Kanban": Crisis Management Japanese Style', *Euro-Asia Business Review*, vol. 4, no. 3, pp. 22–4.

Dore, R. (1973a), *British Factory–Japanese Factory*, London, Allen and Unwin.

Dore, R. (1973b), *Origins of the Japanese Employment System*, London, Allen and Unwin.

Dore, R. (1982), 'Quality Circles and their Transferability to Britain', *Management Decision*, vol. 20, no. 5/6, pp. 8–12.

Dore, R. (1983), 'Goodwill and the Spirit of Market Capitalism', *British Journal of Psychology*, vol. 34, no. 4, pp. 459–82.

Dore, R. (1986), *Flexible Rigidities*, London, Athlone.

Dunning, J. (1986), *Japanese Participation in British Industry*, London, Croom Helm.

Edwards, G. A. B. (1974), 'Group Technology', *Personnel Management*, March.

Egan, J. (1985), 'Quality: The Jaguar Obsession', *EOQC Quality*, vol. 1, pp. 3–4.

Fairbrother, P. (1987), *Restructuring Production, Models of Flexibility and Union Renewal: Japanization in Process?*. Paper presented to the Conference on the Japanization of British Industry, Cardiff Business School, 17–18 September.

Feigenbaum, A. (1983), *Total Quality Control*, New York, McGraw-Hill.

Fletcher, D. (1984), 'Quality Circles at Wedgwood', in Sasaki, N. and Hutchins, D. (eds.), *The Japanese Approach to Product Quality*, Oxford, Pergamon, pp. 79–82.

Ford Motor Company (1984), *Durability, Quality and Reliability*.

Fortune, J. (1986), *Quality of Purchased Supplies*, Pt 619, Unit 2, Milton Keynes, Open University Press.

Fortune, J. and Oliver, N. (1986), *Human Aspects of Quality*, Pt 622, Unit 4, Milton Keynes, Open University Press.

Franko, L. (1983), *The Threat of Japanese Multinationals*, New York, Wiley.

Friedman, A. (1977), *Industry and Labour*, London, Macmillan.

Galbraith, J. (1974), 'Organization Design: An Information Processing View', *Interfaces*, vol. 4, no. 3, pp. 28−36.

Gleave, S. (1987), *How Japanese are Japanese Factories in Britain? A study of Japanese Personnel Management in Japan and Britain*, MBA dissertation, Cardiff Business School, UWIST.

Graham, I. (1988), 'Japanization as Mythology', *Industrial Relations Journal*, vol. 29, no. 1, pp. 69−75.

Gregory, M. (1986), 'The No-strike Deal in Action', *Personnel Management*, vol. 18, December, pp. 30−4.

Guthrie, G. (1987), 'After Japan and Beyond', *Production Engineer*, May, pp. 29−31.

Halliday, J. and McCormack, G. (1973), *Japanese Imperialism Today*, Harmondsworth, Penguin.

Harrington, H. (1982), *Quality Education Rides the Crest of the Third Wave*, IBM internal document, July.

Heller, R. (1986), 'Growth, Profitability and Earnings', *Management Today*, June, pp. 46−63.

Hill, F. (1986), 'Quality Circles in the UK: A Longitudinal Case Study', *Personnel Review*, vol. 15, no. 3, pp. 25−34.

Hirschmeier, J. and Yui, T. (1981), *The Development of Japanese Business*, London, Allen and Unwin.

Hofstede, G. (1980), *Culture's Consequences*, Beverley Hills, Calif., Sage.

Isaac, D. (1984), 'How Jaguar Lost its Spots', *Management Today*, April, pp. 38ff.

Isherwood, M. (1982), 'Japanese Experience of Employee Relations in the United Kingdom', *Management Decision*, vol. 20, no. 5/6, pp. 13−22.

Ishida, H. (1977), *Exportability of the Japanese Employment System*, Tokyo, Japan Institute of Labour.

Ishikawa, K. (1984), 'Quality Control in Japan', in Sasaki, N. and Hutchins, D. (eds.), *The Japanese Approach to Product Quality*, Oxford, Pergamon.

Japan Institute of Labour (1984), *Wages and Hours of Work*, Japanese Industrial Relations Series, no. 3.

Kamata, S. (1983), *Japan in the Passing Lane: An Insider's Account of Life in a Japanese Auto Factory*, London, Allen and Unwin.

Kanter, R. (1985), *The Change Masters*, London, Allen and Unwin.

Kelly, J. (1987), *Labour and the Union*, London, Verso.

Kendall (1984), 'Why Japanese Workers Work', *Management Today*, January, pp. 72−5.

Klein, J. A. (1984), 'Why Supervisors Resist Employee Involvement', *Harvard Business Review*, September−October, pp. 87−95.

Labour Research (1987), vol. 76, no. 8.

Lee, D. (1986), 'Set-up Time Reduction: Making JIT Work', *Management Services*, May, pp. 8−13.

Lewis, J. R. (1987), *British and Japanese Paternalism*, MBA dissertation, Cardiff Business School, UWIST.

Linn, I. (1986), *Single Union Deals: A Case Study of the Norsk Hydro Plant at Immingham, Humberside*, Barnsley, Northern College Research Unit, in association with TGWU Region 10.

Littler, C. R. (1982), *The Development of the Labour Process in Capitalist Societies*, London, Heinemann.

Lupton, T. et al. (1979), 'Manufacturing System Design in Europe', in Cooper, C. and Mumford, E. (eds.), *The Quality of Working Life in Western and Eastern Europe*. London, Associated Business Press, pp. 44−75.

Main, J. (1984), 'The Trouble with Managing Japanese Style', *Fortune*, 2 April, pp. 10−14.

Manpower Services Commission (1987), *Management Development and Technological Innovation in Japan*, London.

Marchington, M. (1979), 'Shopfloor Control and Industrial Relations', in Purcell, M. and Smith, R. (eds.), *The Control of Work*, London, Macmillan.

Marchington, M. and Armstrong, R. (1986), 'The Nature of the New Joint Consultation', *Industrial Relations Journal*, vol. 17, no. 2, pp. 158−70.

Marsden, D., Morris, T., Willman, P. and Wood, S. (1985), *The Car Industry: Labour Relations and Industrial Adjustment*, London, Tavistock.

Matthews, K. and Minford, P. (1987), 'Mrs Thatcher's Economic Policies 1979−87', *Economic Policy*, vol. 2, no. 5, pp. 57−102.

McFadden, A. and Towler, D. (1987), *Nissan − the Challenge to the Trade Union Movement*. Report to the Northern Regional TUC, April.

Mercer, D. (1987), *IBM: How the World's Most Successful Corporation is Managed*, London, Kogan Page.

Merrette, E. (1987), *Industrial Change: A Practical Experience*. Paper presented to the ACAS Wales Conference on Industrial Change, Swansea, 11 November.

Mitchell, T. and Larson, J. (1987), *People in Organizations*, 3rd edn, New York, McGraw-Hill.

Monden, Y. (1981a), 'What Makes the Toyota Production System Really Tick?', *Industrial Engineering Magazine*, January, pp. 36−46.

Monden, Y. (1981b), 'Adaptable Kanban System Helps Toyota Maintain Just-in-Time Production', *Industrial Engineering Magazine*, May, pp. 29−46.

Monden, Y. (1983), *Toyota Production System*, Atlanta, Georgia, Industrial Engineering and Management Press.

Moore, J. B. (1987), 'Japanese Industrial Relations', *Labour and Industry*, vol. 1, no. 1, pp. 140−55.

Morishima, M. (1982), *Why has Japan 'Succeeded'? Western Technology and the Japanese Ethos*, Cambridge, Cambridge University Press.

Morris, J. (1988a), 'The Who, Why and Where of Japanese Manufacturing Investment in the UK', *Industrial Relations Journal*, vol. 19, no. 1, pp. 31−40.

Morris, J. (1988b), *Japan into Europe! The Impact of Japanese Manufacturing Investment in the EEC*, forthcoming.

NEDO (1986), *Changing Work Patterns − How Companies Achieve Flexibility to Meet the New Needs*, London.

Nakane, C. (1973), *Japanese Society*, Harmondsworth, Penguin.

Naylor, L. (1984), 'Bringing Home the Lessons', *Personnel Management*, vol. 16, no. 3, pp. 34−7.

Ohmae, K. (1983), 'Japan's Admiration for US Business', *Asian Wall Street Journal*, 11 October.

Oliver, N. (1986), *Computers and Quality*, Pt 622, Unit 3, Milton Keynes, Open University Press.

Oliver, N. (1987), *The Evolution of Recycles Ltd*, CRU Case Study no. 9, Milton Keynes, Open University Press.

Ouchi, W. (1981), *Theory Z: How American Business Can Meet the Japanese Challenge*, Boston, Addison Wesley.

Pang, K. K. (1987), *Japanese Management Practices in Overseas Subsidiaries: A Case*

Approach, MBA dissertation, Cardiff Business School, UWIST.

Pang, K. K. and Oliver, N. (1988), 'Personnel Strategy in Eleven Japanese Manufacturing Companies in the UK', *Personnel Review*, vol. 17, no. 3.

Parnaby, J. (1986), 'The Japanese Systems Engineering Approach', Lucas Industries internal document.

Parnaby, J. (1987a), 'Competitiveness via Total Quality of Performance', *Progress in Rubber and Plastics Technology*, vol. 3, no. 1, pp. 42–50.

Parnaby, J. (1987b), *A Systems Engineering Approach to Fundamental Change in Manufacturing*. Paper presented to the Ninth Industrial Engineering Managers Conference, New Orleans, 9–11 March.

Parnaby, J. (1987c), *Practical Just-in-Time – Inside and Outside the Factory*. Paper presented to the Fifth Financial Times Manufacturing Forum, London, 6–7 May.

Parnaby, J. and Bignell, V. (1986), 'Manufacturing Systems: Concept Design', *The Structure and Design of Manufacturing Systems*, Pt 611, Unit 6, Milton Keynes, Open University Press.

Pascale, R. (1984), 'Fitting New Employees into the Company Culture', *Fortune International*, vol. 109, no. 11, pp. 62–9.

Pascale, R. and Athos, A. (1982), *The Art of Japanese Management*, Harmondsworth, Penguin.

Paton, R, (1985), *Coping with the Environment*, T244, Unit 12, Milton Keynes, Open University Press.

Peach, L. H. (1983), 'Employee Relations in IBM', *Employee Relations*, vol. 5, no. 3, pp. 17–20.

Pegge, T. (1986), 'Hitachi Two Years On', *Personnel Management*, October, pp. 42–7.

Peters, T. and Waterman, R. (1982), *In Search of Excellence*, New York, Harper and Row.

Pfeffer, J. (1981), *Power in Organizations*, Boston, Mass., Pitman Publishing.

Pucik, V. (1985), 'Managing Japan's White-collar Workers', *Euro-Asia Business Review*, vol. 4, no. 3, pp. 16–21.

Rajan, A. (1987), *Services: The Second Industrial Revolution*. Report by the Institute of Manpower Studies to the Occupational Services Group. London, Butterworth.

Ramsey, H. (1983), 'An International Participation Cycle: Variations on a Recurring Theme', in Clegg, S. et al. (eds.), *The State, Class and the Recession*, New York, St Martins Press, pp. 257–317.

Ramsey, J. (1985), 'Just Too Late?', *Purchasing and Supply Management*, January, pp. 22–3.

Regional Trends no. 22 (1987), London, HMSO.

Reitsperger, W. (1986a), 'Japanese Management: Coping with British Industrial Relations', *Journal of Management Studies*, vol. 23, no. 1, pp. 72–88.

Reitsperger, W. (1986b), 'British Employees: Responding to Japanese Management Philosophies', *Journal of Management Studies*, vol. 23, no. 5, pp. 563–87.

Robbins, S. (1983), 'Theory Z from a Power-Control Perspective', *California Management Review*, vol. 25, no. 2, pp. 67–75.

Sako, M. (1987), *Buyer–Supplier Relationships in Britain: A Case of Japanization?*. Paper presented to the Conference on the Japanization of British Industry, Cardiff Business School, 17–18 September.

Schonberger, R. (1982), *Japanese Manufacturing Techniques*, New York, Free Press.

Schonberger, R. (1986), *World Class Manufacturing*, New York, Free Press.

Sethi, S., Namiki, N. and Swanson, C. (1984), *The False Promise of the Japanese Miracle*, London, Pitman.

Slaughter, J. (1987), *The Team Concept in the US Auto Industry*. Paper presented to the

Conference on the Japanization of British Industry, Cardiff Business School, 17—18 September.

Smith, D. (1988), 'The Japanese Example in South West Birmingham', *Industrial Relations Journal*, vol. 19, no. 1, pp. 41—50.

Spiridion, R. H. (1987), *Personnel Management at IBM: Theory and Practice*, MBA dissertation, Cardiff Business School, UWIST.

Sugimore, Y. et al. (1977), 'Toyota Production System and Kanban System: Materialization of Just-in-Time and Respect-for-Human System', *International Journal of Production Research*, vol. 15, no. 6, pp. 553—64.

Takamiya, M. (1981), 'Japanese Multinationals in Europe: International Operations and their Public Policy Implications', *Columbia Journal of World Business*, Summer, pp. 5—17.

TGWU Region 10 and Northern College Research Unit (1987), *Change at Work*, Barnsley.

Trevor, M. (1988), *Toshiba's New British Company: Competitiveness through Innovation*, forthcoming.

Turnbull, P. (1986), 'The "Japanization" of Production and Industrial Relations at Lucas Electrical', *Industrial Relations Journal*, vol. 17, no. 3, pp. 193—206.

Turnbull, P. (1987), *The Limits to Japanization — Just-in-Time, Labour Relations and the UK Automotive Industry*. Paper presented to the Conference on the Japanization of British Industry, Cardiff Business School, 17—18 September.

Turnbull, P. (1988), 'The Limits to Japanization — Just-in-Time, Labour Relations and the UK Automotive Industry', *New Technology, Work and Employment*, vol. 3, no. 1, pp. 7—20.

Vliet, A. (1986), 'Where Lucas Sees the Light', *Management Today*, June.

Vogel, E. (1980), *Japan as Number One: Lessons for America*, Cambridge, Mass., Harvard University Press.

Voss, C. (ed.) (1987), *Just-in-Time Manufacture*, London, IFS.

Voss, C. and Robinson, S. (1987a), *JIT in the UK*. Paper presented to the 2nd Annual Conference of the Operations Management Association.

Voss, C. and Robinson, S. (1987b), 'The Application of Just-in-Time Techniques', *International Journal of Operations and Production Management*, vol. 7, no. 4, pp. 46—52.

Ward, J. (1987), 'IBM', in Voss. C, (ed.), *Just-in-Time Manufacture*, London, IFS, pp. 365—73.

White, M. and Trevor, M. (1983), *Under Japanese Management*, London, Heinemann.

Whitehill, A. and Takezawa, S. (1978), *The Other Worker*, Honolulu, East-West Centre Press.

Wickens, P. (1985), 'Nissan: The Thinking Behind the Union Agreement', *Personnel Management*, August, pp. 18—21.

Wickens, P. (1987), *The Road to Nissan*, London, Macmillan.

Wilkinson, B. and Leggett, C. (1985), 'Human and Industrial Relations in Singapore: the Management of Compliance', *Euro-Asia Business Review*, vol. 4, no. 3, pp. 9—15.

Wilkinson, B. and Oliver, N. (guest eds.) (1988), 'On the Japanization of British Industry', *Industrial Relations Journal*, vol. 19, no. 1·[special issue].

Wilkinson, B. and Smith, S. (1983), 'Management Strategies for Technical Change', *Science and Public Policy*, vol. 10, no. 2, pp. 56—61.

Willman, P. and Winch, G. (1985), *Innovation and Management Control*, Cambridge, Cambridge University Press.

Wolf, M. (1985), *The Japanese Conspiracy*, Sevenoaks, New English Library.

Wong, V., Saunders, J. and Doyle, P. (1987), 'Japanese Marketing Strategies in the United Kingdom', *Long Range Planning*, vol. 20, no. 6, pp. 54–63.

Woodward, J. (1965), *Industrial Organization: Theory and Practice*, London, Oxford University Press.

Yap, F. (1984), *A Guide to Quality Control Circles and Work Improvement Teams*, Singapore, Aequitas Management Consultants.

Index